RESTAURANT
NEWSLETTERS
THAT PAY OFF

RESTAURANT NEWSLETTERS THAT PAY OFF

Walter Mathews

John Wiley & Sons, Inc.

New York   Chichester   Weinheim   Brisbane   Singapore   Toronto

Book design by Duane Stapp

This text is printed on acid-free paper.

This publication is designed to provide accurate and
authoritative information in regard to the subject
matter covered. It is sold with the understanding that
the publisher is not engaged in rendering legal, accounting,
or other professional services. If legal advice or other
expert assistance is required, the services of a competent
professional person should be sought.

Library of Congress Cataloging in Publication Data:
Mathews, Walter.
     Restaurant newsletters that pay off / Walter Mathews.
          p.   cm.
     Includes bibliographical references and index.
     ISBN 0-471-16912-9 (cloth : alk. paper)
     1. Public relations—Restaurants. 2. Restaurants—Marketing.
3. Newsletters—Publishing. I. Title.
TX911.3.P77M38   1997
659.2'964795—dc21   97-1969

Printed in the United States of America
10 9 8 7 6 5 4 3 2 1

FOR JOANNE BLACK, who has an enviable and intuitive sense of marketing, and who started me on me road to newsletters with *Restaurant Briefing*.

CONTENTS

Acknowledgments

The last 20 years of talking with and writing to some 100,000 restaurateurs across America has provided an invaluable opportunity to appreciate these unique individuals who contribute so much to our social and business lives, our culture and education, our politics and our livelihood. To those who contributed their newsletters, ideas and comments to this book, we're grateful for their generosity and cooperation.

To Duane Stapp, a freelance graphic designer and fine artist, who lives in downtown Manhattan with his wife, cat, and sculptures. The design of this book is all his—all we did was to tell him what we wanted to communicate—he took it from there.

To Paul Swift, a writer and editor, who contributed a wealth of newsletter know-how from his wide experience as managing editor of the *Newsletter on Newsletters,* and *Public Relations Quarterly.*

To Scott Wagendorf, who for six years, has been Managing Editor of *Briefing,* chronicling such trends as low-fat meals, celebrity chefs, the shift to casual dining, fusion cuisine and yes, the rise in popularity of newsletters. As a freelance writer, he also consults with clients in the fashion, travel and entertainment fields.

To all of our friends and helpmates at John Wiley & Sons, but particularly Claire Thompson, our editor; Maria Colletti, who graciously held down two jobs while working with us; and to Diana Cisek, managing editor, production, professional and trade division, who immediately "got it" when we told her the kind of book we wanted to do.

Incidentally, we wanted to publish with Wiley because of the very high ratings its books got from our restaurateur readers when we offered them through the *Briefing* newsletter.

To Jed Mattes, literary agent, who combines eclectic interests in a wide range of subjects, combined with a pragmatic and empathetic approach to both book ideas and contract negotiation.

My appreciation to all of these wonderful people,

Walter Mathews

Introduction

Restaurant goers today have many more choices than they had ten or even five years ago. They may choose a steakhouse to celebrate a birthday, a diner for weekday lunch and join friends at the neighborhood bistro for Friday night out. Occasion, price, convenience, familiarity and location all figure into the formula.

As situations and needs change, it is important to communicate what you intend to provide and stand for.
— *The 1995 Yankelovich Monitor*
(surveying social trends since 1971)

So how do you keep your restaurant top of mind?

More and more restaurateurs are turning to newsletters, according to the National Restaurant Association.

Newsletters come in different sizes, shapes, colors, and cover a wide variety of subjects. What the successful ones all have in common is that they talk about things that their readers will find interesting. (Not necessarily what you, the restaurateur/publisher wants to tell them.) Oh, there's still room to talk about special dinners, new menus and in-store cooking classes, but the information must be presented in a way that makes the guests think they're in the know.

Here are just a few examples of ideas you'll find inside: *Recipes from popular dishes* (Customers will want to visit your restaurant to try the real thing) ... *Information about nutrition* (A good way to announce your heart-smart specials) ... *Recommend restaurants in other cities* (Boosts your credibility at home, and colleagues in other cities may do the same for you).

In the coming chapters, we'll show you how 50 or so of your peers are effectively reaching out to their customers through newsletters. These are real situations and real people. Not theory. They come from restaurants in all parts of the country, representing various types of cuisine and average check. Each one includes comments and suggestions from the restaurant owner or manager.

In addition, we'll examine the other elements that you must consider in publishing a successful customer newsletter: costs, mailing lists, printing, frequency, design and many others.

Keep in mind that people go to restaurants for different reasons: to talk business, to try new foods and drinks, to indulge in the comfort of old favorites, to celebrate birthdays and anniversaries, to relax and get away from it all, to begin—and sometimes to end—relationships. You don't need to tell us all the roles you play, often to the same people who at different times have different wants: confessor, advisor, entertainer, food & wine expert, conversationalist, city tour and shopping guide. You can think of more.

It's only natural for customers to experiment with some of your competitors. But your efforts to keep in touch can be a powerful force to bring them back. Your newsletter can also be a rich source for knowing your customers better, finding out what works and what doesn't, selecting what to write about, menu items, service ideas.

At this point, you're probably thinking a newsletter might be a good idea, but "Can I afford it?" "Who will write it?" and a lot of other questions will need answering. We'll do our best to help.

Your restaurant is a reflection of you and your staff, your personality, your tastes, your experiences, your knowledge and outlook. Your newsletter should be an extension of that, written from your reader's viewpoint.

Your Comments

If you publish a newsletter that we haven't included and are proud of its results, send it along for our next edition.

If you have ideas you'd like to share, send them along, too.

If you have questions, we'll try to answer them.

Best wishes,

Walter Mathews
799 Broadway, #309
New York, NY 10003
(212) 533-9099
FAX (212) 533-9295
E-MAIL WMANYC@AOL.COM

CHAPTER 1

Ten Newsletter Myths

1. The more money you spend, the better your finished product will be.

That's not to say all expensive newsletters don't work—it's just that the expense isn't necessary. In fact, that's the particular appeal of the newsletter format. It doesn't have to be produced on glossy coated paper stock with full-color photos like magazines. Remember that magazines are primarily a means for carrying fancy display ads. Their expensive production reflects that. Newsletters, on the other hand, are designed for personal, targeted communication. The message is the main thing. *(See Chapter 5, What Goes Where: Design & Typography.)*

2. There's only one right way to do a newsletter.

There are as many "right" ways to do a newsletter as there are types and styles of restaurants and restaurateurs. Beyond the basics of looking good in print and writing well and offering your readers something of value to read, the design and content of your newsletter is yours alone to decide and develop. *(See Chapter 6, Getting the Best (for the Least) from Your Printer.)*

3. Keep your personality out of it.

Au contraire. Your restaurant reflects your personality. Adding that to the mix gives the copy life and distinguishes you from your competitors. We repeat: newsletters are a me-to-you communication—much more personal than ads, flyers and brochures. In fact, some restaurateurs tell us that their newsletter is the only advertising they use. *(See Chapter 4, How to Get Your Message Across: Style & Tone.)*

4. Don't promote yourself.

Keep the interests of your customers first, and avoid puffery and shameless, transparent self-promotion. Beyond that, relax. If you can generate excitement about root vegetables and let your customers know your restaurant is *the* best place to find them, that's persuasive writing. The usual newsletter format of 4 or 8 pages gives you room to *engage* the reader in a personal way—in contrast to the quicker read of an ad or flyer. *(See Chapter 4, How to Get Your Message Across: Style & Tone.)*

5. People aren't as important as things and events.

Who says so? It's the people—you, your chef, managers, wait staff, bus boys and dishwashers, even your customers—that form the nucleus of this "thing" people come to experience in your restaurant. Your newsletter is an extension of this enjoyment, a reminder to come back again and to tell their friends about it. *(See Chapter 4, What Makes a Good Story?)*

6. All the conditions must be just right before launching.

That's a myth that will keep your newsletter from ever getting off the ground. We've talked to many of you over the years who say, "If only I had the time," or "I'll wait until I have something important to say." There's no perfect time to start. A newsletter is an invaluable marketing tool, and putting off launching yours is to miss the opportunity to tell your customers and prospects just what a great restaurant you have. In the words of the world's leading sportswear company, Just do it! You can fine-tune the newsletter as you go along. *(See Chapter 7, Who to Write to and How to Find Them.)*

7. Publish only twice a year to avoid information overload.

We recommend publishing your newsletter at least quarterly to develop a reading habit among your customers. Six to eight times is preferable. Once you develop its format and style and put someone in charge of it, your newsletter should become as routine as updating your menu. *(See Chapter 8, Building a Reading Habit.)*

8. If you can't afford to hire a designer and writer, don't bother doing something less professional.

Some of the most effective, compelling newsletters we've seen have few or no graphics. That's the distinguishing mark of newsletters: they're written as personal letters. And who doesn't look forward to getting mail from a friend? Plus, computer software programs for page layout are easily available and easily mastered. Or you can hire— for not much money—a graphics artist to design your newsletter nameplate and page layout (called a template) into which you can incorporate your content each issue from a word processor. *(See Chapter 5, What Goes Where: Design & Typography, and Chapter 6, Getting the Best (for the Least) from Your Printer.)*

9. *The more information you provide, the more likely your readers are to find something they are interested in.*

How many times have you told yourself, "This piece looks interesting. I'll get to it later," only to find it among the recyclables a month from now? Not so with the quick read a newsletter offers. Each short article provides only one basic idea or a description of one person or menu item or coming event. Newsletters are designed to be read immediately—like a letter. Any more length than that, and you're missing the point of the newsletter format. *(See Chapter 4, What Makes a Good Story?)*

10. *Your newsletter will probably end up in the junk-mail pile with all the other direct mail offers.*

Not if you read this book, take it to heart and consult it when you discern a weak spot in your newsletter. Plus, a newsletter differs from other direct mail in that it's more personal: most people at least scan the return address on their mail, and if they recognize something from a neighborhood business, especially one they've patronized, they'll probably open it. How often have people told you, "What I'd really like to do is run a restaurant"? You have personality and curiosity on your side.

QUAVIT

December

Chain

spe

Advance
Ed Goldber

St. L
Cele
Wednesday, D
onight will feature a sp
in addition to our regula
Glögg will be served in th
St. Lucia will make an ap
Read all about it on the fir

St. Lucia at
the James Beard Hou
Wednesday, December 13
Dinner at 7.30pm at the James Beard House
Proceeds will go to
the James Beard Foundation
Please call (212) 627-2308
Advance reservation necessary

AQUAVIT
Restaurant Aquavit of New York
13 West 54th Street, New York, NY 10019
(212) 307-7311

LUNAR
Bella Luna
A Quarterly Publication of Bella Luna Restaurant

A Message
From Karen
& Horst!

There's so
forward to
spring a
summ
do

look   this

morning over coffee and pastries
with a local grower or supplier.
We've lined up experts on mushrooms, local cheeses, herbs,
seafood and more for informal
discussions on specific products,
nutrition, cooking, the restaurant
business and whatever else is on
your mind! We hope that you'll
take advantage of this free
program, and come with questions for our experts.
As always, we value your
input. Let us know which pro-
ns are important to you, and
lcome your suggestions for
ams as well!
forward to seeing
e months, and
healthy,
ring!

Vol. 3.2.
years later. The Convent
is the oldest building in the
Mississippi Valley—25 years
older than the United States
25 years younger than the C
of New Orleans, and the o
structure to survive the F
Colonial period.
After the Ursuline
were named after Sai
were sent from Fra
Orleans, they star
free school for g
and nursery.
people chang
of the nuns
Revolutio
Ursuline
help h
medi
Xav
U

dates to remember
Monday Nights 9/12
join us for Latin Jazz night with Geri
Teresa, accompanied by her guitarist.
Monday 9/25
Marks the beginning of our fall menu
Tuesday 9/26 5-7pm
Cocktail reception for Nancy H.Jenkins'
book signing of "The Mediterranean
Diet" followed by a $25.00 prix-fixe dinner
Thursday 9/28–10/19
join us as we celebrate our Annual
Historical Event. This year we will repeat
last year's "Baronial Dinner", an
extravagant cuisine of the Kingdom of the Two Sicilies
during the baronial court
$50.00

t at bondí
Bondí: Oct 13 to Dec 2
Caffé Bondí is proud to host a show paying tribute to the
Music (BAM) and its "NEXT WAVE" Festival. This show
al artists, as well as the photographers that have contributed in a
hirteen years. Every Festival season is documented in a
Journal, which features portraits of performing artists, as
ated expressly for BAM by a contemporary visual artist.
Festival Artist collection is quite remarkable and includes
Francesco Clemente, Willem de Kooning and Keith
ring October 13th as we exhibit highlights of the "NEXT WAVE"
WAVE" Festival Artist is Jonathan Lasker
t have been featured as part of the "NEXT WAVE"
rs such as Karen Kuehn, Hans Neleman and artist
Bondí will coincide with the premiere of BAM's
E NEXT WAVE" show hosted by Don Byron.

the P
Stree
Ursuli
ed by a
ed t
stands be
of geometri
you enter i
ng hallway le
more tranquil
is the same
Ursuline
and flow
Xavier
pharm
Pfei
di

its with
ucation have
popular, we're
emier our new
Behind the Scenes at
una." Each month,
d a Saturday

What Makes a Good Story?

When developing a general list of story ideas or for a specific issue, keep in mind our operative words: *news* and *letter*. Your newsletter should carry news of interest, benefit or entertainment—ideally, as we say elsewhere, all three. And the best restaurant newsletters also convey the "me-to-you" feeling of a letter. (To achieve this, some writers actually picture a particular, favorite person or group and "write to" them as if they were the only ones receiving the letter.)

In other words, as a unique advertising medium and marketing tool, your newsletter should include:

- Reader benefits (unlike display or broadcast ads)
- Your personal touch

Compiling story ideas

To the many hats you wear as a restaurateur, add that of a reporter (picture those broad-brimmed hats with Press Pass stuck in the band). Keep your eyes open for stories when reading other publications, when going through a routine day of work, when talking with customers.

No need to *write* those stories down immediately. Instead, prepare a stack of file folders and label them in general categories: People, Recipes, Wine, Children, Discounts, and so on. Then when you read something that sparks an idea, tear out the article and file it—or when a customer raves about a dessert she had on vacation, jot down a note about it and file it. Get employees to do the same—jot down specific story ideas and give them to you or the newsletter editor to file.

You'll be surprised how fast the file folders will begin to take shape.

Or, if you're inspired at some point to write a few paragraphs about, say, the autumn specials you're planning, don't worry about creating a complete article—just write what you can at one sitting and then file it in the appropriate folder.

This method serves as an antidote to writer's block and yields a helpful file of story ideas and outlines for future issues of your newsletter. (This is the way many successful authors write whole books—not from beginning to end but building parts of various chapters as the inspiration or information unfolds.)

Brainstorming

In addition to looking for story ideas during your routine work and routine reading of other publications, you might also consider a periodic brainstorming session with a few of your employees. Ask them what they'd like to see in a newsletter. What would they read? What have they read that they liked?

Perhaps even, would they be interested in writing a piece for the newsletter?

Write down all their ideas—good and not-so-good—and file them in the appropriate folders.

At this phase of collecting story ideas, don't be so judgmental that you discourage more ideas. Just go with your instincts and compile as many ideas, leads, questions and comments as possible. Who knows what "themes" may even emerge? After four weeks of this, you find that you've been clipping a number of items and transcribing a number of customer comments that all center on one subject you hadn't even considered for a full-blown article.

Your editorial fare

At the outset, you should probably determine just what kind of articles you are going to include in your newsletter—or, put another way, what kind of articles are you *not* going to include in your newsletter? For example, some restaurant newsletters limit their editorial content to their restaurant alone. Others also include some community news and views. Others report on national trends in wining and dining. Still others reprint articles from food and travel publications (with permission, of course).

See the possibilities? Just try to rein them in at the beginning to develop your own particular editorial bill of fare.

Story ideas

Two pieces of advice:

1. If you ask for ideas, *act* on them. Use them, develop them or explain why not.
2. Always keep in mind your ultimate readers and what *they're* interested in.

Here's a list of suggestions for newsletter stories and features. Each item could constitute a "file" and be broken down into more particular ideas, or repeated to coincide with seasons of the year, for example.

- *Food and wine* Recipes, nutrition, cooking and tasting classes, picnics, trends, regional variations, education (new products), herbs, spices. Every item that appears on your menu could conceivably be the subject of a story—including salt and pepper.

- *People* Interesting customers, famous customers, local dignitaries, birthdays and anniversaries, staff news and employee recognition, customer mail, you and your travels.

- *Special events* and the seasons of the year Community events, special dinners and receptions, museum and gallery openings, contests, discounts and special offers, a calendar of events, upcoming holidays and celebrations.

- *Community involvement* Charities, charity benefits, environmental concerns, recycling, community organizations, promotional tie-ins with other businesses and organizations.

- *Awards and reviews* Recognition you and your restaurant have received from trade organizations and local, regional and national publications.

- *Miscellaneous* Question of the month, recommendations for places in other cities, reprints from consumer food publications, explanation of restaurant policies, puzzles, changes in menu or hours, Internet links, letters to the editor.

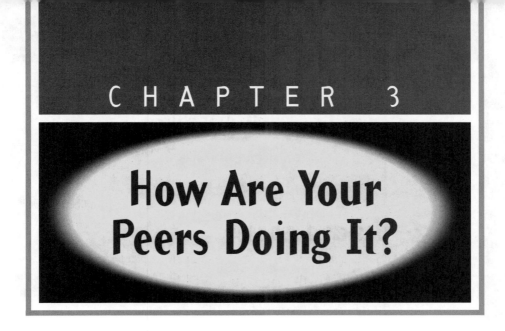

CHAPTER 3

How Are Your Peers Doing It?

In this chapter, you'll find the "heart" of this book. The things, people, ideas, knowledge, experiences, attitudes from a wide-ranging collection of restaurateurs from across the U.S. Of course, we hope that the other chapters will be valuable in bringing the newsletter's "nuts and bolts" from concept and construction to reality, giving it support, helping you to make it happen. But, even standing alone, for this "heart" to beat requires that you determine the personality and qualities of every aspect of the diner's experience, including what role customers themselves will want to play (and pay!).

All of the newsletters reproduced here (actually, two pages from each) are in almost actual size, so you can read what they're saying to their customers. You may pick up some ideas for your own restaurant. The variety of sizes, layout, content, tone, match the variety of personalities who write them. But they will all agree that newsletters are an extremely cost-effective way of producing repeat business or word-of-mouth advertising; of keeping in touch. One refers to his newsletter as being as important as the "bread on the table."

We thank all of the restaurateurs for giving us permission to write about their newsletters. Although people in this business are strong-willed and determined, they are also generous and willing to share with others.

Pasadena, CA

185 seats

Provincial French
and rustic Italian
cuisine/Mediterranean-
inspired decor

Marley Majcher, Dir
of Mktg. & Co-owner

(818) 449-4151

Are you publicizing
all that you have to offer?

Subtle way of saying
families are welcome.

≡ABIENTO≡

110 South Lake Avenue • Pasadena, CA 91101 • (818)449-4151

WINTER 1995

Use and Abuse!

O.K. let's be frank about it. Are you using Abiento to its full potential? Are you taking advantage of all of the products and services that we have to offer? It's all right, go ahead, we won't complain. But please let us remind you:

Abiento is (a):
- Full service catering company!
- The perfect location for your corporate event/private party (with three locations to fit your needs: our front patio, garden and party room)!
- Your one stop shop for custom gift baskets and gift certificates in any denomination!
- Open for Saturday and Sunday Brunch (with live music on Sundays) and is the perfect spot for your bridal or baby shower!
- Unique restaurant with plenty of free parking!
- Open Christmas Eve and New Year's Eve!
- Featuring a special Christmas "food to go" menu!
- Open 7 days a week!
- Very involved in the community!

Program Update!

* Know any new parents? If so, they could be eligible for our "**Postpartum Impression**" program! Abiento would like to extend an invitation to all of the parents of newborns. Visit us on your first night out after the little one arrives. With the purchase of any pair of entrees, Abiento will give you <u>and</u> your partner a glass each of champagne, <u>on us</u>, as a way of congratulating you for a job well done! Call

Black on various light-
colored heavy card stock

5 1/2 x 8 1/2,
self-mailer

4 pages

Published every 8-12 weeks

5000 printed and mailed

Published since mid-1993

10

Co-owner Marley Majcher has a common-sense philosophy about publishing her restaurant newsletter: Keep the editorial style simple and direct, put one person in charge (even though she solicits the staff's input) and make it good looking. "But most importantly," she says, "we really target it to our customers and their needs and try to let our personal style come through."

The entire job is done in the restaurant—with the exception of printing—for about 42¢ each including Majcher's time. "In our operation there is always some down time, so we fold, address and sort then. It works out to be less expensive than hiring a mailing service." But she warns that if you have to bring in staff just to work on the newsletter, it may not be cost-effective.

Special Services!

To Go: Our "to go" business is starting to boom. Everything on our menu is available for take out: yes, breadsticks! our homemade bread, pastas, entrees and, of course, desserts!

Picnic Baskets: We also have a special menu (available at the hostess desk) of additional items that are great to pack in one of our picnic baskets. Perfect for the next USC or UCLA game and very fashionable too!

Rothschild Products: We've brought in a new line of products: a terrific raspberry salsa, exotic vinegars and olive oils - all from one of the world's finest gourmet food companies. They would be perfect to put in a basket along with a bottle of wine, some breadsticks, any of our entrees and a pastry. A great idea for the holidays or for the friend who has everything. We can even custom design one while you eat your meal.

Gift Giving! It seems the holidays will soon be upon us. For that corporate client, hard to satisfy loved one or even as an employee incentive, why not give an Abiento gift certificate? They are available in any denomination!

More Good News!

The Noise Update: Yes, in our constant pursuit of a noiseless environment, Abiento is pleased to report we are making progress. With the installation of four new ceiling umbrellas and one large one in the party room, I think everyone would agree our surroundings have really improved!

Help Hotline: Can't get your soufflés to rise? Your pizza dough too tough? Don't know which wine to serve with that turbot? Chef Steffann does, so call him! That's right, any cooking, menu planning or general inquiries can be answered at Abiento. If he can't take your call right away, someone else will definitely be able to help. Remember to dial 818-449-4151 for all of your cooking

Nice idea. Will probably generate publicity as well.

A recent newsletter on special events not only lit up the phone but generated an $8500 catering job. "Needless to say, our newsletter has paid for itself many times over," Majcher surmises.

A free dessert and a chance to win a dinner-for-two are offered to recipients who correct mailing list errors or who inform Majcher they'd like to be removed from the list.

Our reaction: Unconventional size and heavy paper stock get this letter noticed in a crowded mail box. The caveat is "Does it fit the restaurant's personality?" In this case, absolutely.

Newsletter — Alban's Bottle & Basket

188-190 N. Hunter • Birmingham, MI 48009-5704 • 810-258-5788 • Fax 810-258-DANA
6535 Telegraph • Bloomfield Twp., MI 48031 • 810-646-6484

Vol. 10 Feb. - Apr. 1996

Chile... The Napa Valley of South America

Some say the key to business success is "location, location, location". This may be true for success in wine making, too; consider Chile.

Chile is blessed with ideal soil and terrain at an agreeable elevation for wine growing, all at a close proximity to the sea. This means we can have mountain grown fruit with strong coastal influence: drainage and soil content are excellent! The nights are cooling; and the vines get plenty of sun, but the grapes don't bake in low-land heat.

Since Chile imported French "know-how" and vine cutting some 140 years ago, the dominant players in her portfolio are familiar to most American wine drinkers. Cabernet Sauvignon and Franc, Merlot, Sauvignon Blanc & Chardonnay.

So consider Chile... a location that sends us the classic wines we favor, perfectly grown and well made. You'll be pleased to find the wines are undervalued, too!! Ask any of our experienced clerks at either the Telegraph or Hunter location.

Happy Hour at Alban's...

is Monday through Friday from 3 p.m. to 6 p.m.. Drinks can be enjoyed in either the bar or the lounge. **YOU can enjoy all well drinks for only $2.20 and Fosters and Killian beer can be found on tap and enjoyed for only $2.50 a pint. Along with these bargains you can also enjoy FREE BAR APPETIZERS.** Come join us and check out our great bartenders... LINDA, DAWN, JANE, ANDI, SARA, SALLY, ROB AND JEFF... You may even bump into a group of our regulars, Herb, Jack, Rick, George, Eddie, Laurel and Hardy. THEY REALLY ARE FUN FOLKS!!!

A Bit of Irish Luck... ☘ ☘

will shine down on you at **O'ALBAN'S**, the week of St. Patrick's, March 11th through the 17th. Enjoy our chef's Irish Pot Luck lunch and dinner specials!! Just a few of the things you will be able to find... Corned Beef and Cabbage, Lamb Stew, Oxtail Soup and much more. AND.... If you have an Irish dish you would like to see available during this time, **send us your recipe. We will select one and it will be featured that whole week.** In addition **the lucky winner will be invited for dinner** for himself and his guest and will be able to sample the recipe first hand. Send to: Irish Recipe, c/o Alban's, 190 North Hunter, Birmingham, Michigan 48009. Deadline for entry is March 4th, 1996.

Important Days to Remember

FEBRUARY
1-4	Winterfest
2	Groundhog Day
4	Bill B.'s Birthday
8	It's Charles' Birthday!
12	Happy Birthday, Abe!
13	Happy Birthday, Dwight!
14	Valentine's Day
19	President's Day
21	Ash Wednesday
22	Washington's Birthday

MARCH
17	St. Patrick's Day
20	Spring has Sprung
25	Happy Birthday, Wendi!
28	Birmingham Antique Fest
	Check out the Community House
31	Palm Sunday

APRIL
1	April Fool's Day
4	Passover
4	Pete T.'s Birthday
6	Good Friday
7	Easter Sunday
9	Tiger's Opening Home Game
13	Happy Birthday, Sue!
15	Pay Those Taxes!!
15	Holocaust Remembrance
22	Earth Day
25	Secretary's Day

Stuck in the office and your stomach is growling? Unexpected clients for lunch?? Too tired to cook dinner??? Did you know we Deliver????!!

Call us at
258-5555
or
Fax us at 258-DANA

Visit Our Gourmet Wine Shoppes

Alban's quarterly newsletter is different from almost every other restaurateur we talked to. The difference: Every issue is mailed to a different group of people. The theory: "We target zip codes by looking at the American Express Business Profile report which tells us where our current business is coming from," says Marjorie DeCapite, co-owner. "Then we try to hit those areas." Regular customers can still pick up the newsletters in the restaurant or, if they specifically request it, DeCapite adds them to the "Marjorie File" to receive all mailings.

DeCapite considers herself a newsletter afficionado, reading everything she can get her hands on: "I try to give customers information that they didn't know before or didn't think they needed to know. That's what builds and maintains loyalty and the reason people return."

German Wines...

are suitable for almost any occasion. If the wine is to be served with a meal, remember that the wine and food are partners, and as such, each should complement and enhance... not overpower... the other. In planning your meal, expect to pour about six half-filled glasses from each bottle.

Serve white ones chilled, rosé wines taste best a couple degrees warmer, and red wines should be served about room temperature. Served too cold, a wine looses its fragrance and taste.

When opening a bottle of wine, remove the lead capsule and wipe the rim... then remove the cork.

Pour the wine into a clear, stemmed glass with a tulip-shaped bowl. A glass which is somewhat tapered at the top helps contain the bouquet and allows the wine to be swirled in the glass easily. NEVER fill a glass more than half full at any time.

Party Time in the Lounge

Join Linda and Dawn on Wednesday, February 14th, from 11 a.m. for our annual **Valentine's party**. Good food, fun and prizes, too. Linda and Dawn promise a good time for all!!

We will begin our celebrations for St. Patrick's on the 15th of March, **but the official party is March 17th, Sunday.** Party time starts at Noon. Bring your blarney stone and receive a complimentary beverage. Don't forget to wear GREEN. We promise you'll enjoy food, fun and prizes. You can also join in singing along with our special balladeer. See you HERE!!!

Planning a Party???

Make it easy on yourself so you can enjoy every moment just like all the other people who are having fun. **We can provide you with many options. Our upstairs mezzanine can be rented in its entirety or you may choose to only use half of the area.** If you would prefer more privacy, we are able to utilize rooms at the Village Inn, which is just around the corner.

You can choose your entrees from our buffet menu or our regular lunch and dinner menu. Should you prefer something not there, count on our experienced chefs to prepare it for you. In addition we would be happy to set up an open bar or cash bar if that is your choosing. We want to make your life less complicated!! We're here to please YOU!! Contact any of the managers and we will be happy to finalize all your preparations.

Is it Whiskey or Whisky??

Like everything else in colonial times, the word whiskey was an import. Whiskey, with and 'e' is how the generic word is spelled when unconnected to a brand name. Most American and Irish distillers also use this spelling. BUT, in Kentucky (rebellious as ever)... with the exception of a handful of brands, Scottish and Canadian products are spelled without the 'e' as in whisky.

(Source: Whiskey, by Oscar Getz)

Potato Soup

Ingredients:
1–1/5 lb. Potatoes
1 Onion
1/2 lb. Bacon
1 Tbs. Chopped Parsley
2 Tbs. Chicken Bouillon Granules
1 Tsp. Thyme
Salt
Pepper
1 Tbs. Aromat
Garlic
2 Qts. Water
1 Pt. Milk
2 Tbs. Butter
4 Tbs. Instant Potatoes

Sauté onion with seasonings and half the bacon. Add potatoes, chicken bouillon granules and water. Cook until potatoes are tender. Thicken with instant potatoes. Cook remaining bacon on a sheet pan in oven and chop. Add to soup and also add parsley. Add milk gradually along with butter.

Are you this flexible in your party planning?

Famous Quotes

"The highest reward for a person's toil is not what they get for it, but what they become by it."
Author: John Ruskin

Trivia

How do the roots of Chile's vines differ from those of the Napa Valley???

For the answer, check with any of the clerks in either of our wine shop locations: Telegraph and Maple or Hunter and Maple.

POP QUIZ ANSWER: TRIPLED!

One of the most anxiously awaited features are the customer profiles. "They willingly reveal much more about themselves than I expected," says DeCapite. Other topics: community events, employee profiles and recipes.

Our reaction: Alban's includes both a restaurant and the "Bottle and Basket" gourmet wine shop, so its newsletter does double duty while keeping an upbeat, friendly tone and fostering a "small-town" feeling.

Central Florida
Six locations

Various seating
capacity

Tex-Mex in a lively,
eclectic setting

Nell Hyltin,
Co-owner

(407) 869-8008

Are you alert to
guests' nutritional
wants and needs?

VOL: 2   NO. 3
The Newsletter
Who Cares
JULY – SEPT 95

AMIGOS
◆ ORIGINAL TEX-MEX ◆

SUMMER LITES MENU

Received like a rich cousin

YUM, YUM!
We done good

Vege Fajitas, the Cancun Club and Andy's Big Enchilada are just a few of the new featured items at AMIGOS.

We've squeezed out the cholestrol without sacrificing the flavor. Most of the new items are low--to-no fat.

Vegetable Fajitas are marinated & steamed in fat-free ingredients and served with whole wheat tortillas.

Mom's one disappointment was the Vegetable Tamale. We have temporarily pulled it off of the menu because it just wasn't the best it could be. It WILL reappear on the menu along with additional surprises, just as soon as all the bugs are worked out! Oops, that doesn't sound good!

Our bar-b-que items are finding their way into many appreciative tummies. Bubba done good on that one - and so did Brian Reed, manager of our Winter Park and OBT locations.

ON THE LOOSE WITH TICKETS TO MEXICO are Shanda Carmickle and Greg Rickman - big winners in AMIGOS Cinco de Maya contest. In addition, they received 2 sombreros, 2 serapes, SPAM and enough BEANO to last the trip!

Greg and Shanda were at AMIGOS when The Big Enchilada left the good news on their recorder. Shanda retrieved the message while Greg, a detective, with the OC Sheriff's Office piddled in the car. Shanda screamed. Greg, thinking they had a burglar - went charging in with weapons drawn. We love it! Congratulations!

Black on various
earth-tone papers

5 1/2 x 8 1/2, self-mailer

4 pages

4 issues/year

7000 printed/
6000 mailed

Published since Jan 1994

"I write and type every word [on a typewriter] and take every picture," says matriarch and owner Nell Hyltin. She uses a Polaroid camera specially designed to take black-and-white photos suitable for publication. The only concession to technology are the few headlines stripped in by the printer.

The sizeable mailing list is plumped up each issue with hundreds of new names from "green cards" that guests complete in each restaurant. Hyltin uses a mail house to maintain the list. The service regularly checks for duplicates, but otherwise names are only deleted if a customer asks. The reason: If an addressee has moved, Hyltin is glad for the new resident to have her newsletter.

The newsletter doesn't usually divide its content by individual store location,

COOKBOOK SELLING FASTER THAN DOLLAR DIAMONDS

"If Ya Ain't A Little Fat, Ya Momma Didn't Love Ya", Tex-Mex Cookbook by AMIGO'S Momma Nell and illustrated by Jake Vest, syndicated cartoonist, is selling like mouth wash at a kissing convention.

Orders have poured in from 18 states, 3 foreign countries and 1 third world nation.

Cheap folks everywhere are catching onto this idea for gifts, etc. They are also fun to add to anyone's recipe collection.

Cookbooks are available at all AMIGOS locations for $9. or by mail order for $12.50 ea. We accept American Express, Visa and Master Card.

Call 689-8008

TEXAS CLUB TO HOST PARTY

TEXAS SHINDIG

The Texas Club of Central Florida is sponsoring a SHINDIG on Tuesday, April 9 from 6:30 - 9:30 p.m., in the Winter Park AMIGOS.

Texas Independence And Cinco de Mayo will be celebrated - one early and one late - still a fun gathering.

Happy hour prices will be available on drinks and a light buffet will be served. Drawings will complete the evenings festivities. $3. per person.

Texans, guest, friends and the curious are urged to attend. Please come and help support the efforts of the Texas Club.

Have you thought of doing your own?

WHILE STIRRING THE BEANS, I WAS THINKING... We're entering our 3rd year of publication - continuing our standards in writing void of journalism excellence! Spice up your life - have something new to talk about, add to your world of information by receiving the BEANO BULLETIN (for free subscription call 1-800-257-8650). It's always good to stay informed. The LUCKENBACH MOON is another source of meaningful thought - available for $15 yearly. Call 210-997-3224... So much for reading assignments! Recipe contests everywhere with the surge in popularity for tortillas, salsas, etc. They're grabbing at everything you can think of - it's a hot market.... New on Texas Top 10: When you leave Amarillo turn out the lights; I only feel at home when I'm gone; Don't cry down my back, Baby, you're rusting my spurs! Definition of health terms: CARDIOLOGIST - a dealer in Vegas; PELVIS - a cousin of Elvis; ORGANIC - musical; D & C - where Clinton lives... Bring your ladies hats to Altamonte and trade for food (No, Not your ladies, their Hats!).. Stefan will make you an offer you can't refuse.....

Alerting guests to other worthwhile publications gives you more credibility.

---

but if business is off in a certain restaurant, a 2-for-1 or other promotion is used effectively to boost business there.

When asked where she gets her ideas, Hyltin chuckles, "I'm nutty. I just think of things that have happened to me or things that bother me."

Her advice to others: "Keep it fun, light and simple and don't take yourself too seriously. Try to bring some love and some warmth into your customers' lives."

Our reaction: Typewriter typeface and hand-drawn illustrations give this letter its personality. Even though the chain now has six locations, the owners haven't lost their folksiness or Texas-sized sense of humor.

New York City

170 seats

Elegant townhouse setting, updated Scandinavian cuisine

Marie Barnevik, Dir. of Mktg.

(212) 957-9045

Third party endorsements are always reassuring.

AQUAVIT

Restaurant Aquavit of New York, 13 West 54th Street, New York, NY 10019 Tel. (212) 307-7311   Winter 1995

Celebrating St. Lucia

St. Lucia

Dear Friends,

On September 29th, we were awarded three stars by The New York Times. In case you missed Ruth Reichl's review, we've reprinted it here for you...

Aquavit ushers in the holiday season with a special celebration of St. Lucia. . . at the restaurant and also at the venerable James Beard House...

To toast the Holiday Season, we share a simple recipe with you... traditional Swedish Glögg... perfect to share with family and friends stopping by for a holiday cheer...

Aquavit and Finnair has a gift for you!!! December 11-16, we're giving away five round-trip business class tickets to Scandinavia...

Plan to join us for the Joseph Phelps Insignia five-course wine tasting dinner, on January 22...

We invite you to join us with family and friends as we celebrate the holiday season at Aquavit.

Happy Holidays

Håkan Swahn

Håkan Swahn

Italians who happen to be in Sweden on December 13th are always surprised at the enthusiasm with which the Lutheran Swedes celebrate the Sicilian St. Lucia, who receives no such attention in her native country. In fact, all she has in common with her Italian namesake is the name.

As part of the celebration local newspapers organize a "Lucia competition". That is, the readers select one of a number of girls from photographs (long, preferably blond hair is often one of the main qualifications!). The chosen one, wearing a white gown with a red ribbon round her waist and a head wreath with candles, becomes the star of the Lucia procession. Her attendants are the other competitors, and together they sing the traditional Lucia song while walking with their hands devoutly pressed together in front of them.

Lucia is also celebrated in homes across Sweden, where the youngest girl takes the part of Lucia and the parents are awakened at dawn, by the strains of the children singing the Lucia song and a tray of warm "Lucia cats". (Saffron buns)

What were the origins of this peculiar festival in the winter darkness? It has nothing to do with the Italian saint. Strange as it may seem, Lucia is a manifestation of quite a different medieval saint, Nicholas.

When the Reformation came to Northern Europe, the adoration of saints was prohibited, but some of them, and especially Nicholas, the generous patron saint of schoolchildren, were not easy to do without.

So the Germans replaced the bearded saint with the Christ child and moved the distribution of gifts from St. Nicholas day, on December 6th, to Christmas Eve.

During the 17th and 18th centuries the Christ child, represented by a girl dressed in a white linen tunic and with candle wreath in her hair, played this part in Germany and German-influenced circles in Sweden.

But in Sweden it failed to take root as a part of Christmas celebrations and was transferred to Lucia Day, because early that morning it had been the custom of the Swedes, ever since medieval times, to eat and drink to prepare themselves for the Christmas fast, which began at sunrise on the morning of December 13th.

In the manor houses of Western Sweden during the 18th century, the German Christ child was transformed into a kind of hostess of these festivities. She then assumed the present-day saint's name, but it was not until the end of the 19th century that Lucia became known elsewhere in Sweden. Stockholm held its first Lucia procession in 1927.

If you have ever visited Aquavit on the St. Lucia day in past years, you might have been caroled by the Lucia procession during dinner.

We will also present a dinner at the James Beard House on December 13th. For more information please call (212) 627-2308. Proceeds go to the James Beard Foundation.

Burgundy copy on buff-colored paper

8 1/2 x 11

4 pages

4 issues/year

10,000 printed

Published since early 1995

"We'd been talking about doing a newsletter for years—but not getting it done," says Marie Barnevik, director of marketing. "Until finally I went out and bought the software, wrote a sample newsletter and took it to the owner." That was an inauspicious beginning, but it now enjoys the owner's full support and backing.

"The key is removing yourself from this situation that you know so intimately," believes Barnevik. "You have to put yourself in the place of your customers. What do they want?"

Each issue of the newsletter carries a contest for a dinner for four. A quiz asks simple questions that can all be answered by reading the newsletter. "We want to keep it accessible," remarks Barnevik. Other regular features: Upcoming wine and aquavit tastings, Scandinavian folklore

Glögg

Swedes traditionally serve Glögg on Christmas Eve and St. Lucia. It's a hot drink that warms during the coldest of Northern nights. Recipe ingredients for glögg vary widely. Most call for red wine some for vodka and include a range of spices. Here our chef shares his own secret recipe. This recipe can be adapted to suit your own taste.

1/2 bottle vodka
1/2 bottle red wine (or non alcoholic)
seed of 10 cardamom pods
6 cloves
peel of an orange
1 stick cinnamon
1/2 cups raisins
1 cup caster sugar
1 cup blanched almonds

Place everything except the almonds in a bowl, stir well, cover and let stand for 12 hours. Heat gently, stirring to melt the sugar, without bringing to boil. Add the almonds and serve warm in small cups or punch glasses.

Gunilla von Arbin and Martin Shapiro at the AIWF dinner

Did you miss...

American Institute of Wine and Food...
On October 2, the AIWF kicked off their 1995 Fall Game Dinner series, at Aquavit. Guests included AIWF Chairwoman Anna Herman, Co-chair Martin Shapiro, Swedish Consul General Dag Sebastian Ahlander and his wife Gunilla von Arbin. The evening was sponsored by D'Artagnan and Guenoc Wines.

Baking the Daily Bread...
The kitchen at Aquavit is turning out a moist Lingonberry Bread. The small, tart berry gives the bread a slight pink color.

Aquavit Cooks at IKEA...
More than 4,000 people sampled the Gravlax chef Marcus Samuelsson prepared during the opening three days of IKEA's new store at East 57th Street in Manhattan.

Cooks For Kids...
Chef Samuelsson took part in a cast of celebrity chefs and newscasters on November 13th to benefit The Children's Friends for Life Foundation. Daniel, Oceana, Nobu, Sarabeth's and Union Square Cafe were some other great restaurants that dished up delicacies.

Desire Lundh and Kristin Nyström baking Lingonberry bread at Aquavit

> Seasonal recipes are especially popular for entertaining.

Joseph Phelps Wines

The term "innovative" is often used to describe Joseph Phelps.

Since establishing his first vineyard in Napa Valley in 1972, Joseph Phelps has not only been a leader in proprietary wine production in the U.S., but also a pioneer in bottling grape varietals native to France's Rhône River Valley.

Affectionately dubbed the "Rhône Rangers," Phelps, along with winemakers Bob Lindquist and Randall Graham of Bonny Doon, began to plant not only Syrah, but other Rhône varietals.

Today the winery features a full line of Rhône-styled wines under the Vin du Mistral label, as well as his award winning Insignia.

Join us and marketing director Angelo Brutico on January 22, to celebrate ten years of winemaking excellence.

Call us at (212) 307-7311 to reserve a table.

Win a FINNAIR Business Class Trip to Scandinavia!

Just answer the questions below correctly and you'll be eligible for the drawing on March 1, 1996.

Drop entry off during your next visit or mail to: Aquavit 13 West 54th Street, New York, NY 10019

Which country is home to Finnair? _____

Which medieval saint is the origin of St. Lucia celebration?_____

How many stars did Aquavit receive from The New York Times in September? _____

Name _____

Street _____

City _____ State_____ Zip_____

Telephone _____

> Good example of creative partnerships that add value to both businesses.

---

and culture and a calendar of events.

Aquavit's list has grown from 2000 a year ago to around 15,000 and now occupies one-quarter of their advertising budget. The names come from monthly business card drawings for a lunch for two. Newsletters are also on display near the hostess stand; she offers a copy to guests while they wait for their tables and asks them if they'd like to receive it regularly.

Our reaction: We're glad that the Aquavit newsletter has resisted the glossy, glamorous and yes, impersonal makeovers that tempt upscale restaurants. It's professional, yet comfortable, just like the restaurant.

Two phone lines make
reservations and ordering-
in more efficient.

60th Anniversary Issue!

Food FOR THOUGHT

Holiday Reminders
Closed 4th of July
Closed Labor Day

60 Years of Classic Italian Cuisine

(or ... Who's Celebration is it Anyway?)

60 years in business - it's hard to believe. Does that make it an anniversary or a birthday? In any case it's certainly cause for celebration!

And yet it's strange how we celebrate the major milestones in our lives. Our friends bring **us** presents on **our** birthday. Well wishers bring tribute **to** the celebrants of an anniversary. It seems to me things should be the other way around.

We ought to be grateful to others for the milestones in

our lives. After all, our triumphs, our achievements, our joys are not ours alone, but to be shared by those who have contributed to our lives.

So what's all this mean to **you**? It means that as we celebrate our 60th year in business and three generations of family ownership that I would like to give something back. To return the favor, if you will, to all those who have made our success possible.

On March 25, we had a book signing and four-course dinner "extraordinare"

created in this unique spirit of celebration. This is only the kick off of a year of special events, special values and special features.

Throughout this newsletter you'll find more on the many things we have planned for the year. This is **our** way of saying thanks to **you**, our loyal customers and good friends, for 60 spectacular years of business.

My sincere gratitude and many thanks,

Sam Bacco

Sam Bacco

Reservation Hotlines
Pizza and Orders To Go
- 755-1173
Dinner Reservations -
755-0635

BACCO'S
RESTAURANT

Twelve-Hundred Thirty Thomaston Avenue, Waterbury, Connecticut

Generating new business and reinforcing the loyalty of established clientele was the goal of starting the newsletter "Food for Thought" eight years ago, says owner Sam Bacco, and it's definitely paid off for his namesake restaurant. "It's been a great way to keep our name in customers' minds and motivates them to come back. Plus patrons like the variety of information it provides."

Everyone on the 2500-name mailing list—periodically updated and maintained at the restaurant—receives the four-page newsletter, which contains features on the staff, nutrition information on signature dishes, seasonal menu highlights, special recipes and often a coupon to dinner at Bacco's. With the help of a public relations agency, Bacco creates the list of topics to be covered. After jointly writing the

DOTTING THE "I's" AND CROSSING THE "TEA's"...

is a phrase normally reserved for the process of making sure all the details are attended to. When it comes to something as simple as a cup of tea, Bacco's takes details to unprecedented heights:

• Our Tea is imported in bulk from England and packaged for distribution in Conn. by Harney & Sons Ltd.

• This custom blend is all natural, contains no fillers and is available as either naturally decaffeinated or regular brew.

• This extraordinary beverage is custom "brewed" just for you.

We take this much trouble with a cup of tea because that's just the way we treat **everything** at Bacco's.

TAKE A BITE OUT OF PRIME!

Juicy, delicious U.S.D.A. Prime Rib of Beef ... served just the way you like it. It's Bacco's new **Saturday Night Special**. Thick and delicious, our Prime Rib is served with a hot oven popover, salad and your choice of vegetable or potato. But remember it's Saturday night only and quantities are limited ... so come early.

"Classic Italian Cuisine Since 1931"
1230 Thomaston Avenue Waterbury 755-1173

BACCO'S RESTAURANT

OUR STAMP OF APPROVAL

They're sizzling hot and an overwhelming success.

For over a month, we've been featuring our char-grilled specialties in a special drop-in menu insert.

Your response has been fantastic. Although our char-grill was installed over a year ago, it has taken some time to fine tune all the ingredients necessary to create these superb features. We now have steaks and chops from the area's finest purveyors, cut thick, juicy and grilled to perfection. Some of our features include Loin Lamb Chops for $13.95, Thick Center Cut PorkChops for

$11.95, T-Bone Steak (14-16 oz.) for $15.95 (with or without sizzling butter), all served with baked potato, vegetable or pasta and salad with choice of dressing.

Now it's time to go public. We've created a distinctive new char-grilled "Stamp of Approval" that will be featured on our menu, menu inserts and advertising. We'll be offering unique and special features from time to time. If char-grilled is your thing, look for our "Stamp of Approval".

WHAT'S YOUR BEEF?

It seems that over the past few years beef has received a bad rap. In fact, when it comes to the nutritional advice on beef you've been given a bum steer. Here's the facts:

• **Beef** - America's favorite entree according to a recent Gallup Poll.
• **Beef** - Rich in nutrients, high in protein, zinc, iron and niacin.
• **Beef** - 3 oz. only 76 milligrams of cholesterol.
• **Beef** - A 10 oz. serving has only 222 calories.
• **Beef** - The only meat graded by the U.S. Government.
• **Beef** - In moderation (as should be the case with all things) is good for you.

Creating a logo builds business by menu category.

---

stories, the agency puts the newsletter together. Bacco brings it to a mailing house with labels, and it's mailed to patrons first class.

Bacco measures the newsletter's success by increased traffic counts and customer feedback: "They always come in and offer comments on what they've read. The updates on the restaurant, whether it's food

information or the news on a recent remodeling, gives them something to talk about, and they enjoy feeling like they're a part of the operation."

Our reaction: We'd like to see "Food for Thought" published with more regularity to build a reading habit. While cost may be a consideration, even a one-page, one-color version between more heavily produced issues lets guests know you're thinking about them.

New Orleans

220 seats

Eclectic Continental
cuisine in fine-dining
setting

Karen Pfeiffer,
Co-owner

(504) 529-1583

Food education
always leads to a greater
appreciation of the
job you do.

LUNAR NOTES

A Quarterly Publication of Bella Luna Restaurant   Vol. 3.2 / April 1996

A Message From Karen & Horst!

There's so much to look forward to at Bella Luna this spring and, looking ahead to summer, we're not slowing down!

We've been gratified by your enthusiasm for our special tastings, cooking classes, and guest chefs, and we plan to keep offering fresh and exciting events throughout the year! Several events are highlighted in this issue of Lunar Notes, and you can expect to hear about more in our next issue.

Don't miss our May lawn and tea party at Ursuline Convent ... we can't think of a more appropriate way to benefit this important historic landmark than to host this special event. Delicious food and drink, the music of a string quartet, croquet and badminton are just some of the features planned for this lazy spring afternoon. Chef Horst's herb garden will be at its best, and you can expect to find his herbs in some of the delicacies that he'll be serving!

And, because events with an emphasis on education have been our most popular, we're excited to premier our new program "Behind the Scenes at Bella Luna." Each month, we'll spend a Saturday

morning over coffee and pastries with a local grower or supplier. We've lined up experts on mushrooms, local cheeses, herbs, seafood and more for informal discussions on specific products, nutrition, cooking, the restaurant business and whatever else is on your mind! We hope that you'll take advantage of this free program, and come with questions for our experts.

As always, we value your input. Let us know which programs are important to you, and we welcome your suggestions for new programs as well!

We'll look forward to seeing you in the coming months, and our best wishes for a healthy, happy and delicious spring!

From Medicine to Entrees!

As you walk through the Porter's Lodge off Chartres Street and onto the grounds of Ursuline Convent, you are greeted by a majestic building which stands behind a formal garden of geometrical hedges. After you enter the old building, a long hallway leads you to an even more tranquil garden in back. This is the same garden where the Ursuline Nuns planted their herbs and flowers, where Sister Francis Xavier grew her medicines and pharmaceuticals, and where Chef Pfeifer picks herbs for his delicious dishes.

Ursuline Convent was built in 1745 at the request of King Louis XV of France. Our Lady of Victory Church was added 100

years later. The Convent itself is the oldest building in the Mississippi Valley—25 years older than the United States but 25 years younger than the City of New Orleans, and the only structure to survive the French Colonial period.

After the Ursuline Nuns, who were named after Saint Ursula, were sent from France to New Orleans, they started the first free school for girls, orphanage, and nursery. As the needs of the people changed, so did the duties of the nuns. When the French Revolution broke out, the Ursulines worked as nurses to help heal the wounded with their medicinal herbs. Sister Francis Xavier, one of the original 12 Ursulines and the first woman pharmacist in the New World, started the herb garden for such purposes.

It is not surprising that the herb garden still has a large impact on the Convent. At one point in time, herbs played such an important part in the church that they were used during ceremonies and rituals. For instance, brushes made of rue were used for sprinkling holy water during high mass. The garden's tradition has continued since the days of its medicinal use...now, Chef Pfeifer enjoys the same tranquility that was once shared by the Ursuline Nuns. And rumor has it that Monsignor O'Reilly "borrows" from the garden now and again!

Come and see the convent and enjoy the garden yourself. Tours are Tuesday through Friday every hour from 10:00 till 3:00; Saturday and Sunday at 11:15, 1:00, and 2:00. *Adults: $4.00, Seniors and Students: $2.00, and children: free.*

Black on various
brightly-colored papers

8 1/2 x 11

4 pages

4 issues/year

2500 printed/
2200 mailed

Published since 1/94

"Our customers tend to be sophisticated diners and want to learn about food and wine," says co-owner Karen Pfeiffer, "so you'll see articles about exotic caviars or truffles or herbs that we introduce in our cooking."

The owners are justifiably proud of understanding customer interests and maintaining a diverse mix of articles. Regular features include: "Did You

Know?" trivia for foodies and otherwise; "A Message from Karen and Horst," "Calendar of Events" and "Octavio Recommends," their sommelier's recommendations. "Look at the newsletters and magazines you like to read for inspiration," recommends Pfeiffer.

This is truly an inside job. Pfeiffer writes and designs her letter on a PC running Microsoft Publisher. Then it's

20

The Perfect Summer Picnic

With some of the most beautiful parks anywhere in the country, New Orleans offers a plentitude of romantic spots for a perfect summer picnic — Audubon Park, City Park, the Lakefront, the Fly and Woldenberg Park just to name a few. If you're on the North Shore, check out the park next to the old Abita Springs Brewery.

Once you've decided where to venture to on your next outing, you'll be looking for some special goodies to fill your basket. To offer some exciting ideas, Chef Pfeifer put together his version of the perfect picnic menu. Enjoy!

Sun-brewed Liberty tea* with mint tea-sickles*

Sourdough baguettes with yellow sun-dried tomato pesto*

Grilled polenta* with baby lettuces, marinated olives* and balsamic vinaigrette*

Rack of Sonoma lamb in a mustard-herb crust* with Mediterranean rice*, orange-onion marmalade and a cracked pepper sauce

Assorted fresh fruits

* Indicates products available at Bella Luna's Pasta Shoppe, Gourmet Kitchenware and Food Boutique: Eastern Shore Tea Company Liberty tea blend; Kennedy Gourmet tea-sickles; Fox's Fine Foods yellow sun-dried tomato pesto; Cucina Sorrentis porcini mushroom polenta; California Harvest black olive tapenade; Rustichella D'Abruzzo balsamic vinegar; Nantucket Off-shore Seasonings — Mt. Olympus rub; and Kitchen Del Sol tomato basil Mediterranean Rice.

Of course, most of this can (and should) be prepared in advance. You will need to bring a grill to finish off the lamb for the best results.

(see "Picnic" page 4)

Bella Luna Calendar of Events

Tuesday, July 4 — Independence Day: Happy Fourth of July ... enjoy your holiday!

Tuesday, July 18
Wed., July 19
10:00 a.m. - 2:00 p.m.

Cooking Camp for Kids: Executive Chef Horst Pfeifer shares his culinary skills with children between the ages of 8 -13 years during this two-day cooking camp. Items to be prepared include: pasta, lasagna, breads, grilled vegetable salad, fish, desserts and more. Cost is $100 per person and includes lunch both days. Call Kate Eddington for reservations at 529-1583.

Sunday, July 23 — Bella Luna Closed for Renovations: The restaurant will be closed from Sunday, July 23, until Monday, August 7, when it will re-open for regular business. Sorry for any inconvenience this may cause; thanks for understanding!

Tuesday, Sept. 12
Wed., Sept. 13
10:00 a.m. - 2:00 p.m.

Cooking Class: Step-by-step demonstration in the kitchen with Chef Pfeifer. Menu will include: blackened shrimp salad; penne pasta with roasted chicken and profiterole with ice cream and chocolate sauce. Cost is $45 per person (includes lunch served with wine). Call Kate Eddington for reservations at 529-1583.

Sunday, Sept. 24
11:00 a.m. - 2:00 p.m.

NOCCA Fundraiser: Bella Luna will be the corporate sponsor of a fundraising event for the New Orleans Center for Creative Arts. The event's theme is "Sunday by the River: A Venetian Brunch." For tickets, call Martha McKnight with Friends of NOCCA at 523-7708. All proceeds benefit NOCCA's new building fund.

One more way to keep your kitchen busy during off-peak times.

Good cross-selling retail.

duplicated on 11" x 17" colored paper using a high-speed copy machine, folded and mailed with help from the staff.

"Traditional advertising scares me a little," admits Pfeiffer. "You never know quite how effective it is. With the newsletter, we know the same day it drops and for the next two weeks after." The ultimate compliment she gets is customers telling her that they hold on to past issues.

Our reaction: There's so much to recommend about this newsletter. From the gracious tone to well-researched articles and wide variety of topics, the owners' celebration of food draws readers in.

Bluebird Cafe News * April 1996

APRIL BLURBS

APR 1, 8, 15, 22, 29 **The Bluebloods w/** Mike Henderson, Michael Rhodes, Reese Wynans & John Gardner-Glen is out on the road with Mark Knopfler, so the mighty Michael Rhodes is filling in mightily. This month you have five chances to get your weekly dose of the blues.

APR 2 **Larry Jon Wilson** returns to Nashville with his incomparable tales and tunes. He's one of our favorite troubadours. See him and you'll agree.

APR 3 **Hugh Moffatt & Eric Taylor-** And speaking of troubadours. Here's another pair we're partial to. Moffatt wrote the classic *Old Flames Can't Hold A Candle To You* and continues to tour the globe delighting audiences. Taylor's tunes have been covered by many including Nanci Griffith's great *Deadwood, South Dakota* .

APR 4 **The Chili Shack** is back with special guests Deborah Allen *Baby I Lied*, Fred Knobloch *Back In Your Arms Again*, Dena Michelle & Shane Caldwell. They'll be joining the usual casts of crazies for another night of gastric and musical fun.

APR 5 **Baillie & The Boys** are back too. If you missed them last month you missed a treat. Don't make that mistake again. It's good to see them back in action and back at the Bird. Look for a new album soon.

APR 6 **Phillybilly** is Rich Fagan, Kasey Jones and Joe Collins. And they are a whole lot of music and fun. Fagan has hit the charts most recently with *Sold (The Grundy County Auction)* and shows no signs of letting up. It's always a belly full of laughs so make plans to be here.

APR 7 Sunday writers showcase with special guest Jess Leary, *Mi Vida Loca*; *Ready, Willing & Able*.

APR 9 **D4A$-** A special evening with Don Schlitz-Don came roaring back into action last month with one of his best shows ever. There were new tunes, new guitars and new guests. Same old jokes though. But hey, 3 out of 4 ain't bad. Gather up that loose change.

APR 10 **Bernie Nelson, Craig Wiseman, Kent Blazy & Dave Gibson** ITR- It's another of our "real men" in the round. Real men with real hits. Hits like *If Tomorrow Never Comes, Cadillac Kind, Bubba Hyde* and so many more.

APR 11 **Jim Photoglo Band-** Photoglo puts the band back together and it's about time. From *We Were Meant To Be Lovers* to *Fishing In The Dark* , Jim is always entertaining.

APR 12 **Fred Knobloch, Thom Schuyler, Tony Arata & more** ITR- Yowza! Don't get much better than this. Even with a Lowenbrau. *The Dance, The Change, Back In My Arms Again, Sixteenth Avenue, Why Not Me, Old Yellow Car* ... those are just a quick sample of the hits these guys have penned.

APR 13 **Gerry House, Paul Jefferson, Keith Urban & Beth Nielsen Chapman** ITR- Here's a new group. Everyone's favorite DJ and jokester, Gerry House *The*

River and The Highway makes a rare and welcome appearance. Chapman, Urban and Jefferson all have new albums in the works and we can hardly wait. This will be a night of new country, folk and pop.

APR 14 Sunday writers showcase with special guest Becky Hobbs *Rub -A -Dubbin'*.

APR 16 **Dar Williams** is the hottest new talent in the folk and acoustic world. Folks like Joan Baez are singing her tunes and singing her praises. You will too. Get her first Razor and Tie release, The Honesty Room, and look for her brand new release, too.

APR 17 **Tin Pan South** is Nashville's city-wide celebration of our greatest asset, songwriters. All over town clubs will be packed with the best of the best. Naturally, scientific studies have shown time and time again that the Bluebird is the very best place to experience such festivities. Tonight kicks off with **Rich Fagan, Paul Craft, Kim Williams & Michael Smotherman** at 6:45. They'll be followed by **Bob DiPiero, John Scott Sherrill, Karen Staley & Jon Ims** at 9:45. Tin Pan South tickets are available through Ticketmaster 737-4849.

APR 18 **Tin Pan South** continues. At 6:45 we have **Skip Ewing, Don Sampson, Phil Vesser & Tim Rushlow.** At 9:30, it's **John Jarrard, Ronnie Rogers, Mickey Cates, Teddy Gentry & Randy Owen.**

APR 19 **Tin Pan South:** **Randy Van Warmer, Pat Terry, Brett Cartwright & Parker McGee,** 6:45. **Hugh Prestwood, Gary Burr, Michael Johnson & Julie Gold** at 9:30.

APR 20 **Tin Pan South** wraps up just as hot as it started. At 6:45 it's **Kim Carnes, Vince Melamed, Gary Harrison & Shane Teeter.** Then it's **Matraca Berg, Tim Mensy, Jim Photoglo, Christy Seamans** to close it out at 9:30.

APR 21 Sunday writers showcase with special guest **Steve Seskin** *I Think About You.*

APR 23 **Jaime Kyle & Friends** ITR- Kyle has penned hits like *Stranded* and *Wild One* for Heart and Faith Hill respectively. she also released her own album a couple of years ago. She'll be accompanied by Gary Harrison, Keith Stegall & D Vincent Williams. Stout crew.

APR 24 **Steve Seskin, Dana Cooper, Craig Carothers & Don Henry-** Seskin, *Wrong , For A Change* returns to the Bird and this time he's bringing some writers a little left of the usual Music Row folks. Cooper is a Nashville and folk staple. Sharp writing and passionate performances are his trademark. Carothers hails from Washington state and is one of Blurbman's favorite new writers of the decade. It's just great to have Don Henry back again, too.

APR 25 **R.B. Morris Band-** Morris is also one of Blurbman's favorite new discoveries of the last year or so. Lots of other folks feel the same. The man is a poet, a playwright, a songwriter and singer of rare vision. Get acquainted with him.

APR 26 **The Alex Harvey Band** heats up another Friday night for us. Harvey has just launched a new label, Laureate Records, and we're knocking on wood. And thanking our stars he still finds the time to do

the do for all the dudes and dudettes at the Bird. The man who brought us *Somebody New, Delta Dawn, Reuben James* , and *Rings* is still cranking them out. Brandon Harvey opens.

APR 27 **Chuck Jones, Chuck Cannon & more-** Chuck and Chuck will no doubt have some more great names and talents joining them for this show. *I Love The Way You Love Me* and *Whisper My Name* are a couple of chart toppers from the Chucks. Give us a call or check your papers.

APR 28 Sunday writers showcase with special guest **Alex Harvey,** *Somebody New, Delta Dawn, Reuben James.*

APR 30 **April Barrows Band-** Barrows has just released a brand new album full of her lush ballads and sophisticated swing. It's the next best thing to seeing her live. We suggest you do both.

Amy's sidebars add personality to calendar style.

Reminder of profitable catered events.

Although Bluebird Cafe News is not a conventional newsletter, its success is exceptional. "When we started sending out a calendar, we were the only ones doing it," remembers Amy Kurland, owner. "Now there are at least four other music clubs in town doing the same thing."

Bluebird's mailing list numbers around 10,000 names, however Kurland never mails to the entire list at once. Locals receive it monthly, while those outside the Southeast every other month, unless they send stamped, self-addressed envelopes. "It entices local customers, and is a reminder to those outside of the area. The list had humble beginnings—a drawing to win a Walkman—but its recent expansion includes 2000 names obtained from Bluebird's Worldwide Web site (http://www.hidwater.com/bluebird/).

22

APRIL 1996 AT The Bluebird Cafe

Sunday	Monday	Tuesday	Wednesday	Thursday	Friday	Saturday
OUR INTERNET ADDRESS: HTTP://WWW.HIDWATER.COM/BLUEBIRD/ WE'RE ALSO AT BLUEBRDCAF@AOL.COM (FOR TRIVIAL MATTERS ONLY, PLEASE!) ITR MEANS IN THE ROUND: ALWAYS A GREAT EVENING WITH GREAT SONGWRITERS AT THE BLUEBIRD.	6:00 OPEN MIC HOSTED BY BARBARA CLOYD · 9:30 THE BLUEBLOODS W/MIKE HENDERSON, MICHAEL RHODES, REESE WYNANS & JOHN GARDNER — **1**	6:00 COMMUNITY SHARES 10TH ANNIVERSARY FUNDRAISER DINNER TRACY NELSON & BAND TICKETS: 227-7500 · 9:30 LARRY JON WILSON — **2**	6:00 CLAY DAVIDSON 6:45 JEFF WOOD 7:15 KATHY HUSSEY 7:45 DEBI CHAMPION 8:15 ROY HURD · 9:30 HUGH MOFFATT & ERIC TAYLOR — **3**	6:45 REBECCA MAGNUSON 7:15 GARRISON WHITE 7:45 PAULA HAWLEY 8:15 LORIN BRISTOW · 9:30 THE CHILI SHACK SHOW WITH GUESTS DEBORAH ALLEN DENA MICHELLE SHANE CALDWELL & FRED KNOBLOCH — **4**	6:45 ROGER DAY 7:25 JOHN ENGLANDER 8:05 DANNY DARST · 9:30 BAILLIE AND THE BOYS — **5**	6:45 STEVE KEY 7:25 DAVE MACKENZIE 8:05 MICHAEL KELSH · 9:30 PHILLYBILLY — **6**
6:30 SPOTLIGHT MARK IRWIN BAND · 8:00 WRITERS NIGHT WITH GUEST JESS LEARY — **7**	6:00 OPEN MIC HOSTED BY BARBARA CLOYD · 9:30 THE BLUEBLOODS W/MIKE HENDERSON, MICHAEL RHODES, REESE WYNANS & JOHN GARDNER — **8**	6:45 TNN COUNTRY NEWS TV TAPING: TIM NORTON, LINDY GRAVELLE, POUND LAMB, GENE COOK & RON BELL 7:45 EMILY KAITZ 8:05 TRAILOR PARK TROUBADORS · 9:30 D4A$ A SPECIAL EVENING WITH DON SCHLITZ — **9**	6:45 ITR JOHN ROSE, CAROL ANN BROWN, JILL RILEY & KIM LOE · 9:30 ITR BERNIE NELSON, CRAIG WISEMAN, KENT BLAZY & DAVE GIBSON — **10**	6:30 WRITER SPOTLITE: ALISA CARROLL, BRENDA K. RUSSELL, SHARON CORT, LAINE MARSH, SOUTHERN HEART, SHELLY BUSH & ESSRA MOHAWK · 9:30 JIM PHOTOGLO AND BAND — **11**	6:45 ITR ACE FORD, SUSAN DUFFY, LESLIE SATCHER & TROY JONES · 9:30 ITR THOM SCHUYLER FRED KNOBLOCH TONY ARATA & FRIEND — **12**	6:45 ITR MICHAEL LILLE, HENRY HIPKINS, NORMAN HARRELL & JOHN MCVEY · 9:30 ITR GERRY HOUSE PAUL JEFFERSON KEITH URBAN & BETH NIELSEN CHAPMAN — **13**
6:30 SPOTLIGHT JIM INFANTINO · 8:00 WRITERS NIGHT WITH GUEST BECKY HOBBS — **14**	6:00 OPEN MIC HOSTED BY BARBARA CLOYD · 9:30 THE BLUEBLOODS W/MIKE HENDERSON, MICHAEL RHODES, REESE WYNANS & JOHN GARDNER — **15**	6:45 ALEX FORBES 7:15 JOE BIDEWELL 7:45 MATTHEW KAHLER 8:15 TOM GUARDINO · 9:30 RAZOR AND TIE ARTIST DAR WILLIAMS TICKET: 291-5000 — **16**	6:45 Tin Pan South * ITR RICH FAGAN, KIM WILLIAMS, PAUL CRAFT, MICHAEL SMOTHERMAN · 9:30 Tin Pan South * ITR BOB DiPIERO JOHN SCOTT SHERILL KAREN STALEY & JON IMS — **17**	6:45 Tin Pan South* ITR SKIP EWING, DON SAMPSON, PHIL VESSER, TIM RUSHLOW · 9:30 Tin Pan South* ITR JOHN JARRARD, RONNIE ROGERS, MICKEY CATES, TEDDY GENTRY & RANDY OWEN — **18**	6:45 Tin Pan South* ITR RANDY VAN WARMER, BRETT CARTWRIGHT, PAT TERRY & PARKER MCGEE · 9:30 Tin Pan South* ITR HUGH PRESTWOOD GARY BURR MICHAEL JOHNSON & JULIE GOLD — **19**	6:45 Tin Pan South* ITR KIM CARNES, VINCE MELAMED, GARY HARRISON & SHANE TEETERS · 9:30 Tin Pan South* ITR MATRACA BERG TIM MENSY JIM PHOTOGLO & CHRISTY SEAMANS — **20**
6:30 SPOTLIGHT SUZANNE BURNETTE BAND · 8:00 WRITERS NIGHT WITH GUEST STEVE SESKIN — **21**	6:00 OPEN MIC HOSTED BY BARBARA CLOYD · 9:30 THE BLUEBLOODS W/MIKE HENDERSON, MICHAEL RHODES, REESE WYNANS & JOHN GARDNER — **22**	6:45 ITR SALLY BARRIS, LESLIE TUCKER, PIERCE PETTIS & TOM KIMMEL · 9:30 ITR JAIME KYLE, GARY HARRISON KEITH STEGALL & D VINCENT WILLIAMS — **23**	6:45 ITR GREG CROW, JOHN FOUNTAIN, KEN FORSYTHE & BARBARA CLOYD · 9:30 ITR STEVE SESKIN DANA COOPER CRAIG CAROTHERS & DON HENRY — **24**	CLOSED UNTIL 9 PM FOR A PRIVATE EVENT · 9:30 R. B. MORRIS BAND — **25**	6:45 ADIE GREY 7:25 RICK GORDON 8:05 LISA KEITH & SPENCER BERNARD · 9:30 BRANDON HARVEY OPENS FOR ALEX HARVEY BAND — **26**	6:45 TEXAS ITR CHRIS PERTITTA, STEVE HOOD, DEANNA BRYANT & RONNIE GARRETT · 9:30 ITR CHUCK CANNON CHUCK JONES & COHORTS — **27**
6:30 SPOTLIGHT CLIFF GOLDMACHER · 8:00 — **28**	6:00 OPEN MIC HOSTED BY BARBARA CLOYD · 9:30 THE B[LUEBLOODS] — **29**	6:45 LARIMORE HENLEY 7:15 MARK NARMORE 7:45 PAM WESTON 8:15 DAVID HAMBURGER — **30**	**C**all all Mondays starting at noon for reservations for our Tuesday thru Saturday regular shows. Don't forget our early shows featuring the best up and coming writers with no cover charge! Our …		*Tin Pan South: You can order tickets for all Tin Pan South shows starting today through Ticketmaster: (615)737-4849	

The newsletter accepts advertising but sees it as more of a service than a revenue source. Additional fees are generated by selling their mailing list seven or eight times per year. Kurland advises careful scrutiny of potential buyers. No one has ever complained, she says.

You don't have to look very far to see other signs of the newsletter's effectiveness. It's the only way guests find out about the cafe's popular frequent customer club. "The newsletter really helped us make our name in the marketplace," continues Kurland. "And I'm still thrilled to walk into someone's home and see our calendar posted on their refrigerator."

Our reaction: We're not sure whether this is a newsletter or a calendar of events, but the point is that it's a regular communication to Bluebird's customers and it works.

Chicago

50 seats

American with
ethnic influences in
a cozy bistro setting

Brett Knobel, Owner

(773) 248-0999

Let your personality show.

NEW WORLD FOOD
An Occasional Newsletter from

For weeks I have been racking my brain and pouring over cookbooks, looking for inspiration for New Year's Eve, which I feel must be very special, and nothing moved me until I came across my old Paula Wolfert cookbook on Morocco, and had a "coup de foudre" regarding the menu. Here it is, and I hope you like it as much as I do: The first seating, at a prix fixe of $42, has a choice of sweet and hot sugarcane shrimp(grilled shrimp with a wonderful marinade on a skewer of fresh sugarcane--which lends its own wonderful flavor to the shrimp), or bastilla (bastilla is a Moroccan "pie" of squab and custard laced with cinnamon and almonds. It is a very festive dish, but so time-consuming to prepare that one doesn't often encounter it.

But what better occasion than New Year's Eve?). Then a nice green salad of mixed field greens; followed by a choice of three entrées: a lamb t-bone with everyone's favorite carrot hash, or grilled venison chops with our very special mustard mashed potatoes, or mixed seafood fry with celery root slaw...stop right there. Did I say seafood "fry"? I did--I was writing out a variety of menus with the totally au courant "grilled tuna with two sauces", or "ragout of seafood in a ginger flavored broth" when I had my menu Ephiphany and remembered the seafood platters of my childhood. Delicately pan-fried clams and oysters and shrimp with tartar sauce and hot sauce--where did that go? Well, we're bringing it back for New Year's Eve! If you're like me, you don't really eat fried food anymore--but that doesn't mean you don't still love it. (As Woody Allen said, albeit about a totally different subject, "the heart wants what the heart wants.")

And finally, a special New Year's Eve dessert extravaganza. The second seating, at a prix fixe of $65, gets <u>both</u>, appetizers as well as a sorbet between the salad and the main course, <u>champagne</u>, and a morning breakfast basket so you don't have to move from the house the next day until a reasonable hour. Reservations are necessary, and we need a credit card number with the reservation.

 773-248-0999

I myself am coming as Marlene ("...it took more than one man to change my name to Shanghai Lily..."), something I have been promising to do for quite some time now. I feel dressing up puts one in a festive frame of mind-- but please feel free to dress up or not as you like; after all, it's <u>your</u> party! Happy holidays and happy New Year to all of you from all of us.

Brett

Black ink on white paper
8 1/2 x 11
2 pages
4-5 issues/year
1000 mailed
Published since early 1995

"I try to keep things interesting while not going too far afield," says Brett Knobel of her sporadic self-published newsletter. Topics range broadly from food and wine education to travel to special events, all woven together with interesting tidbits of family history or folklore.

At the same time Knobel is conscious of maintaining balance, refusing to let her easy-going style become too self-promo-tional. "I get newsletters all the time that are really thinly veiled ads. I don't read them and I doubt anyone else does."

Response has been "incredibly enthusi-astic," according to Knobel. Reservations always jump after a mailing: "People say, 'I just got your newsletter and it reminded us that we hadn't been there in a while.'"

Knobel realizes that developing a read-ing habit is important, but is also practical,

I grew up in N.Y. To say that my family was passionate about food is an understatement. Besides a great piece of bread, my Father particularly adored a classic yellow two layer cake with chocolate frosting that hardened on the outside and stayed soft and gooey on the inside, and we frequently made a pilgrimage to a bakery on Long Island owned by some rather remote relatives who made the best example of that type of cake that I have ever had. So when I opened my restaurant, in addition to making great bread, I determined I would make this cake. The bakery had long since gone—but I put my Aunt on the job—and she located those cousins and posed the question: "What is the recipe for the great fudge frosting you used to put on your cakes?" And she came back to me with the answer that they had used a commercially prepared product. Well, of course, that's against my religion—so I had to try and duplicate the taste in my mind by trial and error. And I have. So my holiday gift to you is the classic American layer cake

icing: 8 oz. butter
          3/4 cup cocoa
          pinch salt
          1 lb. confectioner's sugar
          1 tsp. vanilla
          scant 1/2 cup cream

Beat together and spread on cake. Yum!

from:
BRETT'S RESTAURANT
2011 W. Roscoe
Chicago, Illinois 60618
248-0999

A thoughtful anecdote spices up a basic recipe.

publishing an issue only when she has something important to say. "It's hard being a one-man band," concludes Knobel on the lot of the small independent restaurateur.

Our reaction: This quick read does its job and quite well at that. We're always impressed when a restaurateur's integrity and sincerity come across.

LIFE RESTAURANT GROUP

Atlanta

11 Restaurants, various seatings

Various themes

Pano Karatassos, president
Elaine LaMontagne, editor

(404) 237-2060

Buckhead Life Restaurant Group
(BLRG)

Volume XIX 1995

b**u**ckhead
LIFE

★ Celebrity Column ★

Atlanta attracts a diverse group of politicians, professional athletes, and entertainers. Quite often they come to Buckhead Life Restaurants to dine, so you never know who you'll see at any of the locations. Recent sightings include:

103 West assistant manager John Lefkaditis greets Evander Holyfield — Atlanta and America's favorite boxing champ, at 103 West — just 3 days after his comeback fight.

AT PANO'S & PAUL'S
Politicians: Joe Frank Harris, Zell Miller, Senator Paul Coverdel; **Sportscasters:** Fran Tarkenton, Don Sutton; **Sports Stars:** Andrew Lang, Gerald Perry, Jeff George, Dwain Ferrell, Darian Conner, Eric Zaire, Franco Harris, Mookie Blaylock; **Plus:** Mike Landess, Jeff Hamilton, The Lettermans.

AT 103 WEST
Sports Stars: Mookie Blaylock, Stacey Augmon, Steve Smith, Grant Long, Andrew Lang, Jon Koncak, Enas Whatley, Jim Less, Doug Edwards, Coach Lenny Wilkens and General Manager Pete Babcock, Peggy Fleming, Evander Holyfield, Randy Cross; **Plus:** William Gray, Maya Angelou, Robert Hammond, Johnetta Cole, Louis Sullivan, Joseph Lowery.

AT CHOPS
Sports Stars: Richard Todd, Mike Stanton, Kent Mercker, Jon Koncak, Sean Jones, Rich Miano, Jeff George, Irv Eatman, Steve Avery, Lenny Dykstra, Tommy Nobis, Chris Hinton, Bill Fralic, Tommy Gregg, Jeff Gordon, Kyle Petty, Andrew Lang, Andre Rison, Mats Wilander, Ken Venturi, Larry Nantz, Evander Holyfield, Davis Love III, Clarence Jones, Mike Fratello, Ronnie Rothstein, Pat Riley, Lenny Wilkens, June Jones; **Sportscasters:** Skip Caray, Dick Stockton; **Plus:** Frank Charkinian, John Schuerholz, Harry Connick Jr.

AT BUCKHEAD DINER
Actors/Actresses: Martin Mull, Robert Duvall, Sally Struthers, Ellen Degeneres, Jasmine Guy, Raven Simone, Alec Baldwin, Sean Penn, David Cassidy, Jamie Walters; **Entertainers:** Kriss Kross, Elton John, Billy Joel, Robert Plant, Foreigner, Jennifer Holliday; **Sports Stars:** Jackie Joyner Kersey, Kareem Abdul-Jabar, Steve Lundquist, Norm Johnson, Bo Jackson, Rod Laver, Jon Koncak, Edwin Moses, Chris Doleman, KC Jones, Ray Goff, Vince Dooley, Lenny Wilkens; **Authors:** Fannie Flagg, Clancy Woods, Kathleen Kennedy; **Broadcasters:** Dan Rather, Sandra Bookman, Stu Klitenic; **Plus:** Dick Versace, LA Reid, Max Cleland, Buddy Darden, Zell Miller.

AT PRICCI
Sports Stars: Drew Hill, Patrick Ewing, Jeff George, Carl Lewis, Carl Banks, June Jones, Lenny Wilkens; **Broadcasters:** Fred Kahlil, Ernie Johnson Jr; **Plus:** Veronica Castro, Pebbles, Stan Kasten, Dallas Austin, Tony Little.

AT ATLANTA FISH MARKET
Sports Stars: Lex Luger, Kevin Battle, Andre Rison, Harris Barton, Jon Koncak; **Politicians:** Zell Miller, Sam Nunn, Cynthia McKinney; **Broadcasters:** Stu Klitenic, Ted Koppel; **Plus:** Atlanta Hawks Cheerleaders, Eldrin Bell, Bobby Brown.

AT VENI VIDI VICI
Entertainers: John Secada, Felicia Rashad, Ahmad Rashad, Regina Taylor, Jane Powell; **Broadcasters:** Amanda Davis, Don Farmer, Nick Charles; **Plus:** Robert Osborne, Kenny Leon, Patrick Ewing, Council General Myamato, Maynard Jackson, Mayor Bill Campbell.

AT CORNER CAFE
Entertainers: Steve Perry, Greg Alan Williams, Ronnie Dunn; **Sports Stars:** Edwin Moses, Jack Nicklaus; **Plus:** Eldrin Bell, Zell Miller, Ray Goff, Max Cleland.

Powwow at NAVA

MAY 10 MARKED THE GRAND OPENING DATE OF NAVA, AN UPSCALE SOUTHWESTERN RESTAURANT, and the newest from the Buckhead Life Restaurant Group. Substantial research was done and investments made to create an authentic and theatrical Southwest experience — from the flavorful cuisine to the architectural decor and art.

President/Owner **Pano Karatassos** lured renowned Chef **Kevin Rathbun**, formerly of Baby Routh in Dallas, Texas, to direct the hearty cooking in the newly designed NAVA kitchen. Sous Chefs **Scott Serpas** and **Todd Stoner**, plus Pastry Chef **Kirk Parks** were also recruited from popular Southwest establishments to better present the Southwest style to Atlanta and its international visitors.

Chef Kevin comments, *"I love Southwest food because of the bold flavors, vibrant colors, and the textures of food which make for a great presentation. I particularly enjoy using traditional Native American spices and herbs to jazz up the menu."*

NAVA's innovative menu is a collage of seafood, meat, and game dishes with Latin and Native American influences, and ingredients indigenous to the South and Southwest. Examples from NAVA's menu include: Chili Cured Lamb Rack with Red Pepper Chiliquiles; Beef Tenderloin, Cowboy Cut, Roasted Garlic Jus; Sweet Shrimp Relleno with Golden Tomato Butter; and Grilled Chicken Tortilla Tomato Soup. The Southwest fare at NAVA can be prepared as mild or robust as each individual guest desires. Noteworthy, lighter and healthier menu selections are prominent and an important focus. The **Totopos Bar** offers a variety of small dishes and specialty spirits. An extensive beer and wine list consistent with the Southwest cuisine is also a NAVA feature.

To capture the genuine feel of the Southwest, eight of Santa Fe, New Mexico's finest craftsmen were commissioned to come to Atlanta to work on the NAVA project hand-in-hand with restaurant designer **Bill Johnson** of The Johnson Studio. The restaurant reflects the region with natural wood, adobe-like walls and fireplace (made from actual New Mexican plaster with its identifiable reddish-rose hue), and large-scale appointments (such as the Vigas beams that dramatically line the ceiling).

Southwest sculpture and characteristic art are highlighted in "nichos" throughout ("little things of beauty"). The new clean, straightforward, and open layout allows each of the expanded three tiers to have its own unique vantage point of the restaurant while feeling a central part of the energy. NAVA's outdoor dining, literally in the heart of Buckhead, can be enjoyed as the generous Southern seasons allow.

BL 1

Good background intro to new restaurant—giving readers details to look for (and talk about to friends!).

Black ink on white

8 1/2 x 11

6 pages, gatefold

3 issues/year

30,000 printed/15,000 mailed

Published since 1986

Buckhead Life is packed full of information—as it should be since it covers about a dozen restaurants of widely varying menus and themes. Of course, as new restaurants are added to the Buckhead Life Restaurant Group, they are prominently featured on page 1. Plenty of photos with smiling faces characterize the newsletter. Recipients are sure to recognize their favorite chef or maitre d'. A page 1 Celebrity Column lists "recent sightings" at the restaurants.

Nor is the newsletter shy about the honors and press clips the restaurants and their owners receive—as well as the fundraising benefits they stage on behalf of local charities.

Regular features also include recipes from the restaurants and a detailed listing of each restaurant featuring its address

Tips for Private Dining Success

Whether you're planning a small business gathering, a casual engagement party, a wedding reception, or a large birthday celebration, private dining events can be some of our most cherished memories. For such an occasion, here are some helpful tips from experienced professionals from 103 West, considered one of Atlanta's most popular sites for private dining events:

Dean Pugel, Executive Chef, 103 West: *(culinary viewpoint)*
- Make sure that the menu is flexible in order to accommodate all guests, not just a certain group (i.e. men and women, vegetarians and beefeaters).
- Passed hors d'oeuvres are recommended when guests are expected to arrive at different times; and can be done for sit-down or buffet meals.
- Sit-down meals convey formality, and buffets encourage more mingling. Buffets are not necessarily less expensive.
- When planning the menu, feel free to discuss unique, creative approaches with the chef or caterer (i.e. special, exotic ingredients or novel dessert shape to reflect an event theme or logo).

Sia Moshk, General Manager, 103 West: *(service viewpoint)*
- Select two-four locations where you would ideally like to have your event. Meet the manager who would handle your party. Compare prices and all that is included (i.e. service, style, number of courses, food quality, ambiance, beverage options, convenience factor) - you might be surprised that places presumed to be expensive are very similar to "perceived moderately-priced" locations. Make a final choice after these comparisons.
- If you select a restaurant/hotel/club that also has regular restaurant dining during your event, make sure a separate staff will handle your function.
- It is critical that guest hosts have confidence in the people handling their parties, so they may enjoy socializing or attend to other business issues.
- Look for veteran service pros that accommodate special requests (i.e. food preparations to a diet to non-food related needs).
- Complimentary printed menus (incorporating business agendas or social acknowledgements) are a lovely touch.
- Coming through with the little thoughtful details makes the difference between a good and a great time.

Helen Wood, Catering/Sales Manager, 103 West: *(planning viewpoint)*
- Reserve a private room as far in advance as possible, especially for large parties (events are often booked a year in advance).
- Try to find a facility that is willing to work with you and your special needs (i.e. floral arrangements, vegetarian meals, place cards, valet parking, specialty linens, dance floor, musicians, audio/visual) - to lessen your "to-do" list.
- Try to have alternative event dates when initially making plans.
- You should feel at home and comfortable while discussing policies and contracts. Be wary of inflexible, rigid attitudes.

Photographs are from the recent beautiful wedding and reception at 103 West for Larry and Amy Hahn. Decorations for the wedding by Event Designs.

BL 4

CHAR-GRILLED ANGEL FOOD CAKE

A recipe by Executive Chef Michael George of Chops

1/4 cup sugar
1 cup cake flour
1/2 tsp. salt
2 tbl. cocoa powder
10 each egg whites
1 cup sugar
1 tsp cream of tartar
1/2 tsp. vanilla
1/2 tsp. almond extract

- Preheat oven to 350 degrees
- Sift 1/4 cup sugar, flour and salt together.
- Whip egg whites until stiff, add cream of tartar and then 1 cup sugar.
- Fold in vanilla and almond extract.
- Fold in flour and sugar by 1/3's.
- Pour 1/2 of the batter into an ungreased tube pan.
- Add 2 tbl of cocoa powder to remaining batter and pour into tube pan.
- Bake approximately 45 minutes.
- Cool upside down for 2 hours

Topping
2 pints strawberries cleaned and quartered
1 cup sugar
1/4 cup Grand Marnier Liqueur
2 cups whipped cream
- Combine strawberries, sugar, and Grand Marnier

To Serve
- Cut cooled cake into wedges and place on hot, clean grill.
- Turn when browned on both sides.
- Place on plates and top generously with strawberry mixture and finish with whipped cream.
- This one of my grandmother's favorite recipes done on the BBQ after a dinner of grilled steak and potatoes.
- I particularly like this recipe because of the simplicity of the idea. It's a lowfat light dessert - that's done on the grill - my favorite style of cooking.

Personnel-ities

Every season, each of the Buckhead Life Restaurants selects a non-management employee who provides impeccable service worthy to be the standard of his or her trade. This season's honored employees are (back row, left to right):
Oscar Hernandez *Steward* — Chops
James Jones *Line Cook* — 103 West
David Danks *Fish Counter Clerk* — Pano's Food Shop
Adam Bradford *Line Cook* — Atlanta Fish Market
(front row, left to right)
Amy Smith *Lead Hostess/Bartender* — Pricci
Marcie Lefkoff *Hostess* — Buckhead Diner
Melissa Akers *Line Cook* — Pano's & Paul's
Julie Mitchell *Server* — Corner Cafe/ Buckhead Bread Company
Abel Bustos *Steward* — Veni Vidi Vici (not photographed)

"Models?" The dapper chefs at Buckhead Diner were recently photographed to be featured in an upcoming catalogue for "Chefware USA" clothing. Photographed from left to right are *Rob Howell* sous chef, *Dan O'Leary* executive chef, *Gregg McCarthy* executive sous chef.

Obvious but very effective recipe presentation— complete with the chef's mugshot.

The photos in this newsletter are plentiful, varied (in size and style) and always happy! Good employee recognition.

---

and contact information, hours, the chefs and general managers—and logo.

Gift certificates are also enclosed with some issues—either inserted loose or attached to one page with wafer tabs.

Our reaction: An excellent example of a newsletter printed in black and white, but with the depth of color. Good for faxing, too.

Even though they
don't charge for the
newsletters, price
adds value.

FALL 95 NEWSLETTER
VOL.2 NO.3 — $1

dear friends of bondí & bruno bakery...

Thank you for your continuous support and patronage. We are preparing for the autumn with new dishes, delicious pastries and exiting events.

At Bondí, our new Fall Menu will be available as of Monday September 25th. Some of the highlights include: for antipasto "Carpaccio di cervo affumicato," a carpaccio of venison loin topped with slices of Grana Padana cheese served with cucumber & celery pickled in mint vinegar.

Our primi piatti once again features "Ravioli di zucca e salvia", our homemade ravioli filled with pumpkin and ricotta, served with an olive oil and sage sauce. Our secondi piatti is highlighted by the "Costolette di cinghiale all'arabesca", a rack of boar marinated in vinegar and red wine, lightly coated with a mixture of spices i.e. black pepper, nutmeg, ginger, cardamom, cinnamon and fennel seeds. In addition to our regular menu we will have the Baronial menu available from September 28th to October 19th (see article on Baronial Dinner). Join us as we indulge in Chef/Co-owner's Salvatore Anzalone delicious creations!

At Bruno Bakery, autumn is a very special season! Chef-Owner Biagio Settepani and Chef Frank Cordi are preparing for their busiest season. The season begin with the preparation of honey cakes

and coconut macaroon to celebrate and honor the Jewish Holidays, followed by the kiddies cup cakes, Halloween cookies, custard pies and pumpkin pies for Halloween. November 11th, St. Martins' Day marks the day to taste new wine, as the Italian saying goes " per San Martino si prova il vino," for the occasion Bruno Bakery will make the traditional San Martino's biscotti. What better way to taste new wines!!

Finally the climax is reached with Thanksgiving, Christmas, and New Year when a large assortment of pastries and cakes will fill the counters of the bakeries; such as Pumpkin pies, Pecan pies, Panettone, Stollen, Pandoro, Pandolce Genovese, Torrone Siciliano, Struffoli, Homemade chocolates etc. etc...Come and join us in celebrating the holidays!
(see Calendar of events for a listing of upcoming special events.)

baronial dinner

The cuisine of Italy, as much as it is regional is also divided into two distinct categories: La Cucina Povera and La Cucina Alto-Borghese. La Cucina Alto-Borghese was enjoyed by the Bourbons of Naples and Sicily, the French in Piedmont and the Austrians of Lombardy and Venice. The cuisine of the nobility being much more consistent throughout the country, as the ingredients were more accessible to that class of people.

Caffè Bondí once again presents the Baronial menú of the Kingdom of the Two Sicilies. This extravagant menú, researched by our food historian Dr. Luisa di Giovanni and prepared by Chef/Co-owner Salvatore Anzalone will be available September 28th through October 19th. "The Kingdom of the Two Sicilies"* during the 18th and 19th centuries, was a period when French influence invaded the kitchen, as well as the style of the nobility. French Chefs were imported hence ostracizing local cuisine from their households, with the introduction of the French Chefs, the Monzùs emerged. They were the carriers of the French cooking tradition. As it was done with the nobility, the title Monzù was only passed on after...

Menú del Regno delle Due Sicilie
Menú of the Kingdom of the Two Sicilies
(Baronial cooking of Southern Italy in the 18th and 19th Centuries)

Antipasto
Tornagusto di regaglie
vol-au-vent stuffed with chicken livers sauteed with onions and Marsala wine
and
Crostini di pâté delle Due Sicilie
crostini topped with a pâté of mushrooms, black olives, capers and Herbes de Provence
Primo
Timballo di maccheroni alla moda del Marchese
timbale of macaroni baked in crust with meat, mushrooms, livers and chicken layered with bechamel

Secondo
Brioche di crostacei di Monzù Terramoto

"We thought we were misunderstood," says Leah Abraham, about her motivation for starting a newsletter. "We wanted to communicate a message about who we are."

Has it worked? "Better than any advertising we've ever done," says Nino Settepani, co-owner and Abraham's husband. "If we forget to mention a special event in an issue, we accept the fact that it won't be nearly as well-attended."

"We have a lot going on, so we have a lot to talk about," reports Abraham. Every issue highlights the restaurant's everchanging art exhibits, jazz entertainment and special dinners. "Dear Friends" announces changes to the menu or any other special messages for customers. An intellectual article on food or travel is standard and is frequently a result of suggestions from customers.

CAFFÈ Bondí

7 West 20th Street · New York, NY 10011
212.691.8136

Bruno Bakery

602 Lorimer Street · Brooklyn, NY 11211
718.349.6524
506 LaGuardia Place · New York, NY 10012
212.982.5854

Free Membership Offer For Bondí Patrons

You are cordially invited to join the New York Gourmet Society for free (reg. $50) as a customer of Bondí/Bruno Bakery. Enjoy exciting wine tastings and exquisite dining events. Meet new friends who share your interest in fine wine and food. As a new member, you will be invited to a free new member's wine tasting. To enroll call (212) 592-0777 or mail the coupon below to: NY Gourmet Society · 217 E. 86th St. Suite 103, New York, NY 10028

Name _____

Address _____

City/State/Zip _____

Tel. Home _____ Daytime _____

> A co-op effort—both organizations benefit.

art at bondí

B.A.M. II at Bondí. Oct 13 to Dec 2

For the second year Caffé Bondí is proud to host a show paying tribute to the Brooklyn Academy of Music (BAM) and its "**NEXT WAVE**" Festival. This show will incorporate the visual artists, as well as the photographers that have contributed to BAM over the past thirteen years. Every Festival season is documented in a "**NEXT WAVE**" Festival Journal, which features portraits of performing artists, as well as cover art that is created expressly for BAM by a contemporary visual artist. BAM's "**NEXT WAVE**" Festival Artist collection is quite remarkable and includes works by Roy Lichtenstein, Francesco Clemente, Willem de Kooning and Keith Haring. This year's "**NEXT WAVE**" Festival Artist is Jonathan Lasker.

Join us at Bondí starting October 13th as we exhibit highlights of photography and visual art that have been featured as part of the "**NEXT WAVE**" Festival, including photographers such as Karen Kuehn, Hans Neleman and artist Donald Baechler. The show at Bondí will coincide with the premiere of BAM's ALTERNATIVE JAZZ: "**THE NEXT WAVE**" show hosted by Don Byron. Special thanks to Tom Caravaglia, our curator. ✪

music at bondí

Raised in New York City by musical parents, Geri in her youth, was exposed to a large variety of music through her travels all over the world with her parents.

Although her parents were classically trained, it was Jazz, and more specifically, Latin Jazz which most interested Geri as a singer.

Having spent a great deal of time in Brazil while growing up, Geri took to singing Brazilian music. She is best known for her interpretation of Bossa Nova Standards. She says: "the musicality of the Portuguese language makes it so natural to sing." Performing this music with just voice and guitar best shows the beauty of the music and its underlying rhythm, which is based on Samba.

Geri has performed Jazz and Brazilian music with various groups in and around the city for the last several years and continues exploring the many ways to blend Jazz and Latin Rhythms. ✪

book signings

"The Mediterranean Diet Cook..." "Eating in Italy"

dates to remember

Monday Nights
Beginning 9/12
Join us for Latin Jazz night with Geri Teresa, accompanied by her guitarist.

Monday 9/25
Marks the beginning of our fall menu

Tuesday 9/26 5-7pm
Cocktail reception for Nancy H. Jenkins' book signing of "The Mediterranean Diet" followed by a $25.00 prix-fixe dinner

Thursday 9/28-10/19
join us as we celebrate our Annual Historical Event. This year we will repeat last year's "Baronial Dinner", an extravagant cuisine of the baronial court during the Kingdom of the Two Sicilies $50.00

Friday 10/13-12/2
join us again as we pay tribute to BAM (Brooklyn Academy of Music) and its "**NEXT WAVE**" Festival

Tuesday 10/24, 5-7pm
Cocktail reception for Faith Willinger's book signing of "Eating in Italy" followed by a $25.00 prix-fixe dinner

Friday 10/27 7pm
Don't miss our First Annual "Wild Game, Barolo and Barbaresco Dinner" $45.00

> Supports the art community, and guests have another reason to come back.

Peter Kump

It is with great sorrow that we mark the death of Peter Kump, founder of Peter Kump's school and co-founder of the James Beard Foundation.

People who receive the newsletter have had an experience with us," says Abraham, "so we know our audience is interested in what's going on at Bondí." That's because most of the names were obtained from comment cards left with guest checks. But to expand her reach, Abraham also purchases lists by zip code and uses the mailing lists from the artists or musicians whose work she stages in the restaurant.

Our reaction: This letter looks as slick as a magazine, but doesn't seem to get in the way of it being personal. The active layout does a good job of communicating just how much this restaurant has going on.

Virginia Beach, VA

80 seats

Updated Continental cuisine in eclectic, casual setting

David & Pamela Watts, Co-owners

(757) 496-3333

Subtle, yet effective way to introduce praise.

September **Café David** 1996

"Keep creating David, cuz they're always awesome! Marinara is best we've ever had no matter where we've traveled!!" ...Patti & Charlie Fidler, Va. Beach, Va.

NOV. 14 AUSTRAILIAN WINE TASTING   NOV. 20 THANKSGIVING COOKING CLASS

Nov. 14 Australian Wine Tasting - APERTIF - Seaview Sparkling Brut
1st Course: Wynns Estate Chardonnay (Wild Mushroom Soup)
2nd Course: Penfolds Koonunga Hill Shiraz/Cabernet (Warm Gorgonzola with Fall Fruit Chutney)
3rd Course: Penfolds Organic Chardonnay/Sauvignon Blanc (White Bean & Grilled Red Onion Salad over Arugala
4th Course: Penfolds Bin 128 Shiraz (Cassoulet - Duck Confit, Potato, Tomato, Mushrooms and Lentils)
            Penfolds Bin 407 Cabernet Sauvignon (Comparing a Shiraz to a Cabernet Sauvignon)
5th Course: Penfolds Club Port NV (Chocolate Creme Carmel)

Nov. 20 Thanksgiving Cooking Class - David is still thinking! Smell the sawdust burning?
He's talking about Cornish Game Hens with 2 Different Stuffings for the Main Course.

Summer is over! Wasn't it a memory before it even began? "Time keeps on slipping, slipping, slipping into the future." One of the more memorable events was Mary O's review of Cafe David. As timing would have it, August is ALWAYS our busiest month. The good press made it even busier. I must apologize once more to those of you who couldn't get a reservation or who couldn't stand the wait. We know how much we owe (like, everything!) to those who supported us during those lean and mean months. NOVEMBER....now that's a month for a review! At one busy point I saw a car pull up with 4 people and just prayed that they were going to Coastal Grill! You know, that God is going to get me for that one! We all tried the very best we could to make things as wonderful as possible. I'm not sure David and all of us have ever worked that hard before.

Thank You all for the cards, clippings and comments on Mary's article. It amazed us and made us feel so proud that so many cared and took pride in being recognized. Success for us is being appreciated by the most well-traveled and knowledgeable diners in town and that you should feel at home and an integral part of the heart of Cafe David.

It's now the season for Wine Tastings and Cooking Classes. Don't forget that we're open 7 DAYS a WEEK and SUNDAY BRUNCH. We will use one side of the restaurant and keep the other side for business as usual. It then will not lock us into one particular day. Personally, I don't want to do much of anything on Mondays, even for fun. David and I particularly love Australian Wines and the Penfolds Grange Hermitage is our very favorite Wine. There are so many Australian Wines that equal and even surpass many French and California Wines. Come see, find out, teach others and share. It's just too much fun learning about WINE.

1423 North Great Neck Road • Virginia Beach, Virginia 23454 • (804) 496-3333

Black ink on white stationery

8 1/2 x 11, self-mailer

1 page

Published monthly

600 printed and 500 mailed

Published since 9/95

30

"There's not a week that goes by that I don't hear, 'I love reading your newsletter,'" says Pamela Watts, co-owner and editor. "At first I thought, they must not have a life. But then I realized the people making those comments were lawyers, doctors and other professionals—intelligent people."

"I think the reason I get the response I do is because it's easy reading," Watts

chuckles. "I write to guests just as I might talk to them if they were standing right in front of me." Readership—and repeat business—has been boosted by a contest dubbed "Menu Lotto," which allows readers to draw to win a complimentary appetizer, entree or dessert when they bring in that month's newletter.

What started out as a way to talk about husband David's cooking classes and wine

December **Café David** *1996*

"Excellent food, service and atmosphere. We WILL return! Steve & Lyn Owen, Va. Beach"

JAN 16 FRENCH WINE TASTING - APERTIF - Piper Heidseich Extra Dry   7:00 p.m. ($65.00 includes all)
Soup Course- Clos Perriere Sancerre '95 (Cream of Asparagus)
Appetizer Course- Louis Jadot Puligny - Montrachet '94 (Smoked Salmon Mousse w/ White Truffle Oil)
Main Course- Chateau La Grave A Pomeral '93 (Tournedos Nantua)
          Chateau Lynch Bages, Pauillac '93 (Comparing a Pomeral and a Pauillac)
Cheese Course- Chateau La Mission, Haut - Brion '87
Dessert Course- Chateau Doisy Vedrine Sauterne '89 (Napoleon)

FEB 23 SUNDAY 3 - 5 p.m.   ($30.00 includes all)
I hate February! This Tasting gives something to look forward to. We will taste and enjoy in a more casual format. Hors d'oeuvres and 5 great Champagnes. If you're still hungry , hang out and have dinner. We still haven't completely finished details but, we know we're doing CHANDON and that means Moet White Star ! Some really nice Champagnes will be sipped. Broudy-Kantor will host. We'll be home early to prepare for Monday!

Thanksgiving week in New Orleans once again just didn't lend us enough time to eat, drink and be merry. But...we were THANKFUL! We gained poundage and knowledge and lost brain cells and money. Sadly to say and a sick thought too...but...Just our kind of vacation!

There are only so many meals. There were places we just couldn't get to (i.e. Gabrielle's, Randolf's, Christians...). The places that we returned to: 1) The Gumbo Shop (best CHICKEN GUMBO in town), 2) NOLA (just had to have Miss Hay's Stuffed Chicken Wings again) and 3) Cafe Du Monde for Beignets, a no-brainer. For Sunday Brunch, a huge day in New Orleans, we went to Mr. B's Bistro.   We could not get reservations at Commander's Palace for the second year. They seat around 700 too!

Turkey Day was spent at Sapphires, Kevin Graham's new place. Last year we hit Graham's, his signature restaurant, on T-Day. The food was Kevin's usual awesome. I love the artwork and Sapphires even surpasses Graham's. Local artists have paintings but, I love the metal art. The artist forged chairs, a huge chandelier and centerpieces that hold breads and candles.The bright blue sapphire color throughout sent me into major art envy!

The staff (including a Norfolk cook) was most professional and accomodating at the Bistro at Maison de Ville.   The food was incredible but my most noted memory was the '91 Bell Baritelle. The French Maitre'd suggested that this wine was superior to the Opus One. It was at the same price and from Napa as well. The Bell WAS better. Oh! the cool thing about wine...the SURPRISE! That unexpected bottle that you happen upon. There are so many surprises yet to partake.

Chef Anne Kearney at Peristyle lived up to her reputation. Just Superb! Especially the Warm Greens with Goat's Cheese, Port Shallots & Crispy Bacon. We always like to hit at least one old establishment. This year...Galatoires. Sure it was good.. but...the newer chefs just seem to have an edge over the old. No reservations taken...always a line...big- time customers...big-time money. Who can resist? It's history verses the Nouveau.

Now THE place to dine.....Brigtsen's. Frank Brigtsen is a food artisan and darned nice guy too. He's the only chef that I will concede who out-does David. Everything stood out (except the wine list but David brought an '83 Latour). The Grilled Foie Gras in Black Pepper Brioche with Sierra Beauty Apples, Duck Jus and Truffled Honey Appetizer tasted like Paris.

I'd love to include more on all the restaurants...there's no space. I brought menu's back. Come in.....we'll talk. If you're planning a trip to New Orleans...allow me to play Concierge!

1423 North Great Neck Road • Virginia Beach, Virginia 23454 • (804) 496-3333

> Talking about restaurants in other cities often brings the return favor.

tastings, has grown to include recipes, amusing anecdotes and news of the couple's travels. "When you get to a certain point in your culinary careers," says Watts, "travel becomes the best teacher and our customers enjoy hearing about where we've been."

More proof of the newsletter's impact comes immediately after mailing an issue, when the number of covers picks up. "It puts us in their minds," Watts adds.

Our reaction: A nice mix of articles. Travel is the great educator and the owners are generous with their experiences—food and otherwise.

FALL 1995   VOLUME 1, NUMBER 5

fountainside
C H A T

THE QUARTERLY NEWSLETTER OF CARMELO'S ITALIAN RESTAURANTS

CARMELO'S TEXAS TWO-STOMP AT FESTA ITALIANA

photo by Rudi Hohsteiner

Carmelo (lower right) coaches astronaut and artist Alan Bean at last year's "Carmelo's Celebrity Grape Stomp." Bean walked on the "Ocean of Storms" area of the moon twenty-five years ago but this was a crater of a different color!

BOTH CARMELO'S ITALIAN RESTAURANTS UNDERGOING MAJOR RENOVATIONS

Local celebrities and Lucy wannabes will try their foot at "Carmelo's Texas Two-Stomp" at Festa Italiana on September 29, 30 and October 1 at Velvet Park (Southwest Freeway and Buffalo Speedway). The celebrity grape stomping contest always creates some juicy competition between local media celebs, politicos, sports figures and even an occasional astronaut thrown in for good measure!

The contest is judged by the amount of grapes stomped, the duration of time it takes and whether or not the end product even resembles a glass of wine! Commemorative T-shirts are available for participating, bearing two grape-stained footprints.

Carmelo is no stranger to grape stomping and last year he won his own contest - feet down! Growing up in Sicily, Carmelo's uncle raised acres of grapes. During harvest time, Carmelo and the villagers would gather grapes in baskets and load them in a cart pulled by a donkey. When everyone arrived back at the winery, they were seated at long tables placed in the field, given an abundance of food and wine and then they began their stomping.

Enjoy music, dancing, eating, fireworks and stomping at this 18th annual Italian Festival which benefits the Italian Cultural and Community Center. For more information on Festa Italiana, please call the Center at (713) 524-4222.

Carmelo's normally hosts its birthday bash in Houston every year on June 11 but this year the celebration was postponed until the restaurant completes their major renovation project. A triple relief in an introverted space will recreate the Sicilian village of Taormina where Carmelo was born. Clients will find themselves transported to an alley in this village, a hill town that clings to a cliff rising sheerly from the sea on the east coast of Sicily, with sunny skies during the day and the glow of street lights at night.

Meanwhile, Carmelo's is expanding their large private parking lot in Austin which will be secured by exquisite wrought iron and stucco fencing with lighted globes. A grandiose fountain will be the first thing clients see when they enter the lot and turn their keys over to the valet parking attendant. Parking has always been at a premium in the Entertainment District and with the Austin Convention Center near by, Carmelo may have to install his own traffic light!

"Because of the newsletter, people walk into the restaurant for the first time and feel like they've been there before," says Dian Darby, editor. "They already know so much about Carmelo and the staff."

Carmelo and his wife attended an American Express database marketing seminar and knew immediately that a newsletter would be right for them. "We had been upset with the advertising establishment and local media," maintains Carmelo Mauro, owner. "We weren't getting much recognition and the ads didn't do much for us. Our newsletter allows us to reach customers with our message. It's done wonders."

With articles talking about Mauro's background, staff profiles and letters from customers, the focus of the restaurant and newsletter promotes a feeling of family.

photo by Greg Todd

HOUSTON CARMELO'S HOSTS WOMEN'S TENNIS CROWD

During Gallery Furniture Houston Women's Tennis Championship, Carmelo's hosted the following tennis VIPS: Barbara Perry, Tournament Director, Lee Jackson with the Women's Tennis Association Tour and their special guest Stefano Capriati, father of teen tennis star, Jennifer.

Top-seeded Steffi Graf needed only 68 minutes to defeat Osa Carlsson of Sweden 6-1, 6-1 to win the Houston WTC. Graf, No. 1 in the world, extended her unbeaten streak for 1995 to 18 matches and 36 sets. Graf's winner's prize was $79,000. For Carmelo, the prize was submitting the winning bid on an acrylic painting of Graf by famed artist Erik (Opie) Otterstad. The beneficiary of the auctioned item was "Keep Drugs Out of America" and Steffi Graf participated in the presentation to Carmelo and his family. Carmelo and Hilary are both avid tennis players and long-time members of the Westside Tennis Club in Houston.

DATES SET FOR "MARRIAGE – ITALIAN STYLE" BRIDAL SHOWS

Each show takes place in Austin on a Tuesday from 5:00 – 8:00 p.m. with hundreds of brides, grooms, mothers-of-the-brides and friends in attendance. Twenty wedding-related businesses display their wares and everyone enjoys a "rehearsal" Italian dinner. Admission is $6.00 and the next show will be November 7, 1995. Dates for 1996 are March 12, July 9 and November 12.

CARMELO'S FUNGHI CON SPINACI

Celebrating the spring harvest in conjunction with the opening of the new Whole Foods Market in Austin, Carmelo's was one of many restaurants to participate in "What's Cooking in the Park; a Grower/Chef Collaborative" pairing Central Texas produce growers with local restaurant chefs.

Pairing up with Kitchen Pride Mushrooms, Carmelo produced his Funghi Con Spinaci which goes well with sirloin strip or fresh pasta. You can make it at home with the following ingredients and instructions:

- Portabello Mushrooms
- Onions
- Fresh Spinach
- Salt & Pepper
- Garlic
- Olive Oil

Grill Portabello Mushrooms (as many as you wish to serve as an appetizer) and salt and pepper to taste. If you don't have a grill, they can be sauteed in olive oil.

Saute fresh spinach in olive oil with garlic, chopped onion, salt & pepper. Arrange on the plate as a bed for the grilled mushrooms. Add mushrooms and sprinkle with olive oil.

CARMELO'S GOES WORLD WIDE

Carmelo's Italian Restaurants have opened up a new global location on the Internet joining the thousands of businesses who see the potential of serving their customers on-line. The Internet, a global network of computers which has existed over 25 years, has recently expanded the opportunities for businesses to reach new customers. These expanded opportunities come via the World Wide Web. The World Wide Web, which is a part of information structure of the Internet, is being used by businesses because of its ease of use. Using a very inexpensive or free "browser", a potential customer can visit a businesses home page and have a virtual tour.

For example, Internet surfers stopping for a visit at Carmelo's Web site can gather a history of the restaurant, read back issues of The Fountainside Chat, look over Carmelo's appetizing menu, peruse the extensive wine list and find out exactly where Carmelo's is physically located. And that's not all. Future brides or anyone planning a party can find out more information about Carmelo's banquet and catering facilities. We aren't taking reservations or serving food in cyberspace yet, but we bet you will have fun at our new location. Not as much fun as eating at our restaurants though!

The growth phenomena of the Internet and the World Wide Web is being touted by all forms of the media, and we just couldn't pass up the opportunity. The real interesting thing is that when we were doing our research about what kinds of sites restaurants were setting up, the most common type of restaurant we found was Italian. One of our favorite sites will even teach you to speak a little Italian. Turn your browsers to Mama's Cucina at http://www.eat.com/learn-italian.html and learn how to say "There's no one I'd rather share Italy with than you," and how to pronounce eggplant (melanzana) and mushrooms (funghi) in Italian. We've come up with lots of ideas from our net surfing but we are keeping our food earth bound for now.

You can find Carmelo's Web site at this address: Our URL (Uniform Resource Locator) is:
http://www.hyperweb.com/carmelo's/
Don't forget that trailing slash (/) at the end. Carmelo's site was designed for use with the popular Netscape browser, which gave us the ability to use backgrounds and tables for a more elegant "virtual" dining experience. We hope you will enjoy our new location but, of course, we'd much rather see you in person. Now if we could only figure a way to travel to Italy as quickly as our data will.

TOUR ITALY WITH CARMELO!
Carmelo is scheduling food and wine "fun" trips in Italy for 40 people at a time starting this Spring. These 10-day trips will be personally guided by Carmelo so contact him for all the details.

This might be a nice adjunct to your newsletter—to catch all those surfers.

Special events help you to attract new audiences.

"That's what hospitality is all about," says Darby.

Darby researches and writes each issue, then passes it along to a design firm for layout to maintain consistency; the same firm that handles Carmelo's other advertising and direct mail.

Most of the huge mailing list was collected from comment cards left

with guest checks. A completed card enters guests in a monthly drawing for a $100 gift certificate – an effective incentive.

Our reaction: With plans to reduce the number of issues, we hope this attractive, thoughtful letter doesn't lose the readership it's worked so hard to build.

Not only announces international extended family, but adds to image of local group as well.

MICHAEL & ROBERT'S

Melange

WINTER '96

Chez Melange

A CALIFORNIA BRASSERIE
1716 Pacific Coast Highway
Redondo Beach, CA 90277
(310) 540-1222

RESTAURANT CHRISTINE TO OPEN!

Restaurant Christine, the newest of the Michael & Robert's Melange, Inc., is scheduled to open mid-November in Hillside Village in Torrance.

The husband and wife team of Christine Brown and Jordan Funk will operate the new restaurant. Christine, a graduate of The Culinary Institute of America in New York, will dazzle guests with exciting new dishes as the Executive Chef and General Manager. Jordan will serve as Manager.

After several wonderful years, Fino closed on October 26th, 1996 to make way for Restaurant Christine. The old Fino site will remain closed for approximately three weeks for remodeling and upgrading.

Christine and Jordan look forward to welcoming all guests to Restaurant Christine.

CHEZ GOES TO DUBAI!

Chez Melange is currently playing host to two employees of the Taj Group of hotels based in India. Paul and Armit are to be the chefs of a new California style restaurant, called Malibu, in The Princeton Hotel, a small luxury hotel in Dubai, United Arab Emirates.

Michael Franks and Robert Bell were chosen over many other outstanding restaurateurs in Los Angeles to assist the Taj Group in the design of their new restaurants. Both recently traveled to India, Dubai and London as guests of the Taj Group.

In November, Chez Melange will send a team of both Managers and Chefs to Dubai to help their Indian friends. Bill Donnelly and Eric Gay will represent the Culinary Team, with Susan Zimmer as the Front of the House Management Trainer. We wish them all great success!

> The Taj Group of hotels is India's largest and finest hotel chain, offering 44 hotels in 30 destinations across the subcontinent. In addition, the Taj Group includes business hotels, beach resorts, palaces and garden retreats in India as well as key cities throughout the U.S., U.K., Middle East and Africa.

Christine
24530 Hawthorne Boulevard
Torrance, CA 90505
(310) 373-1952

MISTO
Caffé and Bakery
24558 Hawthorne Blvd.
Torrance, CA 90505
310-375-3608

D·E·P·O·T
An Urban Grill Room & Bar
1250 Cabrillo Avenue
Torrance, CA 90501
(310) • 787 • 7501

705 Pier Avenue
Hermosa Beach, CA 90254
(310) 379-7997

The Chez
at the Beverly Prescott
1224 Beverwil Drive
Los Angeles, CA 90035
310-772-2999

Malibu
California Cuisine & Wine Bar
The Princeton Hotel
Dubai, U.A.E.

We've watched this restaurant group grow from the original Chez Melange to Misto, Depot, Pier Avenue Bakery, The Chez, and Christine's (formerly Fino)—Now, Micheal and Robert have joined the Taj hotel group, announcing a new restaurant in Dubai, and another in Bombay.

The newsletter is written by Lisa Franks, and includes a "What's Going On Where?" column covering happenings at all the restaurants. There's plenty to talk about.

Some examples: Caribbean Night, Father's Day, Mother's Day, Academy Award Dinner (big screen), Dinners with winemakers, Passover Specials, Cooking Classes, Benefits.

Chez Melange and the others are known throughout the South Bay area for their events for charities, such as the

... It's a Boy! Misto Manager Cari Dittman delivered a 8 lb. 3 oz., 20 in. baby boy on August 31st. Both mother and son, Blake Dittman are doing great! Cari will return to Misto the first week in December.

... Misto Face Lift. Misto has recently gone through a much needed minor renovation. We have replaced the patio tables, awning, wall paper and upholstery, paint and much more. Please drop by to see our "new and improved" Misto.

... Misto Chef Peter Carpenter has made many changes to always wonderful selection of dishes on the menu. You'll see Peppered Ahi with Wasabi Mustard Sauce, Refreshing Grilled Portobello Mushroom Sandwich, Sauteed Spicy Diced Vegetable Burritos, and three great new Pastas. Our new entree selections available after 5 pm include: Flank Steak, Chicken Piccata, Salmon Braised in Beer, and Turkey Tenderloin with

WHAT'S GOING ON AND WHERE?
BY LISA FRANKS

Cranberry Port Wine Sauce. With Thanksgiving just around the corner, be sure to see the menu from Misto bakery for all your holiday needs.

... Pastry Chef Tracy Ness invites you to come in and sample all of Misto's wonderful Holiday baked goods. Choose from a wide variety of tempting sweets. And remember Misto for all your special occasion cakes, including wedding cakes. Tracy has been making herself known in and around the area for her traditional yet original designs for wedding cakes—and they taste even better than they look! Call (310) 375-2852 for

more information or to set up an appointment with Tracy.

... Depot wishes to thank the many caring people involved in the Halloween Bash Fundraiser for the Children's Health Center. It was a howling success! Our goal of $30,000 was realized. It was so successful that we have already booked next year's party on Monday, October 27, 1997. Our thanks to Toyota, Cathy Stephan of The Enchanted Basket and the entire Depot Staff.

... December 8th is the due date for Baby Shafer #2!

... The Stars are out at The Chez! In recent weeks, we've spotted Andrea Martin, Tom Hanks, Kurt Russell, Goldie Hawn, Liza Minelli, Kirk Douglas, Ellen DeGeneres, Carlos Leon, Tim Robbins, Susan Sarandon, George Hamilton, Sean Connery,

Roger Moore and Julia Louis Dreyfuss. It's a great place for people-watching!

... We now have cigars being sold and smoked in the bar area nightly at Chez Melange beginning at 9:30 pm. They are accompanied by our fine selection of Ports and after dinner drink selections.

... Happy Hour Special at Descanso. Tuesday through Sunday from 4:30 - 6:30 pm, drinks are 1/2 price!

... In the mood for seafood? Descanso features a variety of seafood entrees with nightly dinner specials—a perfect pairing with a wine list with it's own intriguing California flair. Dinner is served Tuesday through Sunday beginning at 5 pm.

... Do you have an idea for a private party or a special occasion, but just can't find that finishing touch? Let Descanso help you plan. We're sure to make your celebration a memorable one. Set up an appointment with the manager, and you'll be on your way!

... As proven in the past two years, New Year's Eve at Descanso promises to be the end of all celebrations!!!

Good example of how to put readers "in the know" on a wide variety of subjects.

Chef Bill Donnelly, Michael Franks and Maureen Clune (Pastry Chef at Chez Melange) at "Sunday by the Sea."

— 3

annual For Our Childrens' Wine and Food Festival, Hospice Foundation.

The Frequent Diner Program encourages its 5000 members to try the different locations Awards range from Team Melange baseball caps to picnic baskets to "Dine Around" for four, complete with limousine and hotel room with breakfast. There's also a "Kids View"

club, with awards of free desserts, special gifts and more.

Mailing list comes from business cards left in restaurant, Chambers of Commerce lists, credit card names.

Our reaction: With several restaurants in the same general area, this newsletter is an ideal way to tell its readers what's going on. Photos and editorial about employees is an excellent way to build and maintain pride and teamwork.

Collector's Choice Restaurant
★ Star Lounge

December 1995   Home of the Swifty Creek Yacht Club

I SAY TOMATO...
From Chef Ganacias

Real tomatoes! Every year, week after week, some of us stalk the local farmer's markets looking for...yes, real tomatoes! I'm not talking about the pink, mealy, cardboard-tasting impersonators we all too often bring home. But the deep, rich garden tomatoes with that aroma and meaty flesh and full, sun-drenched flavor! When you slice one you know you've found one...

Other foods have a season of perfection, like peaches and corn, and follow the same "rules"...the less done to the vegetable the better. Sometimes all that is needed is a sprinkling of salt to heighten their essential flavor. Of course some recipes call for more than just salt but they are designed to feature the salt as the star, with minimal fuss from other ingredients...

FOR MAXIMUM FLAVOR

1. Store tomatoes at room temperature. Refrigeration dulls the taste.
2. Keep tomatoes (not fully ripened) in a closed brown bag until ripe, then use promptly.
3. Cut up tomatoes, sprinkle with salt, toss lightly, let stand. This draws out excess water and intensifies the flavor.
4. For wintertime, make a big batch of fresh tomato sauce. By February "tasting summer" is as easy as

The good things in life are the little, natural things in life. Fresh, quality vegetables, for example, are timeless!

opening a jar and cooking up the spaghetti!

Recipe for
Chucky Tomato Sauce

Good with Fish, Chicken and Pasta
Makes about 2 1/2 cups

1 tablespoon butter, 1 tablespoon olive oil,1 medium, chopped onion, 3 garlic cloves, minced; 3 pounds tomatoes, peeled, seeded, chopped, 1 bar leaf and 2 tablespoons chopped parsley. Melt butter & oil in a sauce pan over medium heat. Add onion & sauté until translucent. Add garlic. Sauté about 5 minutes. Add tomatoes & herbs. Cook sauce until reduced to a chunky puree (About 20 min.) Season with salt and pepper to taste. Add the parsley and...
SUMMERTIME!

1996 !
Resolutions from
"The Choice"

Ready or not...another year! But let's make this the BEST year yet! At the Collector's Choice, we are committed to making still more improvements for our guests...you.

From "the Choice:"

NEW MENUS by late January that you'll find exciting. We mean...really fun, featuring high quality, fresh, perfectly prepared meals!

Our staff is totally committed to providing you with **5 star service!** Food and beverage knowledge, proper serving technique, proper plate presentation, consistency, friendliness with professionalism ...all part of our staff's repetoire.

Our dining rooms will be decorated with interesting **historical artifacts.** The Star lounge will be similarly "out-fitted."

With the influence of Donna and Chef Ganacias, we will soon be having **"wine-maker" dinners** with local wineries! These dinners will be announced when dates and menus are finalized. Reservations needed!

The thing is...the staff at the "Choice" really does care. It makes a difference!

You may also count on **entertainment** on the patio during nice weather. **Stay close, stay tuned!**

Food Trivia: In the eighteenth century, John Montague invented a small meal he could eat with one hand while he continued his non-stop gambling! John Montague..the Earl of Sandwich!

When owner John Hager added a lounge to his ongoing restaurant business, he needed a way to get the word out. A newsletter seemed like the ideal vehicle. He never looked back. It's now also the primary source of information for members of the Swifty Creek Yacht Club, a discount dining club.

A historical setting gives Hager lots of local folklore to draw on for his monthly publication. But one of the most popular regular features follows the ongoing adventures of "Howard at the Star," a character based on an actual customer. Hager is careful about not showing his not-so-fictional character in a bad light and always gets the "real" Howard's okay on the story line.

Hager is proud of his personable staff and often writes about their achievements.

Sounds intriguing, creates mystique.

He recalls the time he mentioned that one of his waiters was training for the Boston Marathon. "Customers began writing messages on payment checks encouraging her endeavor," says Hager. "The whole town got into it. And the newsletter is the only way they could have found out she was running."

Hager is trying to broaden his existing customer base by mailing 500 extra newsletters to new zip code routes each month.

Our reaction: Customers don't expect you to be completely unselfish in your editorial, but if you can be as conscientious as this letter about giving them something to take away, they'll be delighted.

37

Whitestone, NY

50 seats

Authentic Cajun and Creole cuisine in New Orleans-style setting

Steve Van Gelder, Owner

(718) 767-4647

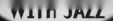

Cajun Quarterly
Cooking with Jazz

Issue #6 May 1996 Copy with permission only

Chef Paul had a great time here on March 24th and so did the other 400 people who came to visit and sample the foods that made Paul famous. We hope to have Paul back in the future so that those of you who were not able to visit with us this time can have a chance. Many of you had said that you thought it would be too crowded when Paul was here but we feel that it is never too crowded.

We Are Now Open on
Tuesday
Thats right 7 days a week !
You can come in and eat until you're full seven days a week from 5pm till 10pm 7 days.
Please call for reservations so we can prepare properly.

!!!!! Events NotePad !!!!!
1) The Crawfish are Here!!
2) Soft Shell Crabs are in and they are great!
3) Logo contest is over see page 4.
4) We are now open on Tuesday starting May 21
5) Monday smokers still smokin'.
6) Prix fixe dinner still available $15-5pm daily.
7) Citywide NY 96 Restaurant days 2pm -6pm.
8) Our long awaited vacation from June 23 until July 10th.Sorry for any inconvenience.
9) NYIT Benefit for Ryan Scholarship fund May 7.

Going above and beyond. Deserves attention.

NY 96 Restaurant Day
If you recall, last year we were invited to take part in the citywide effort to benefit City Meals on Wheels. This year the benefit will be on Friday, June 21 and Saturday, June 22 from 2 pm to 6 pm. We at Cooking with Jazz feel strongly about this type of community involvement, so we will be serving appetizer portions in our temporary sidewalk cafe and, instead of donating 1 dollar for each portion, we will donate all food sales from this event. The mayors office has granted all restaurants a permit to conduct business outdoors for this event so if you do not stop by here, make sure you stop by any of the other restaurants citywide to take part in this event. Last years event raised almost $60,000 dollars for this worthy cause. All you need is an appetite and a wallet!

Black type on white stock

8 1/2 x 11, self mailer

4 pages

4 issues/year

10,000 printed/7800 mailed

Published since June 1994

What's the best way to accumulate a list of 7800 loyal customers? Plead. Comment cards at Cooking with Jazz are vigilantly delivered to guests at the end of their meals. The cards tell guests how much their business is appreciated and ask them if there's anything else they'd like to see on the menu. If guests resist completing these cards, waiters are urged to be good-naturedly aggressive about the task,

pleading if necessary: "Please, we're a small restaurant with a short lease." It's the truth and it usually works.

Articles in the "Cajun Quarterly" range from announcements of new hours and menu changes to clearing the air about guests who don't stick to their reservation times. The restaurant even sponsored a logo contest and received about 130 entries.

Owner Steve Van Gelder is emphatic

Prix Fixe Early Evening Menu
available 7 days

Mon thru Thur
in by 5:30 done by 7

Sat, Sun, Holidays
in by 5 done by 6:30

$15.00 cash only

guaranteed to satisfy the
heartiest appetite!

Appetizers: House Salad
Chicken Wings
Chicken wontons
Cup of soup or gumbo
Caesar Salad
Entree: Grilled Herb Chicken
Roast Vegetable pasta
Herbal seafood pasta or pasta big mamou
Red beans and rice
Grilled or blackened Catfish
Buttermilk Battered Chicken
Chicken Etouffe
Spaghetti squash Primavera
Desserts: New Orleans Bread Pudding w/ whiskey sauce
New York Style cheesecake with Strawberry Glaze
Sour Cream Apple Crumb Pie
Coffee or Tea included

This Months recipe from Cooking With Jazz:
Bananas Foster
2 bananas
1 tb sweet butter
1 tb dark brown sugar
2 t grand marnier
1 t water
1/2 t cinnamon
1 t sweet butter
2 scoops Vanilla Ice Cream
2 rosettes Whipped Heavy Cream

Method: saute bananas until soft, add brown sugar and cirinamon, saute .5 min. then add Marnier and Flambe, then add H2o, bring to boil then add last butter to emulsify. serve around Ice cream and top with whip cream

Election Year 96

Hey now,
Who are you going to vote for? Are you going to vote? Do you think your vote really counts? You bet your vote counts!
Each and every vote counts.
This is a democracy isn't it?
I want you to vote this year , even if you have not voted for the past ten years. Why? It is not only a right but it is also each and every citizens **duty** to vote for the candidate of their choice. Why don't we have much choice is the next question. I feel that voter apathy is the reason we don't have the choice we need. What business can stay in business without a budget besides our old USA. Our politicians have finally voted in a budget 7 months after the fiscal year began. Better late then never. If you still don't feel like voting then you have no right to complain about the way our elected officials act. Please Vote! Let our politicians know that there are people down here who do care about the way our country is being run. It is important to you, me and our children.
Chef Steve

> Overly rah-rah? Not if it's your personality—how you really feel

about the need for cleaning up your mailing list—especially for small restaurants that depend on repeat business. "It may be expensive," he says, "but it's the only way to follow your customers around."

Van Gelder's parting wisdom about newsletters is a tacit endorsement: "Don't tell anyone how well this works. I don't want newsletters to get too mainstream. Or compete with mine in my customers' mailboxes."

Our reaction: We see a trend developing. The more an owner injects his own personality into the copy, the more dedicated his audience becomes.

DAIRY HOLLOW HOUSE

Moos-Letter

Late 1995 - Early/Mid 1996   "All The News That's Fittin'"

Restaurant Reborn

In Which We Bring New Meaning to the Words "Seasonal Cuisine"

As of July 31, 1995, we are no longer offering nightly dinners. But wait'll you see what we've got going on instead! Quarterly pull-out-all-the-stops feasts... soirees... Moos-Letters ...books... room renovations...

Now, we realize that being the Dairy Hollow afficionado you are, you are probably 1) a little sad and 2) wondering "Why?" and "What now?" We think the answers to 2) will cure 1). "Why" is handily discussed by the Neditor himself. And "What now?" details surface in several places; the "Innkeeper's Saturday Sampling" and "Quarterly Feasts at the Inn" stories in our centerfold, the ... well, see for yourself. But please, be reassured *right this second* as to our and the inn's general (if slightly reinvented) well-being.

Bad news doesn't have to sound that way.

A Letter from the Neditor:
The Bridges of "Nedison" County

Every time I drove across the Highway 62 bridge over the King's River, I'd wonder what it would be like to bicycle it. Each time, driving in fact, I bicycled in imagination: pedaling hard, crouched in the alert preparedness which on-road cyclists maintain. With every by-car bridge-crossing, too, I'd cast a quick glance down: gauging the water level, noting the King's depth and potential floatability. As if by looking I might somehow legitimize myself as better than the mere once-a-year canoeist I am in fact... as if the act of having a canoe-floater's thoughts could make me as much a canoe-floater as the act itself of floating.

The bridge itself is an unlikely site for such meditations. It's an arching, poured-concrete bridge, not particularly showy, narrow, shoulderless (hence the

(Continued on Page 2)

Innkeeper's New Saturday Samplings: Strolls, Soirees, Salons & Some Spectacular Surprises (see centerfold)

Three Moos-Letters a Year! Details, page 7.

LOVE That Country Pie!

. . . when it's Dairy Hollow's New South B & B White Chocolate Banana-Cream Pie, a Pecan Crust, that is; one of 5 winning finalists (out of 400+ entries) in a contest sponsored by B & B Liqueur. We didn't win the trip for two to Paris, but did receive a Baccarat decanter, will also be part of some really well-done material they're producing on the five top inns, and developed a recipe that has us all just swooning with delight! More, next Moos.

Friendly New Faces by Night:

Meet David & Jason, your after-hours innkeepers (left & page 2)

Some of the guests at Dairy Hollow House don't return for up to three or four years after their last visit, so the Shanks wanted to remind them of their stay and keep them interested. "We know direct mail works," says Ned Shank, co-owner. "The newsletter is a way to extend our guests' experiences and set up expectations for the next visit." Another goal of the newsletter is to sell cookbooks and children's books written by Co-owner Crescent Dragonwagon.

When DHH decided to limit food service to quarterly themed feasts, the newsletter became the vehicle to issue a highly personal statement explaining their decision. But food will always be an integral part of the establishment and the newsletter, whether its an award-winning pie recipe or recommendations for in-town dining.

Let Us Be Your Dinner Date

ummer 1996: **Soul-of-Summer Supper Soiree**: Saturday, June 29, 7:30 p.m.; $49 per person, 6 burstingly abundant courses. The living's easy, the cotton's high, and the dining is lush, luxuriant, soul-satisfyingly fresh. All the best of the season's bounty inspires new flights of fancy (some from CD's cookbook-in-progress) and the return of old favorites (trout French country-style, black-pepper lamb with garlic and basil, roasty-toasties, from-scratch strawberry shortcake with local berries). And if the night is a hot one, our live but low-key jazz musicians will make it very, very cool.

all 1996: **An Ozarks Autumnal Festival Feast**: Saturday, October 19, 7:00 pm, $49 per person, 6 beautiful fall courses. It's War Eagle Weekend, days are short and cool, the kids are back in school, and the leaves are at the height of their glory. It's time to relax in this, the most joyful turning of the year. Perhaps you'll have spent the day wandering one of America's most famed festivals, the War Eagle Crafts Fair; perhaps you hid from the hoopla, floating the King's River, the vivid leaves reflected in its dark water. In either case, now it's time to indulge in a candlelit dinner of seasonal perfection: pumpkin bisque, pork loin roasted in sweet/spicy onion crust with muscadine demi-glace, caramel-glazed pear cake with inn-made vanilla-bean ice cream, warm granny smith apple dumpling. Traditional acoustic folk music, gentle but spirited, is just right.

Innkeeper's Saturday Samplings: Strolls, Soirees, Salons & Some Spectacular Surprises

A Saturday morning **architectural ramble** along Spring Street with resident historic preservationist Ned, as he informally parleys on Eureka's architectural styles, history, people, and curiosities. **High tea and sherry** with one or both innkeepers in front of the fireplace on a rainy November Saturday afternoon; *so* civilized. What will the invitation be when *you* check in? Now, our feelings will not be the least bit hurt if this is a private-time, hole-up-in-your-room-with-your-companion kind of weekend for you. However, you might just enjoy tasting our prize-winning **New South B & B White Chocolate Banana Cream Pie in a Pecan Crust** (see photo), or taking an "inn-siders" evening **Gallery Walk**. And let's not forget sampling recipes for the upcoming **Crescent Dragonwagon's Vegetarian Cooking: Great Recipes from Dairy Hollow House & Beyond.** It's all part of our new Innkeeper's Saturday Samplings: strolls, soirees, salons, and some surprises. Your invitation will await you at check-in.

No, you can't wheedle out of us exactly what your Saturday's event will be (the weather may dictate some last minute changes; that's why we said "Surprises"). And, there are some weekends, where one or both of us are out of town, and hence, no soiree or stroll, or one with only half our dynamic duo. (Between September and February, however, we have only one trip

Pie-Eyed: Guests Carrie DeCato, Harry Mohrman & Bill Parks at 1st sampling, Sept. 30, with Ned, CD, nighttime innkeeper Jason Oury, Folk Festival musician Crow Johnson, her husband Arthur Evans, and Uncle Phil. (More pies post-pix). "If this came in second," remarked someone, "I'd just like to try number 1, cause this is prettttttty darn good!"

planned, CD is off to tape a television show called "Ready, Steady, Cook!" in New York, but that's another story).

It adds up to that ineffable Dairy Hollow magic chemistry: interesting people, some form of good food, an ever-fascinating historical community, always fun to explore. In a way, we hope to live up to what *Bury My Heart at Wounded Knee* author Dee Brown said of us: that Dairy Hollow is "... a sort of Algonquin Round Table of the Ozarks."

It's part of the post-restaurant "bridge-crossing" reinvention the Neditor describes in his Letter. Of course, not all guests want interaction, but, when we've visited inns as guests ourselves, we've felt an essential part is being able to get to visit with the innkeepers. Inngoers, after all, are travelers, not tourists; they prefer the authentic to the Disney World/ McDonald's versions. If this sounds like you, we think these Saturday Surprises may make you up and holler "I have found it!". In Greek, as you may know, that would be, "Eureka!"

> Can you combine tours of local architecture or history with brunch or lunch at your restaurant?

An upside to the reduced dinner service was more time to publish newsletters: three or four Moos-Letters each year instead of one. To do so, he has begun charging a $10 annual subscription and hopes to convert 20% of the 11,000 names on his existing list. Complimentary subs are still offered to inn guests, however.

Our reaction: We came close to not including this one—since they've limited food service to quarterly themed dinners—but it's just too well-done. Notice how the type and illustrations meld with the overall theme. We don't suggest charging for a subscription, however, unless your writing is as compelling and evocative as this.

The East Bay Express

From The Editor:

Hello again, we would like to thank all our local customers for the great response from our last East Bay Express and hope you keep finding it informative as well as a money saving tool. We hope you had a great summer and thanks to you we did!

A special note, if you haven't been to one of our **Murder Mystery Dinner Theaters**, you're missing out on this areas best entertainment values! The production company, "Elaine's", from Cape May is now performing exclusively here at East Bay! Check for all our upcoming shows in this newsletter.

Hope to serve you soon!

Holiday Shopping Made Easy with East Bay Gift Certificates!

East Bay has just made your holiday shopping a whole lot easier. Our Gift Certificates are the perfect gift since you specify the amount. It can be a stocking stuffer, pollyana gift, a gift for a fellow employee, a gift for the one person who has everything or even a big gift allowing a whole family to enjoy East Bay's Great food and service.

Simply purchase them on your next visit or order them by phone. It's a great gift! Everyone has to eat, so they might as well enjoy it! And remember they're not just for the holidays. They make a great birthday, anniversary, retirement gifts and more.

Holiday Party Dates Going Fast!

Only a few prime dates are left so book your Holiday party now!

Reservations are now being taken for the holiday season which is fast approaching. Book your party now to avoid disappointment. We have private rooms for parties from 20 to 100 guests and, of course, during the entire holiday season we have East Bay professionally decorated with holiday music playing in the background to add to the ambiance of your party.

Remember we also do birthdays, reunions, meetings, anniversaries, rehearsal dinners, showers, weddings, holiday parties and more. Complete packages available from only $7.95 per person. For more information, call Mr. Armstrong at 609-272-7721.

Can be a valuable service for guests.

Inside This Edition...

- ☞ All New Surf & Turf combos
- ☞ All You Can Eat Nights
- ☞ Murder Mystery Dinner Theatre
- ☞ Money Saving Coupons Galore!
- ☞ Micro-Brew Beer Tasting Dinner
- ☞ And Lots More!!

East Bay Crab & Grille
6701 Black Horse Pike
Egg Harbor Twp., N.J. 08234
609-272-7721

With a growing roster of 25,000 readers and color printing, publishing the East Bay Express every three months doesn't come cheap. But it has been absolutely invaluable in updating and refreshing the East Bay Crab and Grille's image, according to Chuck Armstrong. The hefty mailing list was acquired gradually from comment cards and forms the basis for newsletter readership. An extra 5,000-10,000 copies are printed and distributed to local hotels, some of which are delivered directly to rooms.

Armstrong gauges response from the coupons redeemed from each issue and the resulting number of bookings. "We took 450 reservations for our Seafood Buffet without any other advertising," he says.

Armstong is just as enthusiastic about a recently launched Web site (http://www.eastbaycrab.com) which he sees working in

Coupons help track response; like getting an interest-free loan.

tandem with the newsletter. A what's new section, linked with his home computer, can be updated frequently and will contain items from the newsletter. The newsletter, in turn, will frequently talk about his cyber publication.

"If we weren't located in a resort area, I'd probably eliminate all advertising except my newsletter and Web site," says Armstrong. And of those two media, he states his commitment to newsletters in stronger terms: "The Web site may be a fad, but I know the newsletter will always be around."

Our reaction: While not for everybody, the use of color seems to be effective in establishing an image for the restaurant. However, more food and wine information, to supplement the promotions and coupons, would also be welcome.

Omaha, NE

Various seating capacities

Delivery from 25 client restaurants; from ethnic to fast food to upscale

Kristin Tyler, Co-owner

(402) 333-7233

See "Resource Guide", p.186 for Calendar of Events.

Fetchers Food Files

Brought to you by Fetchers Restaurant Delivery | Spring 1995

THE MENU

Fetchers First TWO years!

Jack & Mary's Great Summer Salad Recipe

Grisanti's New Menus!

Choose Little King

Caniglia's Strike Again!

Lights Camara FOOD!

American Express Invited

Our Hours

Fetchers Faculty

Customer Favorites

2 Year Anniversary! Congratulations Fetchers!

April marks a full two years that Fetchers has been serving our great customers! We've certainly learned a lot and enjoyed getting to know you all! We thank you for your patience and understanding through out start-up years and we so appreciate your continuing business. The restaurant delivery industry was very limited before Spring 1993 and so all of our restaurants and their staffs have had to adjust to the added business. And we must say, they have done a fine job!

From you we've heard that the two most important things in food delivery are (*page 2 col 1*)

"A True Marriage of Convenience!"

That's what people are saying about Jack and Mary's and Fetchers Restaurant Delivery. Jack & Mary's famous FRIED CHICKEN, plus the regular menu items including steaks, seafood, salads, appetizers and Nightly Specials are very popular with you, our customers. And Jack and Mary's chef has been kind enough to share a recipe for a special summer salad. (*page 2 col 2*)

Venice Inn's New Dishy Dishes

The Caniglia's have cooked up some great new dishes! Starting with meaty Buffalo Wing appetizers-12 per order. WOW! Or how about the fine Scallops and Linguine in Wine Sauce. Also added is a Creamy Pesto Sauce over Pasta & a Great New Beef Tortelini in their famous Red Sauce. (*page 2 col 3*)

Grisanti's New Menu A Delicious Change

Both the party menu and the individual menu have gone through some revisions and the reviews are in...They are being called "a delicious change". (Lest you bread-snarfing folks are worrying, they have not changed the bread one iota!) The New Party Menu is on Page 4 of this newsletter. It does replace the old party menu, so insert this into your menu guide until our summer guides come out soon.

The new individual menu is quite a treat. The old favorites are, of course, still highlights on this new menu. But, don't limit yourself to just them! For example, for lunch, they've added two traditional Italian calzones- one is stuffed with spicy Italian sausage, sauteed fresh mushrooms and four cheeses. The other calzone is a scrumptious four cheese and spinach calzone. Both are served with Italian Onions and marinara sauce. Also added to the lunch menu is a Shrimp Scampi with Linguine served with salad and bread. Just a sampling!

For dinner, try out the Shrimp Scampi appetizer! Or how about the Mussels (*page 2 col 3*)

Little King Now Available!

Loyal Little King fans can now be armchair quarterbacks and eat their favorite heroes at the same time! Fetchers delivers from this long-time favorite and part of the King's great menu is included on page 3. Check it out!

Order from Fetchers for Mother's Day May 14!

Black type on various pastel papers

8 1/2 x 11, self mailer

4 pages

Published in between menu mailings

7000 printed and mailed

Published since Spring 1993

"Even though we're a delivery service and not a restaurant, our newsletter is just as effective in helping us keep in touch with our customers," says Kristin Tyler, co-owner. Fetchers ordinarily reprints their delivery menu guide twice each year. But they maintain such a stable group of clients that it's often not necessary to reprint so often. In that case, minor menu changes and seasonal shifts in hours can be combined with features such as a Mother's Day reminder, a client's recipe, employee recognition or an informal poll of customers' favorite foods.

"Business always jumpstarts after a mailing," adds Tyler. "So even if we had no changes to announce, the newsletter is a powerful reminder and keeps business from trailing off as it naturally would in the months following a new menu mailing."

44

2 Year Anniversary!

a correct order and timeliness. Getting your order correct is certainly with in our grasp every time and with the cooperation of the restaurants, we think we're getting pretty good at it. All the communication lines your order goes through for the purpose of getting to you correctly are quite amazing. Check out this list:

Family member to Family member to Fetchers phone waiter to Fetchers order form to Restaurant phone waiter to restaurant ticket to cook! WOW! That's lotsa people committed to paying attention to getting your order correct!

The other factor that is important to you is timeliness. And we do our very best to give you accurate estimates. Unfortunately, road conditions, other drivers, restaurant waits, and our lovely interstate road construction☹! make exact estimates quite impossible. You have been so understanding with us when we've been either before or after our estimated time and we thank you!

We've sincerely enjoyed the last two years with you and to show you how important you are to us, we are including the following coupon (only Fetchers customers are receiving this prestigious mailing!): **Two years in business for us means 2 FREE cans of Pop for you** with your next order when you redeem this coupon to the phone waiter <u>and</u> driver.

A True Marriage...

<u>Citrus Chicken Salad</u>
Serves 4

4 Boneless skinless chicken breasts
12 oz. Creamy Italian Salad Dressing
1 Orange
1 Red onion, sliced into rings
1 12 oz. can Mandarin Oranges
1/4 lb red grapes
1/4 lb strawberries
Seasonal fruit
6 oz. Orange Vinaigrette
Mixed Greens (lettuce, spinach, romaine)

Marinate chicken in Italian dressing for 4 hours or overnight in the cooler. Grill chicken until done and cool. Cut into strips and set aside. Chop the assorted greens and place chicken, Mandarin Oranges, grapes, strawberries and red onions on top. Sprinkle with Orange Vinaigrette (recipe following) and garnish with seasonal fruit.

<u>Orange Vinaigrette Dressing</u>
Makes 2 cups

1 c. Cider vinegar
6 oz sugar
1 T. Kosher salt
6 oz. Orange marmalade
Zest of 1 orange
Juice of one orange
1/4 c. vegetable oil

Mix well and serve over salad.

Thank you Jack and Mary's!

Grisanti's New Menu...

Marinara. For salads, a Grilled Shrimp ~~Pasta Salad~~ has been added. Under the chicken entrees, ~~the Grilled Chicken~~ Brochette or Grilled Chicken Alfredo are both very popular. Veal Piccata served over linguine with fresh lemon sauce and capers accompanies fresh sauteed vegetables and is exquisite! Three new pizzas round out the pizza menu: Tomato and Basil, Grilled Artichoke Heart, Country Italian (grilled chicken, pepperoni, prosciutto, fresh green peppers, black olives, mushrooms and onions). Try one! We are also serving Grisanti's Children's menu also through delivery.

For delivery from Grisanti's, there is only ONE number to call, and it's <u>Fetchers! 333-7233!</u>

 Having your outside light on before we arrive certainly speeds up delivery times and gives our drivers fewer eye wrinkles from squinting. They thank you from the bottom of their cars.

Venice's Dishy Dishes

Chicken Marsala is a great new meal available. You may also order the Steak & Shrimp Combo. Three great fish entrees make their debut at Caniglia's also. The Lemon Pepper Catfish Filet is very nice. Rich bay Scallops sauteed with fresh garlic, lemon and wine make up the Scallops ala Siciliana. You may also get a savory catfish filet delicately grilled or blackened to your liking.

All of the meat dishes are accompanied by your choice of potato, pasta or vegetable du jour, fresh green salad and warm dinner rolls. That's a lot of bang for your buck! Food fit for a king and delivered right to your front door.

If customers understand all that goes into it, they'll be more understanding and appreciative.

Helps speed up delivery orders.

"The challenge becomes making sure that the newsletter evenly features all 25 clients," continues Tyler. But she concedes that if a restaurant features Fetchers in their advertising, the restaurant will probably get preferential treatment in the newsletter.

The substantial mailing list is logically composed of previous delivery customers, but Fetchers will add any client's internal list to their own.

Our reaction: No, Fetchers is not a restaurant. That's precisely why we included it. To show how newsletters can be effective in almost any situation. It's targeted, its response is fast and you control the content.

Austin, TX

225 seats

Authentic interior Mexican menu in stylish comfortable setting

Tom Gilliland, Owner/ Dan Fitzgerald, General Manager

(512) 459-4121

Excellent range of articles.

Fonda San Miguel - Serving fine Mexican Cuisine   http://www.fondasanmiguel.com/

Fonda San Miguel

A corner of old Mexico in Austin

2330 West North Loop
Austin, Texas 78756
(512) 459-4121
FAX: (512) 459-5792

Tuesday, January 07, 1997 16:24:27

Take A Trip

Mexican Art

Mexican Cuisine

Fonda San Miguel

Gifts

Cookbooks

Our Menu

Dining in Austin, TX

Our website promotes and educates the public concerning the many aspects of Mexican culture and art, including the traditional and classic cooking of the various regions of Mexico.

News:
Fonda Nominated For National Award Learn about the prestigious Ivy Society.

Features:
Who's got the best grilled cabrito in Mexico City? Here are some fine places to eat this delicacy.

Traveling?
Take A Trip Discover some interesting places to eat in Mexico.

Hungry?
Read **Our Menu** to see what's on our menu this evening.

In the meantime, if you are in Austin or planning to visit, please call us to make your dining reservations at (512) 459-4121 after 3:30 P.M. CST.

You are visitor number 0300

This web site is designed and hosted by **Labnet**.

1 of 1   1/7/97 5:34 PM

Website address: http://www.fondasan-miguel.com

4-5 pages

Updated approximately every two weeks

Published cyber newsletter since late 1995

Fonda San Miguel owner Tom Gilliland takes great pride in the restaurant's authentic cuisine, which offers more faithful versions of the spicy food patrons usually associate with border or Tex-Mex. A year ago, the restaurateur gave the eatery an even more unique niche by going from a traditional mailed newsletter to cyberspace.

Gilliland maintains the Website, which contains about five choices/subcategories to choose from, including a copy of the menu, a report on past or upcoming special events, recipes, a history of the menu's signature dishes and restaurant reviews of establishments in various Mexican regions. "Our Website offers much more than just information on us," notes general manager Dan Fitzgerald, "and for loyal clientele, it's an effective reinforcing technique of the customer's

http://www.fondasanmiguel.com/mainmenu.map?97,31

Fonda San Miguel

Mexico City - Oaxaca - Vera Cruz

Take A Trip To Mexico

Mexico has many interesting regions to visit. These areas of Mexico offer distinct cooking styles. We have found that the best way to make your vacation memorable is to go off the beaten path, beyond the tourist areas. You will be rewarded with delicious surprises.

There are many factors that combine to make an outstanding and interesting dining experience: what you order, the biorythm of both you and the restaurant staff that day, the supplies brought in by the various purveyors, etc.

The important thing is to be creative, receptive to new foods, appreciate what is being done (or not done) and approach your new encounter with a positive attitude, i.e. have fun! Don't have a middle-class mentality (you're not in Kansas anymore); Eat as a peasant or as a King!

Mexico City

There are many wonderful restaurants in this grand city, all price ranges. The following represent some of our favorites for different reasons but don't even begin to represent, even minimally, the diversity of dining in Mexico City.

Hosteria Santo Domingo

One of the better known and authentic regional Mexican restaurants. Worth a trip but not everything is wonderful. We know the following items are outstanding: "Pollo con natas": Chicken with a special sauce (natas) made from the skim of the milk and a chile pasilla sauce. Also, the entremeses ranchero (serves 2-4 persons) is a combination platter of specialties. Don't have the Chiles en nogada, one of the great specialties of Mexico. It is a seasonal dish (July through Sept.). Theirs is not up to the standards of other places, they attempt to serve it year around. Don't order this very special dish out-of-season.

Cafe Rosales

Located in Calle Rosales behind the Lottery Building on Reforma Avenue, very plain and popular in the mornings, this is the best Cafe con leche in the city. Their "pan dulce" is also the best in the city, especially the Magdalendas. Also have their Huevos a la oaxaquena (eggs, Oaxacan-style). This is very plain surroundings and inexpensive and very popular. Seldom in the tourist guides!

El Candelero Restaurant

On Insurgentes Sur, this is a majestic and expensive restaurant with fine art and china, serving "alta cocina" or the haute cuisine of Mexico. Splurge!!!

Charco de las Ranas

A traditional Mexico City taqueria, organized in a large capacity setting with excellent taqueria food. There are 4 or 5 around the city. No credit cards.

Early in their founding, the banks wouldn't provide processing to them; now they're used to cash only, the banks are falling all over themselves to get their business & the restaurant isn't interested. Justice!!

Gueleguetza Restaurant (name of Oaxaca's famous festival)

In Satelite City behind the Satelite Mall, this restaurant features Oaxacan

Mexican Art

Mexican Cuisine

Fonda San Miguel

Gifts

Cookbooks

Our Menu

Dining in Austin, TX

Travel is always a topic of interest.

1/7/97 5:33 PM

---

dining experience—a nice way to continue it."

Customers seem most interested in how the restaurant creates its menu, he says, and the background on each dish. Servers are instructed to inform patrons about the Website when they ask menu-related questions or request restaurant information for future travel.

Waiters answer all questions to the best of their knowledge, and then add, 'Here's a way to stay in touch with our restaurant and learn more,'" Fitzgerald states. "In subsequent visits, guests often tell us about the facts they learned on the Internet."

Our reaction: No one quite knows the future of the Internet, but Fonda San Miguel seems to have a jump on it, especially important in techno-savvy Austin.

Food Services Management Associates • The Abbott Building
235 Alpha Drive • Pittsburgh, Pennsylvania 15238 • 412-963-1695

HOLIDAY 1995   **For Guests • Media • Marketing**

The Classic Liqueurs

iqueurs are having a resurgence in popularity. What better way to take the sting out of being over-stressed than to enjoy the small luxury of a sweet-sippin' liqueur. It's easy on the pocketbook and readily available, so why not?

It's true that most Americans are drinking less hard stuff nowadays and making responsible decisions regarding drinking and driving. But many adults still want the social experience of an enjoyable drink without over-indulgence.

Another reason for the resurgence in popularity of liqueurs is their capacity to play many roles for many people. Some women will order a frozen drink with a wild name like a Blue Cloud or a Razzbarretto just because it's fun. And after dinner, they might choose a cordial instead of dessert. Men sip liqueurs too, but they usually order brands with stronger tastes and often pair them with a second coffee and sometimes a cigar. It makes a leisurely and delightful end to a satisfying dinner. And to a younger generation, tempted from the cradle with sugared cereals, sodas and candy, sweet liqueurs are a natural, especially schnapps.

The creators of the earliest liqueurs were medieval alchemists, and their recipes were originally intended to be medicinal elixirs. Several liqueurs are still made from ancient, closely guarded recipes, and their origins are shrouded in mystery. At one time, nearly everyone drank them. Many cordials were sipped as love potions and aphrodisiacs, some were supposed to stimulate the appetite or aid digestion, while others were tossed back as cure-alls for all sorts of ailments.

Most folks use the terms liqueur and cordial interchangeably. Both are made by combining or redistilling spirits with one or more aromatic flavorings, but there are subtle differences. Cordials are most often made from fruit pulp or juices. Liqueurs, however, can be flavored with herbs, nuts, seeds, roots, spices, chocolate and plants, leaves and flowers.

any liqueurs have withstood the test of time. Sipped slowly and savored, they're the very soul of indulgence and romance. Next dinner out, order one of the classics.

Citrus variations are among the most popular flavors. Many people think that the queen of them all is Grand Marnier. This venerable liqueur is sophisticated, velvety and speaks of the good life. An exquisite pairing of cognac with the essence of bitter orange peel, it is one of the most versatile of all liqueurs. Try it warmed in a giant snifter or order a Golden Margarita.

Grand Marnier's orange-flavored sisters are also popular sippers. Dutch-made Curacao dates from the 1500s; the softly citrus drink is also bottled in a shocking swimming-pool blue color. Triple Sec is a refined form of Curacao and is most often used as the sweetener in margaritas. Cointreau, made from French

(cont'd. on page 6)

Introducing CAFE Juno

Brand new Cafe Juno opens in the expanded Juno Trattoria in One Oxford Centre in mid-December. The Cafe emphasizes quick service and exciting food made in an open display-kitchen where chefs will cook before your very eyes.

A selection of nine antipasto dishes will be featured every day. Dishes like Grilled Polenta with Smoked Plum Tomatoes, Sausage and Hot Peppers in Roasted Pepper Sauce, Wilted Escarole Aglio with Asiago Cheese, Roast Chicken Pasta Salad and Green Beans with Pancetta. You can order three, six or, better yet, all nine.

That's just for starters. We also have Sandwiches...Slow-roasted Portobello Mushroom on a Sourdough Ciabatta Roll, Salads...Grilled Garden Vegetable, and Pastas...perhaps a Barolo Braised Veal-and-Mushroom Pasta tossed with Fettucine in a red-wine brown sauce. To name a few. To see the rest, you'll just have to make a lunch date.

The Juno wine list has been updated and expanded, and we now offer more wines by the glass. The cakes and pies are as tempting as ever, and we've added a few more cookies- Hazelnut Shortbread and Sesame Shortbread. And brought back by popular demand, Pignoli Cookies and Creme Carmel.

The Cafe will be open for lunch and early dinner, and will be available evenings and weekends for private parties. Weekday Hours: 11 am to 7 pm, Saturdays: 11 am to 4 pm.

"What's Cookin'" as the newsletter is called, can sometimes be unconventional. Take the random-dot stereogram that occupied a full page of a recent issue. "Isn't it a waste of space?" we asked Marlene Parrish, former marketing director and editor. "That page has been posted on more bulletin boards in more offices than you can imagine," she replied. "All with our logos plainly in sight."

Parrish had been the strong voice of "What's Cookin'." "I gather the information, write copy and sketch out what I think I'd like it to look like, then let my designer go to work." Once each issue is finalized, it's sent to the printer and then the mailing contractor for distribution.

The 10,000-name customer database was built diligently over 5 1/2 years. First with customer comment cards and a fish-

48

Kid's Club Page

How many words can you spell with the word CAR in them? Taking things slowly and CARefully, can you come up with all 10?

1 The two of clubs is one   CAR____

2 Slice up the turkey   CAR____ ____

3 Wall-to-wall   CAR____ ____ ____

4 Orange vegetable   CAR____ ____ ____

5 Chewy candy sometimes on apples   CAR____ ____ ____ ____

6 Song sung at Christmas   CAR____ ____ ____

7 Former President Jimmy   CAR____ ____ ____

8 Fair with rides and games   CAR____ ____ ____ ____

9 Cinderella's ride to the ball   CAR____ ____ ____ ____ ____

10 Woodworker   CAR____ ____ ____ ____ ____ ____ ____

Santa will be stopping by Dingbats Sunday Buffet Brunch in Ross Park Mall between 10 a.m. and 2 p.m. on December 3, 10, 17. Busy guy.

Breakfast on the Porch with Santa

Santa will visit with the little ones from 9 to 11 a.m. on Saturday, December 16. Besides a personal visit with the bearded one, there will be a Breakfast Buffet of all your favorite foods. The kids will get a coupon for a free "Kids-Come-Back Meal and will take home a special gift. The cost is $3.95 per person.

See the Manager at Abaté to make your reservations. For more information, even though we've said it all, call 781-9550.

Safety Tips...

John Balocik — Manager of Buildings Operations and Safety

Hi Girls and Boys. I know you're going to have a great time playing with all the new toys, games and books that Santa is bringing for you. Please remember, Kids, to put them away or out of the way after you're done playing with them. Toys left on stairs or in the middle of a room could cause someone to trip and fall.

This page involves kids, making you popular with mom & dad too.

Families can help Dingbats adopt a family this holiday season. Contribute a non-perishable household item such as canned food when you visit any Dingbats between December 1 and 18. Each child will receive a FREE POG and a FREE PEPSI. Look for the Community Food Bank Barrel at all Dingbats. And thanks.

Won't you say you Love Me Too!

That's what Barney says. Come see the friendly purple dinosaur at Dingbats City Tavern in One Oxford Centre on Saturday, December 16.

bowl to gather business cards, then by adding media lists and membership rosters of local clubs.

The center spread of each issue features a lively, eye-catching events calendar. "We live in a visual age, " says Parrish. "And this captures the readers attention in a graphic, *USA Today* kind of way."

Photos involve employees and guests in the publication. Each restaurant has a disposable camera on hand for special moments. Employees often comment if their stores are not represented in an issue. "What have you done that's newsworthy?" quips Parrish. That gets them motivated.

Our reaction: Punchy copy and cheery graphics reflect the high-energy theme of these family-style establishments. (And a little humor never hurt anybody.) We like the fact that there's something for everybody—including the kids.

AT THE FOUR
SEASONS

Austin, TX

114 seats inside/
42 outside

Updated classic
cuisine with regional
influences in relaxed
elegant decor

Peter Gregg,
Cafe Manager

(512) 477-0704

Tea service is
gaining popularity
all over the U.S.

This may be true for a
number of restaurants with
an extensive wine list.

Volume 2
Number 1
February, 1996

Newsletter for The Four Seasons Hotel, Austin, Texas

Afternoon Tea—

For Any Occasion

"We are overjoyed with the response we've received from our regular tea patrons who are discovering that this event is a perfect break in the week," said Food and Beverage Director Christina Clifton. Indeed, the success of our Tea Service, from 3-5 p.m. on Wednesdays, has proven that this is an idea whose time has come. With the panache and elegance our patrons always enjoy, this event has quickly gained acceptance. Just imagine taking time out from a stress-filled day and settling in for a lavish selection of teas, coffees, pastries, and hors d'oeuvres while admiring our view of Town Lake.

Texas Hill Country Wine & Food Festival Pours On the Culinary Delights, April 11-14.

Plans are being finalized for the Eleventh Annual Texas Hill Country Wine & Food Festival, scheduled for the Four Seasons, April 11-14. This year's lineup of star chefs includes Cajun master Paul Prudhomme. Begun in 1985 as an event to advance the appreciation and quality of wine and food in Texas, it annually attracts 2000 participants. The 1996 Festival features stars such as Prudhomme, cookbook author, television personality and Cajun chef supreme; Douglas Rodriguez of New York's renowned Patria; Madhur Jaffrey, eminent Indian chef, actress and author assisted by Dawat Restaurant in New York; Horst Pfeifer from New Orleans' Bella Luna; Mark Miller of the Coyote Cafe restaurants in Santa Fe, Las Vegas and Austin; and Mark Militello of Mark's in the Grove and Mark's Place in Ft. Lauderdale and Miami at the Saturday night dinner.

No matter what your taste in wine, food, and cigars, you'll have a time to remember at the Festival. The event's organizers were overjoyed when they heard that Penfold's Grange Hermitage wine had been named the number one wine in the world for 1995 by *Wine Spectator* Magazine, since the "Best From Down Under—Penfold's Grange Hermitage," is one of the featured seminars for Saturday. Also, attendees can go to cooking schools at Central Market, "Shopping With A Chef" at Whole Foods, baking with Daniel Leader at Schlotzsky's Bread Alone, a Friday

Texas Beef Council, Whole Foods, Central Market, Bread Alone, and more. Tickets are available for all three days and individual events as well. It's always a sell-out, so call now for your reservations, at (512) 329-0770. (And of course, for maximum enjoyment, relax and stay at the Four Seasons—call 478-4500.)

Sleep Tight, Four Seasons Style.

Listening to guests' requests keeps the Four Seasons in the forefront of Austin hotel service. And bedding is no exception. Executive Housekeeper Ashley Lester says that now, every room in the hotel will have a fluffy, feathery European style duvet for warm sleeping. Also, guests can have a choice of wool or non-allergenic blankets for those chilly Central Texas nights. And while we're on the subject of hotel improvements, watch for the new and unique decorations on each elevator landing.

Rare Wines Are Commonplace With Us.

Our Sommelier Peter Gregg has looked into some special nooks and crannies in the wine vaults and has discovered some stellar bottles which we think are almost impossible to find anywhere else in Austin. The next time you dine with us and are in the mood for something truly special, let our knowledgeable waitstaff suggest some spectacular wines to accompany your choice of food.

For instance, Gregg points to his Girard Viridian, Staglin Cabernet, and '88 Haut Brion. Also, he has some '88 Pahlmeyer, '90 and '91 Caymus Special Select

Four Seasons Calendar

Jan. 31st   Bordeaux Vintner Dinner hosted by Woody DeLuna. Cafe.

Feb. 14th   Valentine's Day. Please plan early due to limited availability.

Black copy with turquoise accents

8 1/2 x 14, self mailer

2 pages

2 issues/year

6000 printed/5000 mailed

Published since 1994

"The main purpose of our newsletter is to raise overall awareness and maintain top of mind share among our customer base," says Peter Gregg, cafe manager. Beyond that he has other more specific goals in mind: "First it puts a personal face on the restaurant and hotel in general. By using a light-hearted friendly tone, we are helping convince some potential customers that the restaurant and hotel are

not stuffy places. Second, it lets customers know about upcoming events such as vintner dinners, and other news like additions to the menu or wine list.

"It would have been more difficult to launch our new afternoon tea service without the added publicity generated by our newsletter. And we've been seeing some new faces at our vintner dinners." But the newsletter's presence is felt in other equally

ment of restaurants worldwide. *** Speaking of wine, we have several very special vintner dinners in the works for 1996. Be sure to watch for information on them. For instance, there will be a Bordeaux dinner on January 31st hosted by one of the top wine experts in the Southwest, Woody DeLuna.

Que Pasta?
Power Breakfasts Can Warm Up Your Business Day.

Breakfast among friends and business associates is a tried and true Texas tradition. And patrons of the Four Seasons have known for quite a while that we serve one of the best morning meals around. But now, Chef Elmar Prambs is taking things one step further with some creative morning menu additions.

What's for breakfast? Well, starting in mid-January, you'll be able to order migas on toasted muffin, Four Seasons style. And alternative cuisine that's lower in calories, sodium and salt—such as egg white frittata with garden vegetables, mushrooms, and ovendried tomatoes. Want something heartier? Try cajun crabcake with scrambled eggs and tomatillo salsa. Or try Earl Campbell sausage, applewood smoked bacon, a beef tenderloin medallion with eggs and sauce Choron or oat-

bran and banana pancakes with pecans and apricot syrup.

Are you an eggs Benedict fan? Try our version with roasted tomato-onion chutney. Like waffles? You owe yourself a taste of our Belgian waffle with Mascarpone Cheese and fresh fruit salsa. Or our scrumptious brioche French toast with strawberries and maple syrup.

And since we're in Texas, don't miss "Huevos San Jacinto"—scrambled eggs with black beans, ham, and avocado in fried corn tortillas. Honestly, with a beginning like this, how could any day go bad? (And don't forget, with our location in the heart of downtown, you'll be close to that 9:00 meeting right after breakfast.)

Profile— Peter Gregg

One afternoon around 3:00 a few months ago, Cafe Manager and Sommelier Peter Gregg realized something that made him ponder for a moment. At one table, sat Meg Ryan. At another, was Denzel Washington. And on the patio, the Beach Boys were enjoying fresh air and fine food, Four Seasons style.

Peter says that he had to stop, think for a moment, and then ask himself, "did I just go through some space warp and land in Los Angeles?"

No doubt, the cosmopolitan nature of our Cafe is a huge part of its appeal. And Peter Gregg is an integral part of the ambience. Peter laughs when someone asks him if he's from Scarsdale or the tony suburbs of Virginia. Actually, he's an "Austin boy," who just happens to have an encyclopedic knowledge of wine and a pleasant manner perfectly suited to The Cafe. Speaking of his background, he says that much of his aplomb comes from his father, who was a University of Texas professor. After earning his business degree at The University

of Texas, Peter opted for a career in food service, because it combines a great deal of what he had learned—accounting, people skills, management, and more.

Peter's background in the business expanded when he worked for Austin's University Club. There, Peter started developing his wine knowledge, customer service finesse, and the rudiments of cooking.

His in-depth background has paid off in his ability to relate to all parts of the dining process for the ultimate pleasure of Four Seasons customers. And when he refers to the Four Seasons philosophy, Peter remarks that is why he enjoys working here so much. "The first thing you learn here is that people come first. With an orientation like that, you know that things will go right for everyone—employees and customers alike."

That all fits in with the trend Peter sees happening. "Maybe it's a nineties kind of thing, but people seem to be spending more time indulging themselves these days. We've seen sales on premier wines like Caymus Special Select and Margaux increasing steadily. And people seem to be taking more time to eat now. Recently, we had over fifty reservations for afternoon tea. We like that—because helping people relax and enjoy themselves is what the Four Seasons is all about."

As for the ultimate indulgence at the Four Seasons, the remarkable series of vintner dinners that have graced the Cafe are about as good as it gets. Peter says that 1996 will take the dinners to an even higher level. "We've been contacting the top vineyards in the United States for months now, lining up only the most prominent names for our patrons," he notes, quickly listing an honor roll of American wineries. He is projecting twelve to fourteen wine events for 1996, plus some surprises.

All the parts of his job please Peter, but what ranks at the top? "At the end of a long day, you can't imagine how satisfying it is to see a happy party of diners leave the restaurant with smiles on their faces. At that point we know that we've provided them with an experience that they couldn't have found anywhere else," he says. It all gets back to the Four Seasons' philosophy of putting people first—something Peter Gregg and the Cafe team do every day.

FOUR SEASONS HOTEL
Austin
A FOUR SEASONS · REGENT HOTEL

98 San Jacinto Blvd.
Austin, Texas 78701

rewarding ways as well. "It's gratifying to see employees featured in an issue being approached by restaurant patrons with comments like 'I grew up in such-and-such place, too' or 'that article about your philosophy on preparing food really clicks with my thinking.'"

Regular features such as employee profiles are mainstays of each issue,

but Gregg has no shortage of story ideas. "We could fill up most of the newsletter just with upcoming events," he enthuses.

Our reaction: The somewhat formal-looking layout and heavy high-quality paper are in keeping with the Four Seasons attitude, but offset nicely by spot-color accents and tasteful illustration.

AND THE
REDNECK

Richmond, VA

145 Seats

A converted ware-
house with a
sophisticated edge.

Jimmy Sneed, owner

Adam Steely,
restaurant manager/
partner

804/648 FROG
(3764)

See "our reaction" below.

The Frog and the Redneck NEWSLETTER

SECOND ISSUE EVER   ●   WINTER 1995/96

SAY WHAT YOU WANT, BUT JULIA THINKS I'M MANLY!

It's hard to believe that It's been almost three years since we've opened and boy, **DO WE LOVE RICHMOND!**

Concerning the timing of this newsletter I think I'll take the humble approach. I'm very, very sorry for those of you who have so patiently waited for this issue. I promise to get the next one out soon.

One of my biggest problems is that every time I produce a newsletter, WordPerfect issues a new version for me to learn...

Anyway, I hope you enjoy it and I'd would love to hear from you! In the meantime, **HAVE FUN EATING!**

JIMMY SNEED

All right, so she's 83 years old. She probably thinks Richard Simmons is manly. But still, this is Julia Child we're talking about; culinary legend, queen of cuisine, grande dame of... well you know who she is. She's the person most responsible for bringing French cooking into the home. Why, my kids even know who she is. And they were **most** impressed that I was invited to her house to shoot a TV show.

It began with a phone call in June of '94. Geoff Drummond, the producer of Julia's shows, wanted to know if I would be interested in going to Julia's house in early August to film a show for her newest series "In Julia's Kitchen with Master Chefs".

I can't believe it! Julia Child wants me?!? You're darn right I'll do it. I'll close the restaurant if I have to.

"OK, but first we'll need a video of you for her to see, since she personally picks all of the chefs. Can you come up with one?" Come up with one? Sure! There's that Discovery Channel thing I did. And some stuff from Channel 12. Hell, I even considered having a buddy film me jumping out of an airplane with a sign that said PICK ME JULIA♡! Fortunately I didn't have enough time to arrange it. **She picked me anyway!** In fact, I'm told that here exact words were "I like him. He looks so manly!" Manly!

That done, they now want to know what I'm going to cook for my two main dishes. That's tough, I have so much awesome seafood from the Chesapeake Bay to choose from. Of course I'll do soft shells but what else; rockfish, speckled trout, sugar toads, crabcakes, cobia, or hey, maybe even bluefish. Yeh, bluefish is so underrated, that may be just the ticket.

"**Jimmy**, listen," the producer says. "You can't do seafood."

"Whaddya mean I can't do seafood?" I'm panicking. "Without seafood, I'm nothing!" I protested. "C'mon guys, I **gotta** be able to do seafood. Somebody, **HELP!** Get reasonable. **I MUST DO SEAFOOD!**"

"It doesn't sell cookbooks," came the economic reply. "The more seafood dishes in the cookbook, the fewer copies we'll sell." So, this is about money is it?

(see **manly** p. 7)

Black on various colored papers

8 1/2 x 11

8 pages, stapled self-mailer

4 issues/year

11,000 mailed

Published since
Winter/Spring '94

This newsletter is as unusual as the name of the restaurant. Sneed writes every word, giving his opinion on a wide range of subjects: explaining why he took steak off the menu; praising his staff; offering portraits by the artist who does the graphics on the newsletter and the murals and cartoons on the walls of the restaurant; staging contests, quizzes, puzzles; calendar of upcoming events.

Sneed and partner/manager Adam Steely share with readers their delights and disappointments in tasting hundreds of wines, brandies, rums, tequilas, single barrel bourbons and premium vodkas. They believe their selection of two dozen single malt scotches is the largest in Virginia. The "Whine of the Day" discusses the popularity of Pinot Noir and the difficulty of finding good price/quality

✈ FIVE COUNTRIES IN FIVE DAYS

Adam and I eat out almost every day for lunch. In so doing we've discovered that Richmond is home to some awesome ethnic restaurants. Though we love 'upscale' food as much as anyone, we find great pleasure in simple, unique and, usually, very cheap food. So we're sharing our five favorite places to eat cheap, but great. Here they are, in no special order:

Saigon - We've eaten more meals here than anywhere. Mom cooks and Dad works the room. Daughter #1 also helps out when she's not in school. (She leaves for medical school (NYU) next fall). (903 E. Grace St. • 355-6633)

Jamaica House - Really, really good. Only four small tables but open all afternoon. Only the brave order the Cow Cod Soup. (1215 W. Broad • 358-5793)

V. I. P. Restaurant - Authentic Korean (we think). We've tried most of the dishes and especially love the stonepot Bi Bim Bap. (7437-B Midlothian Turnpike • 675-0511)

India House - We love eating with Ram (as in CD) and Saguna. In fact, we're having our Xmas party there. (2313 Westwood Ave. • 355-8378)

Full Kee - Authentic Cantonese and more. Order the specials on the wall or go for the Dim Sum on Saturdays and Sundays until 3 o'clock. If you're hungry, don't get the chicken feet. (6400 Horsepen Road. • 673-2233)

Mamma Zu - Ok, this makes six. But it's funky enough to be called ethnic, even if it is already known by Richmond's dining public. It's also a personal favorite (aren't they all?). Adam probably eats dinner there twice a week. Watch out for the huge portions. (501 S. Pine St. • 788-4205)

"REDNECK RISOTTO"
-6 Servings-

STONE GROUND GRITS
1 cup Awesome Stone Ground Grits • 1 T. Butter • 4 Cups Stock (chicken or veggie) • 3 t. Sea Salt -- Heat the grits and stock, while stirring, to a simmer. Cook for 30-35 minutes. Stir in butter and season with sea salt.

SAUSAGE
12 oz. Cooked High Quality Sausage (we use Edwards & Sons) cut into cubes

SAUTEED SHIITAKE MUSHROOMS
2 # Fresh Shiitake Mushrooms • 2 Cloves Fresh Garlic, peeled and finely diced • 2 Fresh Shallots, peeled and finely diced • 2 oz Unsalted Butter, cubed • Sea Salt • Freshly Ground Black Pepper • Extra Virgin Olive Oil • 2 oz Stock (chicken or veggie) -- Remove the stems from the mushrooms and discard. Slice the caps into ⅛ inch slices. Shiitakes are generally very clean and may need only a slight brushing off. Heat a heavy pan till very hot, cast iron if possible, and put in ¼" of olive oil. Add the mushrooms and cook for 30 seconds. Salt and pepper to taste while they are cooking. Add the garlic and shallots but keep stirring the mushrooms so that the garlic and shallots do not color or burn. After 1 minute add the stock to add richness and stop the cooking.

6 oz PARMESAN CHEESE
Mix the grits, sausage, shiitakes and add half of the cheese (grated). Spoon the "risotto" into heated soup plates and sprinkle with the rest of the cheese.

Smart promotion— unselfish and appreciated.

RELEVANT QUOTE OF THE DAY
Simple and chaste in design, properly proclaiming its value by substance alone, not by meretricious ornamentation, as all good things should do.
(O. Henry describing his meal.)

(OK, he was talking about a platinum fob in **The Gift of the Magi**. You remember, Della sold her hair so that she could buy it for her husband Jim's prize pocket watch, which he sold in order to buy her a pair of tortoise shell combs.

---

values. They believe that much of the fun in dining out is to be able to try something new and different.

Sneed's aim in teaching cooking classes is to finish the six-week course with his students having the same passion about food as he feels: textures, freshness, colors, combinations, chemistry, more. When asked for their evaluation of the class, all 42 students gave it a 5, the highest rating.

Our reaction: Sneed does too much at one time. He tells us that, when he gets the urge, he sits down for five hours at a time to write. Our experience is that "less is more." What he writes is fascinating, but a two-or four-page newsletter published regularly usually has the greatest impact with readers.

FRONTERA GRILL

VOLUME 4 ISSUE 1 -- *noticias* -- **SPRING 1995**

FESTIVAL VERACRUZANO

THE FIRST TIME I ASKED A CAB DRIVER to take me to Azcapotzalco, that northwestern quadrant of Mexico City little known to visitors, it took some convincing. Perhaps he knew its utterly urban character—concrete grey, well worn industrial. Perhaps he was remembering that it's the handed-down Aztec word for "place of the enormous ant hill."

What he didn't know was **Restaurante Carnitas El Bajio** or the tropical-warm welcome of the Veracruzana Carmen Ramírez Degollado, culinary visionary and proprietor. Stepping past the enticingly aromatic, front-window display of golden *carnitas* (a leftover from the restaurant's earlier regional incarnation) and griddle full of fresh-baked tortillas, you've moved from dusty, arid Tenochtitlan to the color-washed lushness of the Veracruz coast. The food simply radiates the tropical lilt and sway that makes Veracruz the enticement that it is.

Never having had a meal short of thrilling at Carmen's, I began working to get this ebullient Veracruzana to perform her culinary magic in Chicago. On Monday, June 12th, she'll be at the stove, cooking up a classic Veracruz feast that starts with those infamous, puffy, black-bean-stuffed *gorditas infladas* (anyone had the great fortune of a breakfast plate piled high with *gorditas* at Samborcito in Veracruz?), then on to an exotic fresh shrimp *huatape* flavored with *epazote*, capon in sesame-thickened, red-chile *tlatonile* and a consummate confection of guavas and *camote*.

CARMEN RAMIREZ DEGOLLADO with RICHARD JAMES, Frontera cook.

Come listen to the *Jarocho* music and sip *toritos* (that creamy, flavored *aguardiente* libation that everyone has at Fonda El Recuerdo, Mexico City's liveliest Veracruzano restaurant). There'll be plenty of Mexican beer and warm-weather wine. And of course Mexico's best coffee—Veracruz coffee—as we all wind down.

Rick Bayless

Monday, June 12, 6 PM, $45 (including all beverages) Call us at 312-661-1435 for reservations. ◆

Get ZAPped!

YOU'VE HEARD ABOUT Cabrini Greens, the project that involves teaching Cabrini kids to raise organic vegetables and market them to restaurants. Well, they need a greenhouse, and we've volunteered to help get it for them. Together with our sibling restaurant **Zinfandel** and the zinfandel producers organization (ZAP), we're putting on a dinner that'll show what fun it is to pair that wide range of zin styles with the best international cuisine in Chicago. With 100% of the proceeds going to Cabrini Greens, it'll be a delectably gratifying way to make a big difference for these kids.

Five courses from five Chicago favorites: French from Jean Joho (Everest, Bistro Jo), Italian from Peggy Ryan (Va Pensiero), Thai from Arun (**Arun's**), American from Susan Goss (**Zinfandel**) and Mexican from Rick Bayless (**Frontera/ Topolobompo**). Each course will be accompanied by a couple of zinfandels, poured by the vintners themselves. A great opportunity to savor, chat, query, and learn.

Sunday, June 25, 1995, 6 PM $75 (all inclusive), 100% going to Cabrini Greens. This event is held at Zinfandel; please call 312-527-1818 to make reservations.

Cooking with CARMEN RAMIREZ DEGOLLADO

THE EFFERVESCENT CARMEN HAS WON loyal fans in San Francisco and New York. Last year, I invited her to represent Mexico with me at the "Cuisines of the Sun" festival on the Big Island in Hawaii, and our classes were a big hit. Now, she'll be teaching the flavors of Veracruz in Chicago (I'll be translating for her) at **Frontera**. Her class will include the classic fresh crab *chilpachole*, shrimp in smoky *chipotle* sauce (those ever-popular *chipotles* are the chile of Veracruz), a cold gulf snapper in *adobillo* and a refined, prune-filled cake that's the specialty of Papanteco. Enjoy tastes of everything with sparkling limeade, wine, and Veracruz coffee.

Sunday, June 11, 11 AM, repeated at 3 PM, $45. Call us at 312-661-1435 for reservations.

NAPOLEON BONAPARTE, DUDLEY MOORE,

Wine Ruminations with Henry Bishop

E.T.—sometimes big things do come in small packages. Consequently, we are happy to mention the recent addition of small bottles to our award-winning wine list. Mostly half bottles (375 ml) some half litres (500 ml), these little guys will supplement our kaleidoscopic wine-by-the-glass program for a more intriguing dining adventure dining alone. You want *blanc*, your date wants *rouge*? *No problema*.

Yes Virginia, there is a chardonnay (the lovely Qupe from Santa Barbara) and a merlot (the coveted Shafer from Napa Valley). But we also laid hands on small portions of slightly less main-stream flavors. The half bottle of 1989 Grand Cru "Altenberg" Gewurztraminer from Gustave Lorentz has enough flavor to fill a magnum. The 1988 Brunello di Montalcino from Castello Banfi is twelve ounces of sangiovese perfection. The visionary diner may wish to experience the half litre portion of 1988 Tokaji Szamdrodni Dry, Hungary's unique aperitif that is not unlike a Manzanilla sherry.

So, during your next visit to **Frontera** or **Topolobampo**, please feel free to think small. ◆

topolobampo

"Mexican culture is our passion and it comes through in everything we do, including our newsletter," says Pat Schloeman, manager. "It lets customers experience the restaurant more fully."

Owner Rick Bayless and company started the newsletter with two goals in mind: To find a way to notify guests of special dinners and to instill the same feeling among guests that he felt within his "fam-ily" of employees. "There really is a family-oriented atmosphere here," he says, "and we wanted our customers to feel a part of that by knowing and understanding what goes on."

Regular features include "Wine Ruminations" with sommelier Henry Bishop, a recipe, schedule of special events, flattering press clippings and often an in-depth look at regional

OAXACAN Black Bean Soup

SOPA DE FRIJOLES NEGROS
Serves 6

- 2 cups (about 12 ounces) dried black beans, picked clean and rinsed
- 4 avocado leaves or 1 rib fresh fennel
- 1/2 cup (4 ounces) *chorizo* sausage, casing removed
- 1 small white onion, diced
- Salt, about 1 teaspoon
- 1/3 cup vegetable oil
- 4 to 6 corn tortillas (preferably stale, store-bought ones), cut into 1/4 inch strips
- 6 to 8 ounces medium-size shrimp, peeled and deveined
- About 1/2 cup crumbled Mexican *queso fresco* or salted farmer's cheese

1. Cooking the beans. Place beans in a medium stock pot, cover with 6 cups water, remove any beans that float and let soak 4 to 8 hours, until you see no dry core when you break one open. (Or, alternatively, bring to a simmer, turn off the heat and let stand 1 hour.)

If using avocado leaves, toast them briefly directly over a gas flame or on a hot griddle. Add the avocado leaves or fennel, *chorizo* and onion to the beans. Heat slowly to a simmer, Partially cover and simmer over medium-low heat, stirring occasionally, until they are fully tender, 1 to 2 hours. If you see the beans peeking up through the liquid, add hot water to cover them by 1/2 inch.

2. Finishing the soup. Coarsely puree the soup in small batches in a partially covered blender and return to the pot. Add enough water to thin the soup to a medium-thick consistency. Season with salt.

Heat the oil in a small skillet over medium-high heat. In batches fry the tortilla strips until crisp, about 1 minute. Drain on paper towels.

3. Serving the soup. Five minutes before serving, heat the soup to a boil, add the shrimp and cook about 2 minutes. Ladle warm soup into bowls. Top with a few of the crisp tortilla strips and sprinkle with a little cheese.

¡A PRIVATE PARTY ROOM!

After 8 years and thousands of requests, we've finally whittled out a festive spot that'll hold groups up to 30. Come take a look, then start making plans! Call Pat at 312-661-1435 for details.

GOODIES: Besides the hand-dyed, hand-printed one-of-a-kind T-shirts that Monique King has created for **Frontera/Topolobampo**, take a look at several new books with chapters that feature chef Rick Bayless's real, robust Mexican fare: *Home Food: 44 great American Chefs cook at home on their night off*, a beautifully produced fund-raising book done by the hunger advocacy group Share Our Strength; *In Julia's Kitchen with the Master Chefs*, the companion volume to the television series (Rick's show will be aired in early fall); and two exquisite volumes—one from the Art Institute of Chicago, another from the National Gallery of Art—with recipes inspired by works from these two museum's collections. All are (or will be) available at the restaurant; Rick will gladly inscribe your choice.

MARK YOUR CALENDARS

SUNDAY, JUNE 11, 11 AM & 3 PM: Veracruz cooking classes with one of the warmest, most talented cooks in Mexico: Carmen Ramírez Degollado, of **Restaurante Carnitas El Bajío** and **Mama Titita** in Mexico City. With translation by chef/owner Rick Bayless, Señora Carmen will share tales and delicacies from her Veracruz childhood: classic *chilpachole* of fresh crab, shrimp in smoky *chipotle chiles* cold Gulf snapper in *adobillo* and Papanteco-style cake with prune filling. $45

MONDAY, JUNE 12, 6 PM: Carmen Ramírez Degollado is preparing a traditional Veracruz feast from the infamous black-bean "puffs" (*gorditas infladas*), to *huatape* of fresh shrimp, capon in sesame-thickened, red-chile *tlatonile* and a classic *confeccion* of guavas and *camote*. *Jarocho* music, *toritos* (creamy, flavored *aguardiente*), beer and warm-weather wines fill out the festive picture. $45 (including all beverages)

⚔ BRAGGING ⚔

Without doubt, the greatest honor bestowed on **Frontera/Topolobampo** has been Chef Rick Bayless's place as was one of the five national finalists for the coveted James Beard Foundation's "Chef of the Year" awards. At the nationally televised awards in New York, Rick was also inducted into the Foundation's prestigious "Who's Who of American Food and Drink". In April, Rick was honored as "Chef of the Year" in San Antonio at the annual convention of the International Association of Culinary Professionals, an organization of food writers, culinary instructors, chefs, and caterers. And we hope you saw Todd Purdum's article in the *New York Times* on our last tour of Oaxaca—he eloquently captured both the remarkable essence of that Colonial gem and the joyful satisfaction we all gained as we explored Mexico through its cuisine. (By the way, if you're interested in being on the mailing list for next year's trip, call Pat at 312-661-1435.)

Mexican cuisines. "We have plenty to say," reflects Schloeman. "I just wish we had more time to devote to saying it."

The newsletter, mailed two times a year, works in tandem with postcard mailings. "When special dinners fall too far in between newsletters, we announce them by postcard to the same group of customers," adds Schloeman.

Two hundred of the approximately 3500 names on their mailing list are press. The rest are customers who added their names and addresses to a drop box at the front of the restaurant.

Our reaction: Our reaction "Noticias" is an earthy concoction, enticingly designed and written in an appealing, upbeat style, befitting two of the country's premiere Mexican dining rooms.

New York

45 seats

French-Italian inspired cuisine in stylish, bistro setting

Andrew Nathan, chef/proprietor; Anthony Connolly, maitre d'/manager

(212) 387-0898

More evidence of the continued popularity of cigar dinners.

Personal signatures are a touch that most newsletters lose along the way.

FRONTIÈRE

**MON. FEB. 5TH
VIEUX TELEGRAPHE
DINNER WITH
DANIEL BRUNIER**

**WED. FEB. 14TH
A VERY SPECIAL
VALENTINES
DINNER**

**MON. FEB. 26TH
MONTHLY CIGAR
DINNER**

**MON. MARCH 11TH
MARCH WINE
DINNER**

199 PRINCE STREET
NYC, NY 10012
212.387.0898

Ahh Winter...

We love this season-- Pheasant, Venison, Cassoulet, and Big Hearty Red Wines. The soulful cooking of the French Italian border warms our hearts and bellies with our winter specials. Pheasant in red wine and our Venison with cabbage and pears are just a few of our winter specials. We are also very excited for the return of one of our favorite wines (missing for a few months): The *1991 La Courtade* that Ruth Reichl mentioned in her October revue of *Frontiere*. *Paolo De Marchi* of *Isole E Olena* stopped by to bring us his *1993 Chianti*. Since it's been added to our list, we can't seem to keep it on our shelves.

We are pleased to announce the debut of our monthly wine dinners. On February 5, 1996, we have the honor of hosting *Daniel Brunier* of *Vieux Telegraphe*, who will be pouring and discussing his great wines. This will be a night to be remembered. Please reserve in advance as seating is very limited. Seating is at 7:00 PM. The menu and wines that will be presented are inside the newsletter.

Valentines Day is always a special night in our romantic, candlelit restaurant, and this year plans to be even more. We have a special menu planned to make this Valentines Day the most romantic ever for lovers and friends. See inside for details.

Once again, *Frontiere* and *Gotham City Cigar Society* team up to bring you an evening of cigar tasting, single malt and blended scotches, cognac, ports and a special menu to enhance the cigar selections.

March brings us our second wine dinner featuring the following wines: *Meursault, Verget 1994, Bandol, Le Galantin 1991*, and *Chateau Graud Larouse 1989*. See back for complete details and menu.

As we enter our fourth year, Belinda, Andrew and the staff would like to thank you for all of your support and patronage.

Belinda & Andrew Nathan
Proprietors

Black type on buff-colored paper

8 1/2 x 11, self-mailer

4 pages

4 issues/year

2000 mailed

Published since 1995

Database marketing is one of Frontière's most successful business strategies. "We're very proud of the sophistication of our mailing list," enthuses Andrew Nathan, owner. "We can target individuals based on a number of special interests." Those include at least the four categories listed on an information retrieval card given to customers: Monday Night Food & Wine Tasting Dinners, Winemaker's Menu Series, Holiday Events and Seasonal Menu Updates.

Everyone on the list of 2000 names receives the quarterly newsletter which includes a calendar of upcoming events. Supplemental letters announcing special events in greater detail are mailed to those customers who have expressed an interest in that topic.

Recently, a Thanksgiving Day feast sold out within a few days after it was

FRONTIÈRE

FOR IMMEDIATE RELEASE
CONTACT: ANDREW NATHAN, CHEF/PROPRIETOR (212) 387-0898

THANKSGIVING AT FRONTIERE
4 Course Dinner - $ 35.00 per person

Andrew and Belinda Nathan, Owners of Frontiere in Soho, have found a very special way to thank all their friends, new and old, for their unending support this past year. In Ruth Reichl's column of October 27, 1995, Ms. Reichl wrote that the Nathan's have " perfected the art of making their customers feel at home. " There's no better holiday for sharing with loved ones the warmth of home and hearth than Thanksgiving. Andrew and Belinda's home is Frontiere and on Thursday, November 23rd, the Nathans' door will be open to welcome guests for what promises to be a perfect day of feast, drink and friendship.

Chef Andrew's menu will be served from 1PM on. A choice between Wild Mushroom & Barley Soup, Thanksgiving Vegetable Potage or Spicy Tomato & Mussel Soup with Garlic & Saffron Aioli will begin the day's fare. To follow, choose between a Salad of Autumn Greens, Warm Roast Beet Salad with Goat Cheese or Grilled Wild Mushroom Salad with Warm Potatoes & Goat Cheese. Of course the Turkey is next--let it be Organic with Frontiere's famous Mashed Potatoes, Brussel Sprouts and Bourbon Pecan Yams with a choice of stuffings (Wild Mushrooms, Dry Fruit & Port Wine or Sausage & Sage). For those wanting a less traditional main course, Grilled Atlantic Salmon with Autumn Carrots, Leeks and Red Wine Sauce or Rack of Lamb with Black Pepper Mashed Potatoes, White Beans, Tomato, Roast Garlic & Nicoise Olives will also be served.

No Thanksgiving would be complete without the array of fresh pies and the aroma of fresh coffee wafting from the kitchen. Will it be Pumpkin Pie, the Pecan Pie, or the Apple Pie (all a la mode, of course). No pie? Perhaps a refreshing sample of Andrew's Thanksgiving Sorbets might be your fancy. American Coffee Service will help bring this wonderful meal to a close--of course, later seatings can linger to reflect on all that there is to be thankful for--we're certain that the meal which Andrew and Belinda served to their friends will be high on that list!

Thanksgiving at Frontiere is $35.00 per person for four courses and coffee (excluding tax & gratuity). A children's menu is available for $12.00 per child. Special accomodations for vegetarians will be made.

"We hope you have as many things to be thankful for this year as we do. You have made this year a wonderful year for us and we would like to share this special holiday with you and yours. Hope you can join us."

Belinda and Andrew Nathan

199 Prince Street NYC 10012 212.387.0898

announced in a letter and before any mention appeared in the local press. "I can't tell you how many people we had to turn away," says Anthony Connolly, manager. "The response was gratifying, but it's always frustrating to turn away new customers. At least we were able to accommodate most of our regular guests."

Prior to publishing the newsletter, weekends were booked solidly, but early- to mid-week business needed a boost. A comprehensive direct marketing program, including the newsletter, have made Frontière a popular destination most nights of the week.

Our reaction: Frontière is a good example of how a small independent restaurant can attract and nurture a diverse clientele.

GRILLE

East Setauket, NY

84 seats inside,
46 outside

Innovative fusion-
American cuisine
in upscale casual
setting

Joseph Felicetta &
Daniel Giannini,
Co-owners

(516)751-2200

Asking for input
gets guests involved,
makes them feel part
of something.

Fusion newz

Intro-Issue Spring

The First Six Months

Welcome to our premiere issue of the Fusion Grille Newsletter. We are very happy to be in the Three Village area and by all signs, the community is glad we're here! We envision this newsletter as informal, chatty and helpful. We all have so much on "our plates" these days (sorry for the pun) - what with work and family - there's always so much to do! So, we hope this publication will help you to plan ahead for future Fusion events and provide you with articles of interest. This Newsletter will include a list of current events and upcoming promotions, profiles on the staff, recipes and food and wine articles. We hope you enjoy this publication and please let us know if you want other topics covered.

Many people ask us about the name "Fusion Grille." Some researchers at Brookhaven Labs thought we were serving nuclear waste! But the reality is Fusion is an experiment in defining "American Cuisine". No other country in the world has so many cultures and backgrounds represented in its populace. The idea behind "Fusion" is to define a true "American Cuisine" by utilizing the many different cooking styles and spicings of our people. We take fresh fish, produce, and meats and spice them to reflect Americas wide variety of cultures such as Asian, European, Caribbean and South American. For instance, our crabcakes are made with Capellini (Italian angel hair pasta) and we serve it with an avocado-tequila relish (Mexican/Spanish) and serve it on a plate with Dijon mustard sauce (French) and black sesame seed (oriental). The combinations are fantastic and we are proud to be a

country (and restaurant) of such creativity and diversity. To complement our cuisine, we offer a 150 bottle "all American" wine list and 17 different wines, champaigns and ports by the glass.

Our first six months have been very exciting and hectic. I'd like to highlight for you what has been going on at the Grille :

1. We opened on August 5, 1994, and within the first 10 days we had been visited by the food critics from both the New York Times and Newsday. We, of course, don't know who the critics are and were a bit concerned since it takes any restaurant some time to get up and running. To say the least, we were very happy with the "three stars" we received from Newsday and the "Very Good" from the New York Times. Newsday has only given one other restaurant a 3 star rating in the last year in a half. In December, we also received recognition from Newsday and named "Best of 1994" and made the list of "Best L.I. Restaurants". We are the **only** restaurant in Suffolk County to achieve all these honors!

2. In October we offered our tribute to the South with our Cajun/Creole festival. Some of the authentic dishes we made fresh were seafood gumbo, crawfish bisque, jambalaya, blackened salmon, pan-seared catfish and southern pecan bread pudding.

3. On November 30, the daughter of famed wine maker Robert Mondavi, Marcia Mondavi, hosted our first wine dinner. For those not familiar with a wine dinner, it's an opportunity to learn about certain wines and foods. We close the restaurant to the general public and,

Continued Page 2

Where we believe life should be:
· the best of food
· the best of wine

Black copy with royal blue (same as logo) accents

8 1/2 x 11, self-mailer

4 pages

4 issues/year

2600 printed and mailed

Published since spring 1993

"Our goal was to keep the advertising budget manageable and still reach a broad range of customers and potential customers," said co-owner Joseph Felicetta. "So a newsletter seemed like the logical solution." Of course it helps that stories from the newsletter are regularly picked up by the local press. A recent mention of cooking classes garnered more than 75 responses.

"Fusion News" is put together in-house using a Macintosh computer and Pagemaker software. Felicetta gets design help from a staff member. 2600 copies of each issue are printed at a cost of about $1500 and mailed bulk rate. Although bulk usually takes longer to be delivered, if your news is not time-sensitve, it's a sensible alternative.

Felicetta isn't afraid to tackle thorny

Don't be afraid to get things off your chest—just be tactful.

Constant reminders!

subjects such as tipping and no-shows but most often sticks to announcing promoting wine tasting dinners, recipes and menu changes.

How do you make sure your mailings are being received and read by the right people? Ask them. Reply cards inserted in Fusion Grille newsletters annually warn, "This could be your last issue." If readers don't complete and return the cards, they're taken off the list.

Our reaction: We were most impressed by the first issue which detailed the restaurant's first six months in existence. It was open, honest and personal.

GOLD COAST
230 CALIFORNIA STREET
SAN FRANCISCO, CALIFORNIA 94111

PRESORTED
FIRST CLASS MAIL
U.S. POSTAGE PAID
SAN FRANCISCO, CA.
PERMIT No. 2352

China bans eateries' cooking with opiate

Dealing With Floss

Charleston, W.Va.

The escape of an inmate who used a rope made from dental floss prompted a state agency to vote yesterday to place razor wire above the recreation areas in its regional jails.   *Associated Press*

McDonald's Wins Fight

London

Hamburger giant McDonald's has won an 11-year fight against local intellectuals and conservationists for the right to open a fast-food restaurant in the exclusive London suburb of Hampstead.

Nuggets..

...in for dinner on a Saturday night with his family, and friend **Ed Hopple**, was **John Farrer** maestro of the Bakersfield Symphony Orchestra. John conducted the **San Francisco Symphony** in a fabulous performance under clear skies at Stern Grove the next day...
...from the grove to the prairie - **buffalo roast** was on the menu last month and a what a taste sensation. leaner and more flavorful than most beef it is also environmentally correct.

A cross between **Leroy Nieman** and **Rip Torn** is **Bechtel's** own Kelly McCloud, who apparently knows his cigars. Kelly strolled in one afternoon recently and preferred up **Royal Butera Vintage Cedro Coronas** to all so inclined. A short time later the aroma of burning peat began to fill the front bar. The stogies were extinguished but the burning smell continued. After a quick investigation it was discovered that some miscreant had set the peat moss in our outdoor planter boxes afire...if heaters are your bag we now stock a **selection of fine imported cigars**, just be careful where you plant them.

We've had a run on **Skyy vodka** recently due no doubt to its proclamations of being hang-over proof. the cobalt blue bottle and stylish key chains don't hurt. local rep **Dave Stoop** is in Russia working on a deal to bring Skyy, a San Francisco product, to the Muscovites. Talk about coals to Newcastle...

Our mezzanine was the site for a **Royal Insurance** mixer hosted by **Greg Locher** and co. while mixing and mingling some of the crowd hung over the balcony and shouted words of encouragement to the crew hard at work installing **vintage sheet music from the '40s** in our main dining room.

Gentlemen: if your looking a bit shaggy these days by all means call **Steve's Alley Cuts** on Minna.. He'll tonsoralize you in a hurry and leave a little in your wallet. Steve can be reached at 541-5335

Congratulations and felicitations to **Mark Jennings** and his bride, the comely Claire. he of the celebrated **Shanghai Kelly's** and **Mick's Lounge** and she of a prominent family socially. They had their rehearsal dinner in our rod & gun club room Saturday night and we wish them all the best...
...old, old friend **Eliot Chait** is finally tying the knot himself this fall. And why not? Formerly of **Barclays Bank** and currently with **National Australia Bank** out of New York City, the once fabled **bulldog outfielder** will pay us a visit later this month.

Supporting fellow merchants can be good business.

Subtle reminder that restaurant hosts business gatherings.

The monthly newsletter at Gold Coast doesn't have a name, but it could be called "Stream of Consciousness." That's the rambling approach owner Jim Brandt takes as he weaves upcoming events among outrageous news clippings, gossip and birthdays, promotions and anniversaries. "I pepper the letter with customer names to pique their interest," he says. And Brandt manages to namedrop a vendor or two as well, making an argument for "buying local."

Brandt's dedicated readership now nears 2000 in a dozen states, culled entirely from customers who have dropped a business card in the restaurant's fishbowl. That also enters patrons in a monthly drawing for a complimentary dinner for two. "People I haven't seen for months and sometimes years tell me they

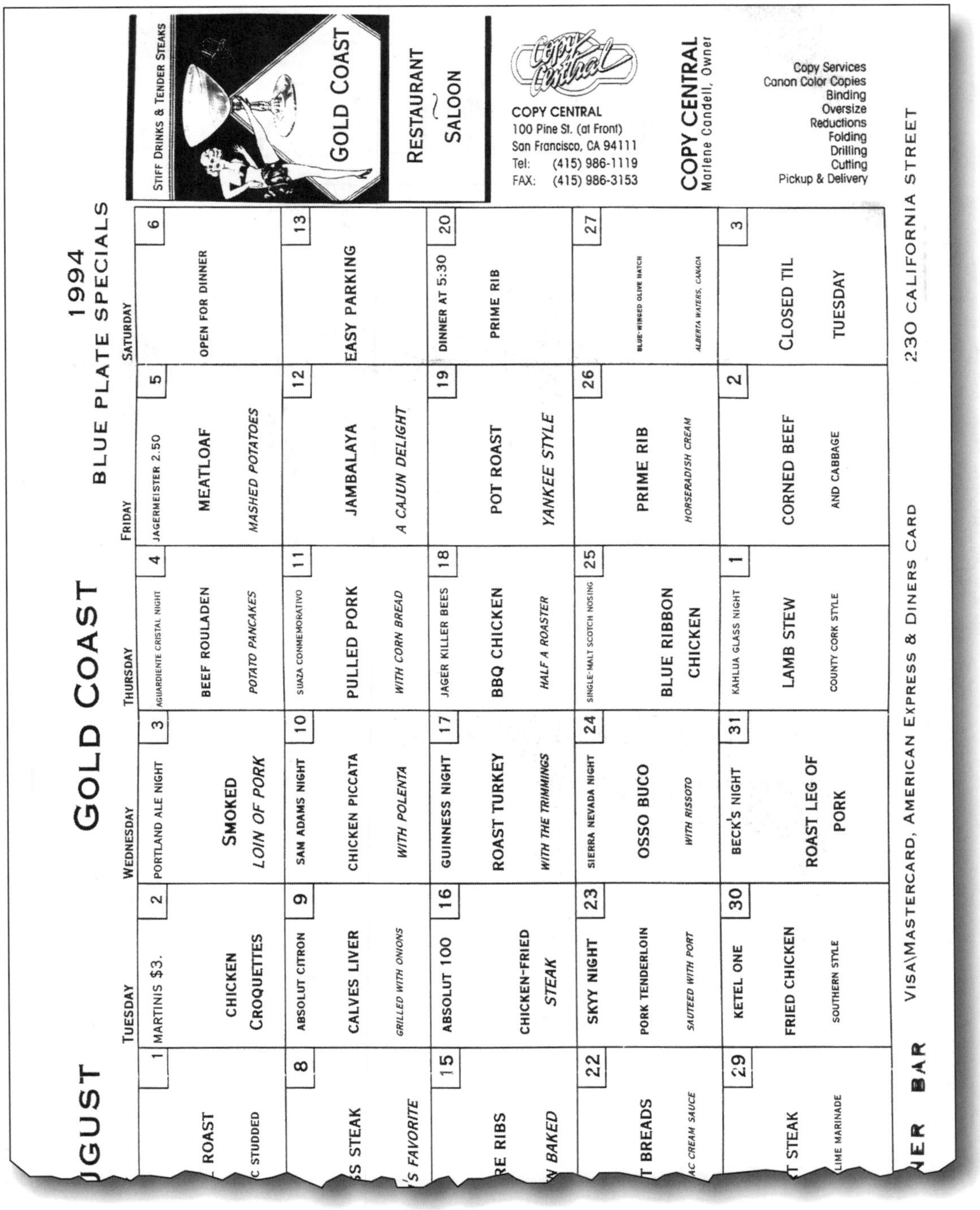

GOLD COAST

1994 — BLUE PLATE SPECIALS

AUGUST

Stiff Drinks & Tender Steaks

GOLD COAST RESTAURANT ~ SALOON

TUESDAY	WEDNESDAY	THURSDAY	FRIDAY	SATURDAY
2 MARTINIS $3. — CHICKEN CROQUETTES	**3** PORTLAND ALE NIGHT — SMOKED LOIN OF PORK	**4** AGUARDIENTE CRISTAL NIGHT — BEEF ROULADEN / POTATO PANCAKES	**5** JAGERMEISTER 2.50 — MEATLOAF / MASHED POTATOES	**6** OPEN FOR DINNER
9 ABSOLUT CITRON — CALVES LIVER / GRILLED WITH ONIONS	**10** SAM ADAMS NIGHT — CHICKEN PICCATA / WITH POLENTA	**11** SUAZA CONMEMORATIVO — PULLED PORK / WITH CORN BREAD	**12** JAMBALAYA / A CAJUN DELIGHT	**13** EASY PARKING
16 ABSOLUT 100 — CHICKEN-FRIED STEAK	**17** GUINNESS NIGHT — ROAST TURKEY / WITH THE TRIMMINGS	**18** JAGER KILLER BEES — BBQ CHICKEN / HALF A ROASTER	**19** POT ROAST / YANKEE STYLE	**20** DINNER AT 5:30 / PRIME RIB
23 SKYY NIGHT — PORK TENDERLOIN / SAUTEED WITH PORT	**24** SIERRA NEVADA NIGHT — OSSO BUCO / WITH RISSOTO	**25** SINGLE-MALT SCOTCH NOSING — BLUE RIBBON CHICKEN	**26** PRIME RIB / HORSERADISH CREAM	**27** BLUE-WINGED OLIVE HATCH / ALBERTA WATERS, CANADA
30 KETEL ONE — FRIED CHICKEN / SOUTHERN STYLE	**31** BECK'S NIGHT — ROAST LEG OF PORK	**1** KAHLUA GLASS NIGHT — LAMB STEW / COUNTY CORK STYLE	**2** CORNED BEEF / AND CABBAGE	**3** CLOSED TIL TUESDAY

(Torn left-hand Monday column, partially legible: ...ROAST / C STUDDED; ...STEAK / 'S FAVORITE; RE RIBS / N BAKED; T BREADS / AC CREAM SAUCE; T STEAK / LIME MARINADE — labeled "...UST" at top and "...ER BAR" at bottom.)

read it religiously and use it as a way to stay in touch.

Brandt's advice for the uninitiated: Start small and work hard to build your list and readership. "I've never bought or sold names," he affirms. "As your list grows it becomes more and more valuable to you." Brandt says if he had to cut back on everything else he does, "the newsletter would be the last to go."

Our reaction: The unorthodox layout and clippings á la Jay Leno make for an interesting read. There's little danger of this being ignored or forgotten.

GOTHAM

Bar and Grill

Fall 1996

This Issue

Profile:
Joseph Nase, Gotham's Wine Director

Profile:
Jacinto Guadarrama, Gotham's Sous Chef

Staff Diary:
Escape to Wine Country

Holidays on the Horizon

Fall Dessert Recipe:
Poached Winter Fruit Compote in White Wine Syrup

Do Try This at Home
Alfred Portale's Gotham Bar and Grill Cook Book

Dear Friends,

For each time that you've returned to our restaurant, whether frequently or once in a blue moon, we've tried to repay your loyalty with consistent devotion to refining the Gotham experience, further defining our own rhythm, personality, and humor. As we enter our twelfth year, I hope that we're settling into a greater confidence and dependability than ever before.

Much of this effort is carried out by veterans of this establishment, most especially our Service Director, Laurie Tomasino, who has been the backbone of the dining room since before I arrived. Today, Laurie is as firmly in charge of the service team as ever -- which should be as much of a comfort to you as it is to me. From knowing a diner's favorite table, to remembering special occasions, to designing and running a service system that the *Times'* Ruth Reichl recently described as a "model for service in America," Laurie's touch is felt by every diner who passes through our doorway.

And, as we enter a time when we become nostalgic for Gotham's beginnings, we're looking forward to reviving some old favorites this fall, such as Pheasant with Poached Lady Apples, Cider Sauce, and Sauerkraut. We're also tweaking some popular traditions, such as the $19.96 lunch that brought so many new faces to us this year. (If you haven't been in for lunch in a while, drop by -- it's become a bona fide "scene.")

Some of the most exciting developments in years have been provided by two additions to our Gotham family. Our new Wine Director, Joseph Nase, brings a young lifetime of passion and experience to his role and has already begun expanding our wine list by several hundred bottles. Joseph loves, loves, loves wine and his enthusiasm will be palpable on the new list when he unveils it later this year.

We've also enlisted a new General Manager, Michael Bergman -- formerly of the Dock's seafood restaurant organization -- a financial and technological wizard who quietly modernized our entire computer and bookkeeping systems within a few short months. Michael also oversees the physical maintenance of the restaurant, bringing an energy and enthusiasm that have fostered an incredible sense of teamwork within the restaurant. Both he and Joseph have swiftly established themselves as invaluable members of our Gotham family.

Other, crucial Gotham traditions roll on. We were honored to receive another nomination from the James Beard Foundation (as the nation's Best Restaurant) this year, as well as our fourth consecutive three-star review from *The New York Times*.

Finally, in addition to all of our commitments to quality and service, we've made one to geography -- we've recently signed on for several more years at 12 East 12th Street, where we look forward to seeing you soon and for many years to come.

Thank you for your continued support.

Alfred Portale

*Alfred Portale,
Executive Chef/Co-Owner*

An important purpose of any restaurant newsletter is to tell your readers what you are about. Chef Portale says, "I work to offer dishes that are intensely flavored and accessible. Each plate should have a clarity that gives the customer the satisfaction of readily identifiable flavors. Plate design is also important to me for I am looking to please on a number of levels. Most importantly though, at the Gotham we are working to understand the ways tat people like to eat, things like time factors, degrees of elegance, and nutritional concerns. In responding to these needs, we create an environment where each diner enjoys their meal in a rich and lively atmosphere.

To make it easy for customers to give their reactions and ideas, they're encouraged to use "Gotham—on-Line" E-mail. (See newsletter above.)

Do Try This at Home

Visitors to the Gotham Bar and Grill kitchen have wondered about the modest, four-burner home stove that occupied a corner of the kitchen for the last nine months. An incongruity in a professional setting, this was the stove on which Executive Chef/Co-Owner Alfred Portale tested and adjusted Gotham recipes for home use for his first cookbook -- *Alfred Portale's Gotham Bar and Grill Cook Book* -- due out from Doubleday in fall 1997. To further ensure "home-accuracy," Portale used apartment-sized pots, pans, and spoons in determining the proper measurements and cooking times. In addition to working with a top professional tester and his team of sous chefs to adapt more than 100 restaurant favorites for the home cook, Chef Portale worked closely with renowned Japanese food photographer Gozen Koshida, whose simple style proved the perfect foil to Gotham's complex dishes, many of which have been depicted in rare "family style" form.

How will this cook book differ from the other chef-authored books that have proliferated over the years? "Chef books are often inaccessible for home cooks," explains Portale. "This book will allow the reader to freely adapt my recipes, making more complicated dinners when they have the time, or using components of dishes in more casual, everyday settings. The book will also encourage, and give tips for experimentation."

The manuscript has been completed, the editing process has begun ... and the stove? It was donated to God's Love We Deliver after the last recipe was tested.

Profile: Joseph Nase

*Joseph Nase,
Wine Director*

Joseph Nase's earliest childhood memories are of crawling over wine barrels in his grandfather's cellar. In fact, the Gotham's new Wine Director hails from a long line of grape growers whose roots may be traced to the vineyards of southern Italy.

Joseph boasts formidable experience in restaurants that have widely respected wine portfolios including San Francisco's L'Etoile, Ernies, and Stars. He has overseen the cellars at the Stanford Court Hotel (*Wine Spectator* "Grand Award" winner) and at Attwater's restaurant in Portland, Oregon. In New York City, Joseph served as sommelier at Tse Yang and as General Manager at Huberts. Most recently, he served as Restaurant Manager at The Pierre Hotel in New York City (*Wine Spectator* "Best of Award of Excellence" winner).

As impressed as we are with Joseph, he was equally impressed with our backstock of hundreds of cases of red and white Burgundies that are stored in our warehouse facility. Due to on-premise space constraints, the restaurant has never been able to offer these selections to our clientele. Under Joseph's direction, we recently gutted our existing wine cellar in order to rebuild it and double its capacity, enabling us to keep an additional 200 selections on-hand beginning this fall. We will have a selection of all the great Burgundies -- the best years from the best producers, and all very well-priced. So wine lovers, take note -- those cloud-like parachutes over the dining room will confirm the Gotham as a *real* wine heaven in just a few weeks.

In addition we will debut an extensive collection of Bordeaux that Joseph has rounded out at auction, as well as a selection of fine German wines which will be available by the bottle or in our expanding by-the-glass program.

Joseph is also selecting a new roster of champagnes and microbrews, offering the most diverse selection from the bar we've ever featured.

He has also expanded and refined the service program here to include weekly wine tastings as well as notes on pairing and wine history, as well as the incorporation of wine "homework" and pop quizzes. So, on those rare occasions when he isn't on the floor himself, you can be confident that your wait person will be able to answer any wine-related questions.

If you're a wine lover, ask to meet Joseph on your next visit to the Gotham.

Interesting. Sells book and shows "heart".

GOTHAM ON-LINE

As former Mayor Ed Koch used to ask, "How are we doin'?" Please E-mail us with comments, questions, suggestions or special requests. General Manager Michael Bergman (**Gothamgm@aol.com**) can answer general queries about the restaurant, while Service Director Laurie Tomasino (**LTMaitred@aol.com**) will be happy to respond to comments about a particular experience, or to help make arrangements for a special or private event.

Layout and writing is done by Gotham's PR staff. Cost, including postage, is about $7 000, using a fulfillment house for mailing.

Recipes, employee profiles and wine articles vie for popularity.

Our reaction: Chef's photo, "Dear Friends" salutation, and "Thank you for your support" set the tone for this interesting and informative piece that customers will look forward to receiving.

Rosy Reviews

GYPSY ROSE RESTAURANT & BANQUET CENTER – GAIL A. MITCHELL, *Innkeeper*
Route 113 (2-3/4 miles south of Route 73) Collegeville, PA • 610 • 489-1600 • FAX: 610 • 454-9789

TAIL END OF WINTER ISSUE 1995
VOLUME XXXI

Our Innkeeper greets the Senior PGA Tour's Rookie of the Year, Jay Sigel at a recent Sigel Insurance Group reception at the Gypsy Rose. Jay received several tour distinctions throughout last year's campaign (SEE PAGE 2) and we look forward to more great news this year.

Headquartered in nearby Schwenksville, the Sigel Insurance Group boasts more than 30 affiliate locations across the U.S., Canada and Puerto Rico. Through long standing relationships and quality performance, the Sigel Group has earned "Preferred Agency" status with many of the companies with whom they place business.

SINCERE CONGRATULATIONS, JAY!

NEED A REASON TO CELEBRATE?

MARCH	17	ST. PATRICK'S DAY
	20	NATIONAL AGRICULTURE DAY *Honor America's Farmers by Savoring their Bounty at the Rose*
	26	MOTHERING SUNDAY (U.K.)
APRIL	2	DAYLIGHT SAVING TIME BEGINS — *YES, SPRING AHEAD!*
	9	PALM SUNDAY
	14	GOOD FRIDAY
	15	1ST DAY OF PASSOVER
	16*	EASTER SUNDAY
	17	FEDERAL INCOME TAX FILING *(Delayed 2 Days), Compliments of the Inkeeper*
	17-21*	NATIONAL SECRETARY'S WEEK
	21*	TERRACE OFFICIALLY OPENS
MAY	1	MAY DAY
	6	SIGMUND FREUD'S BIRTHDAY (1836)
	9	NATIONAL TEACHER DAY *(Purchase a Gypsy Rose Gift Certificate for your Son's/Daughter's Favorite Teacher*
	14*	MOTHER'S DAY
	22	CANADA'S VICTORIA DAY
	29	MEMORIAL DAY
	31	106th Anniversary - JOHNSTOWN FLOOD
JUNE	14	FLAG DAY
	19	FATHER'S DAY

*Denotes Newsletter Article

The Gypsy Rose Quality Commitment
The success in meeting our high quality standard is based on the dedicated initiative of all our employees who are encouraged and trained to meet their responsibilities as vital members of our restaurant's team effort.

Black on buff-colored paper

8 1/2 x 11, self-mailer

8 pages

4 issues/year

5800 printed/5000 mailed

Published since Spring 1986

"Make sure you have something interesting to say, recognize and appeal to all of your different audiences. Inject humor to keep things moving." Those are Owner Gail Mitchell's not-so-secret secrets to publishing a customer newsletter.

Mitchell frequently gets ideas from customers and even publishes their recipes. In addition, a trademark photograph of Mitchell always appears on the front page:

"Customers like the idea of recognizing their host when they come in," he says.

Mitchell is sold on newsletters because he has repeatedly tried other forms of advertising without equally positive results. "The first two weeks after the letter goes out I always experience a surge in business," he says.

Cost per newsletter is about $2300 ($1700 on printing, $600 on postage and

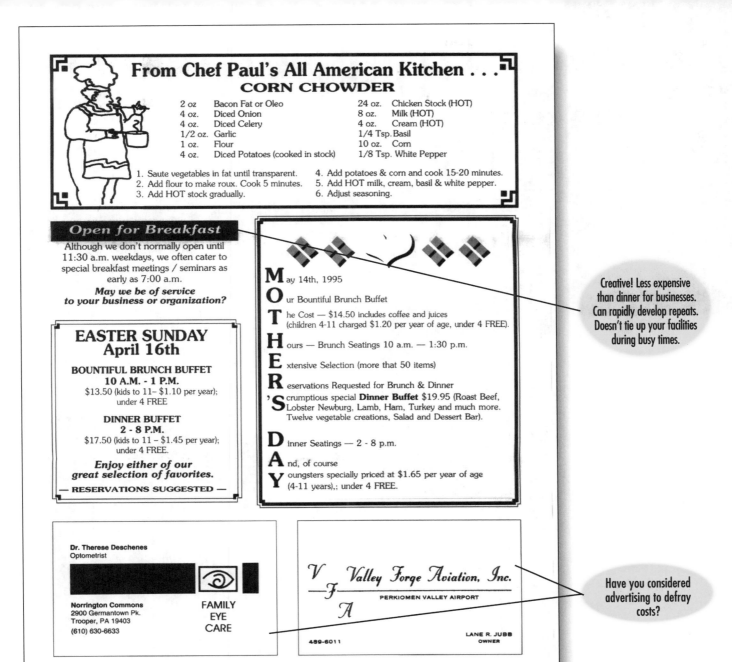

From Chef Paul's All American Kitchen . . .
CORN CHOWDER

2 oz	Bacon Fat or Oleo		24 oz.	Chicken Stock (HOT)
4 oz.	Diced Onion		8 oz.	Milk (HOT)
4 oz.	Diced Celery		4 oz.	Cream (HOT)
1/2 oz.	Garlic		1/4 Tsp.	Basil
1 oz.	Flour		10 oz.	Corn
4 oz.	Diced Potatoes (cooked in stock)		1/8 Tsp.	White Pepper

1. Saute vegetables in fat until transparent.
2. Add flour to make roux. Cook 5 minutes.
3. Add HOT stock gradually.
4. Add potatoes & corn and cook 15-20 minutes.
5. Add HOT milk, cream, basil & white pepper.
6. Adjust seasoning.

Open for Breakfast

Although we don't normally open until 11:30 a.m. weekdays, we often cater to special breakfast meetings / seminars as early as 7:00 a.m.

*May we be of service
to your business or organization?*

EASTER SUNDAY
April 16th

**BOUNTIFUL BRUNCH BUFFET
10 A.M. - 1 P.M.**
$13.50 (kids to 11– $1.10 per year);
under 4 FREE

**DINNER BUFFET
2 - 8 P.M.**
$17.50 (kids to 11 – $1.45 per year);
under 4 FREE.

*Enjoy either of our
great selection of favorites.*

— RESERVATIONS SUGGESTED —

May 14th, 1995

Our Bountiful Brunch Buffet

The Cost — $14.50 includes coffee and juices
(children 4-11 charged $1.20 per year of age, under 4 FREE).

Hours — Brunch Seatings 10 a.m. — 1:30 p.m.

Extensive Selection (more that 50 items)

Reservations Requested for Brunch & Dinner

'Scrumptious special **Dinner Buffet** $19.95 (Roast Beef,
Lobster Newburg, Lamb, Ham, Turkey and much more.
Twelve vegetable creations, Salad and Dessert Bar).

Dinner Seatings — 2 - 8 p.m.

And, of course

Youngsters specially priced at $1.65 per year of age
(4-11 years),; under 4 FREE.

Creative! Less expensive than dinner for businesses. Can rapidly develop repeats. Doesn't tie up your facilities during busy times.

Dr. Therese Deschenes
Optometrist

Norrington Commons
2900 Germantown Pk.
Trooper, PA 19403
(610) 630-6633

FAMILY
EYE
CARE

Valley Forge Aviation, Inc.

PERKIOMEN VALLEY AIRPORT

489-6011

LANE R. JUBB
OWNER

Have you considered advertising to defray costs?

---

mailing), but $300-400 is recouped from advertising which appears in each issue.

"When you've been in business as long I have, your database develops in many different ways," Mitchell explains. Among them: House accounts and business card drop-offs. He admonishes keeping your list clean by always adding an "address correction requested" tag. "It costs 32¢ for each return, but if you don't do that, you'll be wasting money every issue," he concludes.

Our reaction: "Gypsy Reviews" is unique among our featured newsletters. Not only do they accept advertising, but unconditionally guarantee it. The extra income helps offset costs and the ad space may even "legitimize" the news carried inside. But the ads could also be seen as intrusive and not right for every clientele, so monitor guests' comments closely if you try this.

The Crew's News

Are you giving back to the community?

SUMMER 1996
VOLUME VI
NUMBER 1

The HOBEE'S HERALD

YOUR SOURCE FOR WHAT'S NEWS AT HOBEE'S CALIFORNIA RESTAURANTS, ESTABLISHED 1974

Sunnyvale's success gives manager Lynne Moquin (above) plenty to smile about. (Below) A peek inside.

Twenty Years Later, Hobee's Back in Sunnyvale

Two decades have passed since the first **Hobee's Sunnyvale** closed (the old site was sacrificed to make room for **Hobee's Palo Alto**). While we were confident that our friends in "America's Best Managed City" would welcome us back at our new location on Ahwanee and Mathilda (formerly Baker's Square), the daily lines out the door since our March 4 opening have exceeded our most rose-colored projections. Team Sunnyvale's stellar performance early on has added to our good fortune: "I'm so proud of this crew", says vice president **Connie Durant.**

Peter Taber (left) and Sunnyvale councilman Stan Kawczynski preside over a March ribbon cutting.

"They've responded beautifully to the huge crowds we've had since day one!" Many thanks to General Manager **Debra Villasenor,** Kitchen Manager **Javier Chijate,** and all of our customers and indefatigable employees — especially those rookies who received our very special "accelerated" training course — for making Hobee's Number Twelve an instant success. Sunnyvale, it's great to be back!

SAVE THE DATE: "CLUB HOBEE'S AT THE HYATT" RETURNS ON JULY 27

Club Hobee's At The Hyatt, the annual fund-raiser benefitting **ARIS** (AIDS Resources, Information and Services of Santa Clara County), will be returning to the Peninsula on Saturday, July 27. Now in its fifth year, the popular dance party / benefit drawing / silent auction has raised over $45,000 for the vital charity, with 100% of all proceeds going directly to ARIS. For the third straight year, **Hyatt Rickeys in Palo Alto** is graciously donating party room accommodations. Tickets to this year's event are $35.00 per person, $65.00 per couple ($40 at the door). Tickets for the benefit drawing, which features prizes donated by over 40 local retailers, are $2.00 each. For more information, call **Edward Fike** at (415) 493-7823, extension 105.

HOBEE'S PRESIDENT IS FINALIST FOR ENTREPRENEURIAL AWARD

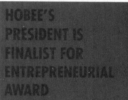

The San Jose Business Journal has selected Hobee's president Peter Taber as a finalist for one of its First Annual Entrepreneurial Awards. Peter will be among fifteen individuals honored at a May 16 ceremony held at the Fairmont in San Jose. Winners will be announced in five categories, with Peter vying for Silicon Valley Retail Entrepreneur of the Year. Win or lose, Peter, who has enjoyed a twenty-two year career with Hobee's, says that he's "enormously gratified" by the nomination. Says the prez, "Considering the tremendous depth of talent in the Valley, it's an honor just to be included on the short list of nominees."

Question: Can a chain of casual American eateries benefit from a customer newsletter as much a single-unit independent operator? An emphatic "yes" according to Edward Fike, v.p. & editor. Started by Fike in 1991, The "Hobee's Herald" has proven itself time and time again.

"Eighty percent of our business is repeat," comments Fike. "So even though we're a chain, we're still a neighborhood

restaurant." Hobee's prides itself on its participation in local charities and other fund-raising events. And the newsletter has been critical to getting the word out about those activities and fostering a sense of community.

Fike gets every restaurant involved in the process by asking them to submit at least one bit of news: "Usually the items [called 'Hobee's Happenings'] are light

HAPPENINGS

Care to share that brilliant idea with the rest of the class? Call Hobee's customer comment line at (800) HOBEES(6), extension 2, or e-mail us at XBRV09A @PRODIGY.COM

Palo Alto customers: World Wide Waiter founders Michael Adelberg (left) and Craig Cohen are standing by for your on-line orders.

HOBEE'S HAPPENINGS

Our apologies that this quarterly rag suddenly became annual in '95. We kept waiting for our deal in Sunnyvale to close so we could give our faithful readers the good news. Trouble was, the deal took more curves than Lombard Street. We plan to see more of you in '96!...... **Hobee's** latest offering to its friends in the tech set: on-line ordering. **Hobee's Palo Alto** (4224 El Camino Real) has been piloting the **World Wide Waiter** program for the past several months. The Web site allows customers to browse the **Hobee's** menu and to place a takeout order quickly and efficiently. To gain access, type in: **www.waiter.com** .....Congratulations to **Hobee's** marketing diva **Karen Cabello** who was recently appointed to the board of directors of the **Mountain View Chamber of Commerce**....A collective pat on the back to the 250+ employees of the six Hobee's locations owned by **Taber Food Services, Inc.** That sizable lot has gamely met the challenges posed by an ambi-

tious upgrade: the switch from manual order-taking to a computerized format. The new point of sale system ("Squirrel") speeds up orders and eliminates the need for the kitchen crew to decipher server hieroglyphics......Kudos to the crew at **Hobee's Cupertino** for continuing to move that store's sales into all-time, record-breaking territory with each passing month. The restaurant, the first franchised location, celebrates its 10th anniversary this October ....We've become accustomed to **Hobee's Montague Expressway** server **Warren Ramsey** accomplishing great things. (You may recall his nod as 1994 Server of the Year by the **California Restaurant Association**). Warren's latest feat, however, is pure inspiration: at age 69, he has successfully kicked a 55

year smoking habit!...... Over at **Hobee's Fremont,** they're still talking about the commotion caused by surprise visitor **Clint Eastwood** several months ago. It seems that

(Continued on pg. 4)

If you want customer interaction, ask for it.

Interesting idea if cost can be justified.

Hobee's Heroine: Kim Chase made headlines when she saved a customer's life in March.

media BITES

"Edward Fike, vice president and general counsel for **Hobee's California Restaurants**, was included in the '30 under 30' list compiled by the editors of the *San Jose Business Journal.* The list highlights 30 individuals under the age of 30 who are likely to become the Silicon Valley's future business, political and social leaders."
- *Mountain View Business News, 12/95*

"Kim Chase of Hobee's on El Camino performed well under pressure and in front of a full house in the restaurant when a customer was choking on some food. Quick action by Kim prevented any serious injury. Kim, we will always sit in your section."
- *Palo Alto Daily News, 3/18/96*

"For the past 16 years, (Jerry) Meyers has eaten all his dinners at Hobee's....The staff, who know his habits well, note every deviation. If he doesn't show up, they call him at home to see if he's OK. If he sneezes, they inundate him with fresh minced garlic and homespun remedies."
- *Palo Alto Weekly, 4/10/96*

The Crew's News

---

and whimsical, but we also use this space to recognize the achievements of our employees and customers."

Just over half of the 13,000 letters printed each quarter are mailed to Hobee's constantly growing and evolving mailing list or stapled to employees' paychecks. The rest are available at each restaurant. The list was accumulated through

HobeeGrams which ask guests to comment on their dining experience; and sign-up offers in the newsletters themselves.

Our reaction: Talk about inclusiveness. We can't believe how many different names—customers and employees—are worked into each letter.

New York City

32 seats inside/25 outside

American neighbor-hood cooking in a handcrafted intimate setting

Barbara Shinn & David Page. Co-owners

(212) 243-9579

A Letter From Home

Home Restaurant
20 Cornelia St.
NYC, N.Y. 10014
(212) 243-9579

Greetings from HOME!

We first want to thank every one of our loyal and wonderful customers who have visited us this past Summer and Fall! We think it was a memorable summer for great corn and tomatoes. Here at Home, we took full advantage of the long harvest, having delicious tomatoes until the end of October.

Now that there is a welcome chill in the air, we hope you will put on your favorite sweater and have Breakfast, Lunch, Brunch, or Dinner in our heated garden! The garden stays cozy even when the temperature dips below 40°. Like alot of our local customers say, "These heaters kick!". Along with the new season, David has added new items to our menu such as a Roasted Root Vegetable Salad with Beets, Turnips, Carrots and Roasted Red Peppers, a main dish of Grilled Lamb Sausages with Cabbage, Barley, and a Juniper Scented Mushroom Sauce, and now, with the Trout, he is serving Garlic Greens, an Artichoke Pancake, and a Warm Lemon Parsley Dressing. Chris, our lunch chef, continues to make his Chicken Dumplings and has added a Barbecued Rabbit Sandwich to the menu. So for any of you who haven't brightened our doorstep lately, come in for a bite!

Our bustling kitchen has also taken on a new project - announcing Home Canning! David and our dinner chef, Robert, are putting up Home Ketchup, Home Green Ketchup, Home Barbecue Sauce, and Home Apple Maple Syrup, and for Thanksgiving, Home Cranberry Sauce. They are all for sale at the restaurant, or, if you need only Home Ketchup, pick it up at Gourmet Garage, Murray's Cheese Shop, or Faicco's Pork Store. All of our Home Canning goodies are perfect for holiday gifts and holiday meals! Especially festive is a 2 pack of Home Red and Home Green Ketchup.

And speaking of the holidays, Home will be open for Thanksgiving, Christmas Eve, Christmas, and New Years. Call ahead for reservations! Lastly, here is a recipe of one of our desserts that we hope will help keep you warm on these coming chilly evenings...

HOME BAKED APPLES
6 red baking apples such as Rome or Cortland
1 cup raisins
1/2 cup cranberries
1 tablespoon sugar
1 teaspoon cinnamon
butter
wax paper or parchment paper

Core the apples but don't peel them. brush the outside of the apples with butter. Combine the cranberries and raisins and sprinkle the mixture with the sugar and cinnamon. Stuff the apples with the mixture and individually wrap in wax paper. Bake until tender, about 45 minutes to one hour. Serve warm with ice cream.

We hope to see you soon!
Love,

David AND *Barbara*

P.S. Hi Mom

HOME RESTAURANT *fine wine, fine ketchup.*

With so few seats inside, it's important that guests know the garden will be comfortable.

Relationship marketing works—and not just with customers.

Black ink on buff-colored or craft-style papers

8 1/2 x 11 (letter) or 5 1/2 x 4 1/4 (cards)

1 page

4 issues/year

2500 printed/2000 mailed

Published since 1992

Home mails their unconventional "newsletters" four times a year, but only one is actually a letter from Home. The other three are thoughtful recipe post-cards. "Customers hold on to the 'Recipes from Home,'" says Barbara Shinn, co-owner, "so the payoff comes throughout the year as they reference the recipe card and are reminded to come back to Home. "We're one of the few truly neighbor-hood restaurants in Manhattan," believes Shinn. "As such, we do all we can to pro-mote neighborhood businesses such as our local meat market, grocer and even brew-ery to customers. I think that 'home-grown' flavor comes through not only in the newsletter but everything we do." The Home mailing list includes media and names acquired by dropping address forms with guest checks. The press por-

A RECIPE FROM HOME

HOME RESTAURANT
20 CORNELIA ST. NYC, NY. 10014
212-243-9579

SHRIMP and HOMINY STEW

1 CUP DICED YELLOW ONION	2 CUPS WHITE WINE
2 TSP. MINCED GARLIC	2 CUPS FISH STOCK
1 CUP DICED CELERY	1 TSP. MINCED LEMON ZEST
2 T. SWEET BUTTER	1 LB. PEELED ROCK SHRIMP
2 T. OLIVE OIL	½ TSP. CAYENNE PEPPER
½ CUP DICED RED PEPPER	2 T. CHOPPED PARSLEY
1 CUP DICED SHIITAKE MUSHROOMS	COARSE SALT TO TASTE
2 CUPS COOKED HOMINY	

IN A 5 QUART POT, GENTLY COOK THE ONIONS, GARLIC, and CELERY IN THE SWEET BUTTER and OLIVE OIL. ADD THE PEPPERS and SHIITAKE MUSHROOMS. ADD THE HOMINY, WINE STOCK and ZEST. BRING UP TO A BOIL. ADD THE SHRIMP and SEASON WITH CAYENNE and PARSLEY. SERVE IMMEDIATLEY.

HOME RESTAURANT
20 CORNELIA ST.
NYC, NY 10014 212-243-9579

SPRING IS FINALLY HERE!
COME JOIN US FOR THE MANY
CHANGES ON OUR SPRING MENU
and ENJOY THE FRESH AIR IN
OUR GARDEN.
A SPECIAL DATE:
ON THURSDAY, APRIL 25TH,
RAYMOND SOKOLOV, AUTHOR OF
"WITH THE GRAIN" WILL BE JOINING
US FOR A FIVE COURSE LUNCHEON TASTING and BOOK SIGNING
TO BENEFIT THE GREENWICH HOUSE. DAVID HAS CREATED A
MENU INSPIRED BY RAYMOND'S BOOK, INCLUDING SEARED SEA
SCALLOPS WITH BASIL GRITS and FRESH CORN, AND LAMB
SALAD WITH QUINOA STUFFED GRAPE LEAVES, ASPARAGUS and
RAMPS. CALL US FOR DETAILS and RESERVATIONS. David
and Barbara

---

tion of the list was compiled by gleaning the names of editors and writers from the mastheads of every magazine and newspaper that had some application to food and dining out. Shinn makes two very important points about any press list: "Make sure you include more than one editor or writer from each publication to be sure you're reaching the right person and to get them talking in the office. And, don't forget to include lifestyle and women's magazines on your list. Many have regular food columns."

Our reaction: The recipe note cards are considerate and appropriate reminders. They really do evoke memories of home cooking and a place of comfort and hospitality.

Atlanta: Vail, CO

500 seats Atlanta/
120 seats Vail

Healthful Moroccan
cuisine served in a
lively, comfortable
setting

Rafih and Rita
Benjelloun, Owners

(404) 351-0870:
web site address:
http://www.mind-
spring.com/~rafih

FEZ

Good reason to have a least a few low- or no-fat items on your menu.

THE IMPERIAL FEZ
Authentic Moroccan Cuisine
FEZ NEWSLETTER

Summer 1993 Issue

2285 Peachtree Road, Buckhead, Georgia 30309 * 1000 Lionsridge Loop, Vail Colorado 81657
(404) 351-0870 - Fax (404) 351-1272   *   (303) 476-1948

FEZ NOTEPAD

With all my respect and consideration, I like to remind everyone that dining and wining are not meant by no means for crushing hunger or to over come thirst and keep going.

Whenever we sit down at the table to eat some food, what we are about to do is restore some energy, some protein, some fibres, minerals, vitamins and all other molecules that are yet to be discovered. Basically, all we are doing is restoring vitality.

Here I urge you all our readers to pay serious and close attention to the food you eat. You are what you eat. By that, I mean every element absorbed by your body becomes part of your body that is use for cell reconstruction.

Modern Science based upon research tells us that every eleven months the human cells are recycled. If every one of us take this fact seriously, and we start building or rebuilding our body with proper food with awareness and nutritional values; understanding of what cholesterol, vitamins, minerals, HDL, LDL means, we

Rafih Benjelloun

will end up being healthy persons that are young in body and in spirit. Longevity will be one's own claim. And when the time comes for the spirit to return home, you will head back with no pain - home sweet return.

FEZ MANAGEMENT

Chef/Owners
Rafih & Rita Benjelloun

Restaurant Manager
Fouad Salbi

Assist. Restaurant Manager
Tony M. Marsid

Kitchen Manager
Fouzi Shenet

Catering & Sales Coordinator
Tajuddin M. O. JarAllah

Rita Benjelloun, Chef, Hostess and Co-owner of Imperial Fez dressed as a Berber from Morocco.

CONTENTS

Layout And Design By:
Tajuddin M. O. JarAllah

Black type with single-color accents on white coated paper

8 1/2 x 11

4-8 pages

4-6 issues/year

10,000 printed/5000 mailed

Published since late 1989

Cultural awareness and proper nutrition are just two worthy themes echoed throughout the pages of the Fez Newsletter. But always within the context of hospitality and always bearing the flavor of owners Rafih and Rita Benjelloun. Readers are exposed to colorful descriptions of far-off places as well as a few next door; snapshots of guests having a wonderful time and regular lessons on how to eat healthfully.

The Benjellouns do much to foster understanding of their native Moroccan culture and cuisine, yet recognition of their peers flows just as freely. Believing that "as Atlanta (or Vail) goes, so goes his restaurant," Rafih is the first to applaud the successes of other restaurateurs. But that doesn't mean he shies away from subtle self-promotion, reminding readers of catering services and the restaurant's inno-

OUR CULTURE

We speak so many languages and yet we can understand them all. We come in so many colors and shapes and we could become mirrors of one another. It would be interesting if we take time to know that person that is different from us.

Yes, we develop in different geographical areas, in different climates, we see life differently, we celebrate differently, despite all of this, we are positive people that are aware of our "grand entrance" and our "exit". The journey in life is what culture is all about.

I like to give meaning to the word "culture" that's not new - I am what my ancestors are, I am the fruit that tastes and smells like every bit of my past. Honor, pride and integrity are my vehicles that carry me through difficulties. I enjoy and even feel more vividly by observing other people's culture in form of expression, celebration and being. I love other cultures.

From this land, as far as our deep rooted trunk resides, our roots scream to the tree that its branches reach up high into the heavens - I am alive, I am here, I am well, I am culture among other cultures here I reside in America. I celebrate Life.

- Rafih Benjelloun ■

Blues Harbor Moved To Buckhead

Ann Butler, Owner Blues Harbor

Blues Harbor has moved from underground Atlanta back to Buckhead. Imperial Fez restaurant and other Buckhead Businesses, along with Buckhead Business Association welcomed it back.

Blues Harbor is a perfect place for after dinner evening relaxation with the best Jazz and Blues music. Don't miss **Taj Mahal** at the Blues Harbor on November 17 - 18, 1993. Will also feature **Chris Cain**, July 6 - 12, 1993.

Blues Harbor is opened for entertainment at 9.30 p.m. daily.

Festival Of Cultures

Festival Of Cultures is organized by Ken Chapman, the President of Creative Events & Services, Inc. as an Atlanta, Georgia celebration of ethnic and cultural diversity which is planned for July 24 - 25, 1993 at the Atlanta City Hall Plaza. The event times are Saturday, July 24, 1993: 11 a.m. to 9 p.m. and Sunday, July 25, 1993: 1 p.m. to 8 p.m. The event is expected to draw about 100,000 to 200,000 people.

Creative Events & Services, Inc. has in the past served as project designers and managers for The Festival Of Cultures sponsored by The Coca-cola Company in 1990 and 1991 which draw over thirty-five ethnic and cultural groups from the Atlanta Community.

Creative Events & Services, Inc. now owns the trademark for the "Festival Of Cultures". They believe that this "Festival Of Cultures" will provide perfect opportunity for Atlantans to learn more about the cultures and diverse ethnic heritages in preparation for Atlanta's hosting of the 1996 Summer Olympic Games.

This event receives the support and sponsorship of the city of Atlanta, Georgia. Mayor Maynard Jackson will be issuing a Proclamation declaring the week preceeding the Festival as "International Awareness Week"

Highlights of the event will include Endorsement by Atlanta Mayor, Maynard Jackson; International Music and Dance; Ethnic Arts and Craft, and Exhibitions; Ethnic Food and Beverage Tasting; Ethnic Cultural Cooking Demonstrations; Parades of Cultures; Authentic Berlin Wall Exhibit; International Business Showcase/travelFest; Kidsfest (children's Area); Sports and Lifestyle Demonstrations; and Fashions and Native Costumes.

See You At the Festival.
- *Tajuddin JarAllah*

Do your customers feel good about what you stand for?.

---

vative rewards program.

"The newsletter opens customers' eyes," says Rafih. "Through our 'Take time to dine,' message, we're trying to communicate that dining enhances our lives in so many ways. It restores vitality, nurtures friendships and builds bonds."

Because so much of the newsletter content is based on health and nutrition, customers hold on to issues for months after they're published and pass them along to friends. "People use the newsletter as a guideline to better eating," he says.

Our reaction: Researchers now credit dining with much more than sustenance. And few places promote that idea—in word and deed—more than The Imperial Fez and its Fez newsletter.

West Bloomfield. MI

55 seats

Basic French. but
often with Asian and
other influences

Jim Lark. Owner

(810) 661-4466

Lark "blows his
own horn" but with
good reason.

the Lark

Tel. (810) 661-4466   Fax (810) 661-8891

6430 Farmington Road, North of Maple Road
West Bloomfield, Michigan 48322

September, 1995   The First Restaurant Newsletter   *Food For Thought* ™   Vol. XV   No. 9

 FLASH!

The Lark Tops Zagat Survey. The long-awaited **Zagat Survey of Restaurants of Michigan & Detroit** will be released in late September or early October. This persuasive compilation of the opinions of "regular restaurant-goers" began in New York City and proved so popular that it has been expanded to cover 26 major regions of the country including (at last) Detroit and Michigan. Zagat's Survey of our area summarizes reports from some 1,200 frequent diners on about 400 restaurants. We are gratified to learn from a well-placed source that The Lark did extremely well and is the "walk-away winner" as Michigan's favorite restaurant. Given that, it is not surprising that The Lark also has the highest total cumulative score for food, decor, and service – 83 out of a possible perfect 90. Paired with **Condé Nast Traveler** magazine's Readers' Restaurant Poll, the dining public now has two creditable rankings of America's restaurants.

Hawaiian & South Seas Dinner. Warm summer breezes bring dreams of distant shores and inspire a Hawaiian and South Seas dinner, an appetizing blend of Pacific, Oriental and French influences. Join us at 7:00 p.m., Monday or Tuesday, September 25 and 26.

The Menu
Tuamotu Atolls
Savory Baked Oysters in the Shell
Macadamia Nut Muffins
•
The Society Islands
Miniature Crabmeat-Stuffed Cheese-Topped Baked Avocado
•
Hawaii
Seared Red Snapper with Szechuan Shrimp & Snow Peas
•
Tahiti
Champagne & Passionfruit Granité Cocktail
•
Fiji
Whole Roasted Teriyaki Sirloin of Beef
Candied Pineapple
Saffron Rice
Hawaii
Piña Colada Cheesecake with Tropical Fruits
•
Hawaiian Kona Coffee
•
Macadamia Nut Bonbons

There will be live South Seas music, and each lady present will be presented with an orchid lei flown from Hawaii especially for this dinner. The price of $75 per person does not include other beverages, tax or gratuity. A variety of tropical cocktails and an appealing wine bouquet will be available. The last date for cancellation or reduction of reservations without charge is September 16.

Brown on ivory

8 1/2 x 11–3-hole
punched

4-8 pages. №10 envelope

12 issues/year

2500 printed

Published since 1981

Food for Thought ™ is the "First Restaurant Newsletter." This simple, informative, four-pager has something for everyone. Its articles demonstrate Jim and Mary Lark's interest in their readers, sharing travel experiences, people they've met, restaurants visited, son Eric's wedding, co-sponsorship of Michigan's Official Chili Cookoff.

Lark tells us that the articles about travel experiences with their "wish you were here" tone are the most popular with readers, who are always asking for more information. Lark's newsletter announces his various "Special Menu" series that feature foods of places visited. Example: Hawaii and South Seas, complete with South Seas music, Hawaiian orchids for ladies, tropical cocktails.

A popular off-hour promotion is

New Menu & Wine List. Enclosed is the new menu and regular wine list for September and October. When I can snare a table, my only problem is that I want every main course listed. With this menu, I think I'll have my favorite freshwater fish, walleye, with Chef Marcus' great Sauternes sauce. On the other hand, I love fresh figs, so perhaps I'll order the duckling with figs, almonds and a brandy sauce. However, I grew up on an island in Georgian Bay picking and devouring quarts of blueberries every summer, thus I'm drawn to the veal chop with sweet and sour fresh huckleberry sauce. But, you can't go wrong with the other choices such as Maine lobster or rack of lamb Genghis Khan, and there's also the daily outdoor-wood-grilled specials. The revised wine list is almost too good to be true, with too much new to detail here. Ask me for suggestions on your next and every visit.

Up North. Talk about roots. The maternal side of my family came from France to Cap Santé on the St. Lawrence upriver from Quebec City in 1687. They migrated to the Canadian side of the Detroit River in the 1730s, shortly after Cadillac's founding of Detroit in 1701. I've always considered these to be the very early dates and was surprised to learn the French were established even earlier at the locale of our lodge Up North. An elm bark structure named Anamiewatigoing (Prayer place near the Cross) was erected at the Odawa Indian's Cross Village in 1691. A wooden church was raised in 1695. Cross Village is six miles north of Middle Village (now Goodhart) and 20 miles north of Harbor Springs, all on Lake Michigan. Monte Bliss, who built our lodge near Goodhart, was obviously a student of history, since its exterior is local rock and elm bark – the only contemporary elm bark structure to our knowledge.

All of these connections somehow made fitting the decision of our son Eric and his fiancé Mandy Walts to be married Up North, choosing the Church of the Holy Childhood in Harbor Springs for convenience over the churches of Cross Village and Goodhart. Their reception was at **Stafford's Bayview Inn,** a quaint old wooden hostelry in the venerable Methodist resort of Bayview, immediately north of Petoskey. On a beautiful summer day, the wedding party sipped Bollinger Champagne as they made their leisurely way from the Church to the reception in an antique trolley converted to travel by road. Fine weather permitted the cocktails and hors d'oevures part of the reception to spill out of the inn onto its porch and lawn, both with views over Little Traverse Bay. The reception and wedding banquet under the supervision of Reggie Smith (son of Innkeeper Stafford Smith) were everything we had hoped for – excellent. Because this Methodist resort is dry, we brought wines from The Lark to serve – Bollinger Special Cuvée Champagne, 1993 Chalk Hill Chardonnay and 1993 Kunde Merlot.

Mandy & Eric Lark

Equally atmospheric was the open house Mary and I hosted the next day under a tent-top on the lawn of our lodge overlooking Lake Michigan, Beaver Island, and the local lighthouse named Skilligalee. This affair was catered by Mike McElroy of **The Crow's Nest** of Cross Village, Michigan's best roadhouse with the finest food and service of any casual restaurant Up North. Mike and his wife Linda (chef of The Crow's Nest) are great friends and outdid themselves, not only with food ranging from shrimp, beef tenderloin, chicken salad, honey baked ham, pastas, sundaes and truffles, but in service by Mike, daughter Meagan and their experienced and dedicated staff.

Since the week following the wedding was The Lark's summer vacation, Mary and I lingered Up North, scouring beech woods for golden chanterelle mushrooms with great success! Some eight hours of forag-

2

Travelogue, history, food and son's wedding weave together to make a good read.

"Cooking & Dinning at the Lark with Chef Marcus Haight."

Participants are invited to join the chef (10:30 Saturday mornings) in the Lark's kitchen while he demonstrates his preparation of the culinary feast. Then into the dining room for the feast with wine.

The Lark is known throughout Michigan and, because of its prox-imity to Detroit, many guests are "out-of-towners." The mailing list is an important way to keep in touch.

Lark monitors the list carefully against reservations. If a name fails to respond, it's dropped.

Our reaction: We've read this newsletter for many years. It's a consistent reminder of all the good things the Lark family has to offer. Always entertaining and educational.

LaSalle Grill Gazette

VOLUME 3, NUMBER 4   ALL THE NEWS THAT'S FIT TO EAT   WINTER, 1995

219-288-1155   115 W. Colfax Ave., Downtown South Bend   800-382-9323

The Four Way Test - Good Simple Guidelines for Doing Great Business

Some of our readers know, but probably most do not, that I am a Rotarian. I have been a proud member of the downtown South Bend Rotary Club since 1983. I have enjoyed the opportunity to serve our community through the Rotary Club's many hands-on philanthropic projects. I am thankful for the privilege to serve the Club in the past as President and a member of the Board of Directors. I plan on being an active member for as long as possible.

I'll bet you're wondering, "What has all this got to do with LaSalle Grill?" Well, I'm here to tell you that if I had not been a Rotarian, I would not have been able to successfully open the Grill.

Why? Being a Rotarian has helped to foster a solid sense of community, stability and business ethics that I otherwise might not have developed. You see, we Rotarians have a simple set of rules that we strive to abide by in our business practices. To wit: *The Four Way Test*.

The Four Way Test was

developed in the 1930's by a young businessman named Herb Taylor. In the depths of the Great Depression, his small aluminum company was $400,000 in debt. His only asset was a $6,100 loan from the bank. Taylor also possessed a devout faith in God. As he pondered what to do with his business he decided to incorporate something new into his business plan. He wrote down four questions:

1. Is it the truth?
2. Is it fair to all concerned?
3. Will it build goodwill and better friendships?
4. Will it be beneficial to all concerned?

Simple, pure & straight forward! Herb went to his employees and asked them to memorize the questions and use the test in their relations with others. Gradually it became a guide for every aspect of the business.

Herb went to his ad agency and asked them to measure his ads in the light of *The Four Way Test*. Superlatives in copy were eliminated. Words like "best" and "finest" were dropped and replaced by facts. All adverse comments about competitors were dropped.

You can probably guess the rest of the story. Herb Taylor's *Club Aluminum Company*, manufacturers of quality aluminum cookware, paid off the $400,000 debt with interest in 1937. The company went on to become a leader in the industry. Herb Taylor credits his success to the use of *The Four Way Test*.

I have *The Four Way Test* posted on a wall at the Grill. I have attempted to run my business based on those four questions. What I have not done is share this wonderful guide with my employees and customers. Sounds like a good New Year's Resolution. January 1 will be here before you know it.

Thanks for a great 1995!

Reservation Policy for Special Event Dinners

Each year LaSalle Grill sponsors at least 10 special event dinners. These dinners highlight specific wines, cigars or occasions such as Mardi Gras or New Year's Eve. As most of you know, we send invitations to these dinners to any of you who request to receive them.

We go all out for our specialty dinners. Only the finest foodstuffs and wine are ordered. Only a certain number of reservations are taken. Then, at the last minute the worst of all things happens. People call at 4:00 p.m. to cancel. Or they don't call at all; they just don't show up. Then we are left with an overabundance of product and an under-abundance of guests. For that reason we have instituted the following reservation policy for special dinners only.

When you make your reservation you will be asked for a credit card number to "guarantee" the space. Your credit card will be billed within 24 hours for the total amount. If you prefer, you can drop by and pay in person. We will hold your reservation for two business days.

Any cancellation prior to 72 hours before the event will receive a full refund. Cancellations between 24 and 72 hours will receive 75% refund. No refunds will be made for cancellations less than 24 hours before the event.

"We had high hopes when we began," says Mark McDonnell, owner. "I wanted to build a core customer base that we could count on for repeat business; involve and educate people in food and wine; and do all of this with subtlety and in an entertaining manner." It was also part of a broader effort to shift advertising dollars to direct marketing.

An IBM PC and Pagemaker software are the instruments of McDonnell's creativity. He gives camera-ready copy to a printer who also applies labels and sorts and mails bulk rate. The newsletter is mailed out first class once a year to purge bad addresses.

Customer reaction has been very satisfying. "This puts us out in front of the competition and lifts us to a different level," believes McDonnell. "Our guests

One of our priorities at the Grill is keeping our guest areas neat and clean. As with any public place, the task of keeping things up is a tough and thankless job. We at the Grill are thankful to have Tony Kuzmits on our staff.

Tony, or Kooz, as he is affectionately known, is one of our original employees. He is also a very special person. Tony has had Spastic Cerebral Palsy since his birth in 1959. In spite of his disability, Tony delivers what our customers have come to expect of all of our employees - a job done right!

He spent his early years in South Bend. The old Logan Center was his first school. After his parents moved to Elkhart, Tony was enrolled in the Beardsley School Special Education program.

Tony has never allowed his disability to keep him down. While in junior high school, he convinced his physical education teacher to let him participate in regular classes. Tony gave it his all. He amazed himself and the teacher.

In 1980, Tony graduated from South Bend Riley High School. He immediately entered the work force by landing a job at McDonalds. He remained there for twelve years before coming to the Grill.

An avid sports fan, Tony also counts coin collecting and ham radio among his hobbies.

We salute Tony Kuzmits for overcoming major disability.

Thanks, Tony, for being one of the Grill gang.

BY CHARLIE RYDE

Real Zinfandel Is Not Pink!

Of all varietal wines, red Zinfandel is my favorite. It constantly amazes me how many people, even some who consider themselves quite knowledgeable about wines, do not know about Zinfandel. When you suggest a bottle to them they comment, "Oh, not that sweet pink stuff," or "We really wanted a decent wine".

On the other hand, people often ask for a glass of Zinfandel thinking that it will be the "pink stuff" or white Zinfandel.

Zinfandel is one of the oldest grapes grown in California. Although it's history is sketchy, the modern belief is that the Zinfandel grape originated in Eastern Europe and was brought to California in the mid 1800's. It has been grown there ever since. Long before Cabernet, Chardonnay or other varietals were grown, Zinfandel was the primary California grape.

White Zinfandel is actually a pink, or "blush" wine. It can be 100% Zinfandel or Zinfandel may be blended with white grapes such as Chenin Blanc or French Colombard.

In any event, the skins of the grapes (which are responsible for the color and tannin content of red wines) are removed from the juice quite quickly when making white Zin.

Real Zinfandel (the red one) comes in many varieties and styles. Generally dry with a hint of spice, Zinfandel's fruit comes out in the middle. Sometimes jammy cherry, strawberry, plum or blackberry, the fruit really shines through. A peppery finish is common.

My favorite food matches include all wild game (especially venison and pheasant) and

duck. In fact, Zinfandel and our seared breast of Indiana duckling are a match made in heaven. Zins are good with any red meat; try one with a steak or even pork (especially with fruit sauces).

We currently have seven Zins on our regular wine list and two offerings on the reserve list. My favorites are the Nalle Dry Creek, Renwood Amador County Old Vines and the recently acquired Chateau Potelle VGS.

The holiday season is upon us and while you're rushing around for the perfect gifts I have a couple of suggestions for the wine lover.

First is a new book from IDG Books Worldwide, Inc. This publisher is best known for the series of computer books "... for Dummies". In their own style, they have now published Wine for Dummies.

A good read for both wine novice and expert, Dummies is concise with a touch of humor and packed full of interesting information.

I would be remiss not to mention Grill Gift Certificates. The gift of the ultimate fine dining is sure to please the most discriminating recipient.

Remember, 5% of all certificate sales are donated to the South Bend Regional Museum of Art. A gift of food, a gift of art ... LaSalle Grill is the Art of Fine Dining.

LaSalle Grill Gazette
LaSalle Grill
Volume 3, Number 4
115 W. Colfax Ave.
Downtown South Bend, Indiana 46601
219-288-1155   800-382-9323
Fax 219-234-8207
Office Hours 9:00 a.m. - 5:00 p.m. Mon-Fri
Proprietor & Publisher
Mark McDonnell
Editor
Charlie Ryder
This publication is dedicated to giving the news, educating our readers, and providing critical comment.
© 1995, M & H Food Ventures, Inc.
Anyone wishing to use information in the Gazette is hereby granted that right ... please reference your source.

Clearing up common misconceptions is good use of space.

tell us they feel good that they have a resource like this." Guests are also instrumental in driving content. He says they often remark "You piqued my interest, tell me more about such and such."

McDonnell's entire customer base of 3000 receives the LaSalle Grill Gazette. However, the list is segmented by interests such as cigar smokers or wine tasting, so additional information can go out to those customers preceding special events. The list is gleaned from several sources: Staff members ask guests, "Would you like to be on our mailing list?" targeted credit-card mailing lists and local and regional Chamber of Commerce business lists.

Our reaction: McDonnell's democratic approach regularly gives his beverage manager and chef a voice vis a vis the newsletter. Why wouldn't diners feel good about supporting LaSalle Grill?

New York City

230 seats

Northern Italian,
casual elegance

Pino Luongo,
owner

(212) 727-8022

Travel tips are a
popular feature, nice tie-in
to regional dinners.

Dear Friends,

This newsletter is the promised, **Italian Travel Issue**, filled with suggestions for restaurants, trattorias, hotels, inns and shopping. Some were sent in by our readers, and others were gathered from our Chefs and Maitre'ds who either grew up in Italy or have experienced Italy as frequent travelers or culinary students. Addresses and phone numbers have been included where possible, but please remember that things change, and these suggestions are the personal opinions of the writers.

If travel is not possible for you this winter, visit ten of Italy's most important culinary regions by having dinner at Le Madri. During January, February and March, we will offer a prix fixe menu based on a particular region's cuisine, in addition to the regular menu. Chef Gianni Scappin has exceptional knowledge of regional cuisines and the gastronomic history of Italy, so I think you will find this regional eating adventure to be as authentic as being in Italy, at least for those few hours at Le Madri.

Believe it or not, New York City has a definite advantage over eating in Rome. Because of the high cost of labor in Italy, restaurants may have only one waiter for every 12 tables. In NYC, two waiters and two busboys would provide service for that many tables. Of course, Italy has the advantage when it comes to ingredients; produce, fish and game and the settings. But, if you compare the decor, service and price, in my opinion, New York wins!

Whether you go to Italy or Le Madri, we hope you enjoy our efforts to provide you with a memorable culinary experience.

Best Regards
Pino Luongo

READER'S TRAVEL TIPS:

"We would like your readers to know about two restaurants we discovered: **"Il Pozzo"** in Umbria, in the small (60 people!) town of Monte Riggione near Siena and **"Il Buono Tavola"**, a place we discovered on our drive back to Rome, 45 to 60 miles outside the city, which was exceptional—both a country club and restaurant with superb food and gracious hospitality! Try the Gnocchi Schiaffa in a light pink sauce and the roasted lamb shank with oven roasted potatoes. Finish with the homemade Biscotti and Vin Santo."

Mr and Mrs Gambardella, New York

Il Buono Tavola Via Nepesina Kilometer 1, 1480 Nepi Viterbo Tel. 0761571362
Il Pozzo Piazza Roma 2 Monte Riggione Tel: 0577 304127

"One of the most outstanding experiences of our recent trip to Italy was in the hills of Sicily at a pensione where we discovered **"Villa Greta"**, located on the hillside above the town of **Taoramina**. The grounds were covered with wild vines and colorful flowers. While the rooms were very basic, the small marble porch with two metal chairs was all we needed to be convinced. Watching the sun set over the most amazing view of the town, the Ionain Sea and Mt. Etna for just 77,000 lire ($42), was a steal!

Another wonderful hotel we found, with a rooftop garden, was the **Hotel Hermitage** off the Ponte Vecchio in **Florence** for only $140 a night. The most incredible dining experience we had was in Naples, once again on the top of a hill. A friend of ours who lives there took us to a restaurant that was owned by two brothers...he told us that whenever he had been there he never saw another diner. We drove up a winding hill which opened onto the very small Piazza dei Martiri, where we parked. The restaurant looked closed, but we saw a light and knocked. One of the brothers finally answered the door and led us to a table in a warm inviting room with a fireplace and rustic decor. There was no menu, instead we were served a multitude of appetizers in tasting portions, brilliantly prepared pastas and marvelous desserts. Strangely enough, no other diners joined us the entire time we were there!"

Alysa J. Goodman, New York

Dai Cappellani Ristorante Vico S. M. a Capella Vecchia 30 N.

"There is a marvelous restaurant simply called **Locanda** in the tiny hill town of **Amelia** in south–central Umbria, which dates back to 1134 B.C. The dining room is in a vaulted medieval space built over catacombs and excavated pre–roman roads. We recommend the prix fixe family style menu. After dinner, they will take you on a tour of the old tunnels that honeycomb under the mountain, some leading two kilometers out to the countryside so one could come up behind the besieging enemy's lines!"

Diane Ramo, New York

Locanda Ristorante Tipico Via Angeletti, 7 Amelia 05022 Tel (0744) 978079

Montalcino: Ristorante Rattoria Dei Barbi, Edgardo Ristrante

4-color process
8-1/2 x 25-1/2, 3-fold
80lb. paper
3-4 issues/year
15,000 names
Published since 1993

This newsletter has six sides, allowing great flexibility in cross-selling Toscorp Inc.'s different restaurants: Le Madri, NYC; Il Toscanaccio, NYC, Chicago; Sapore di Mare, Wainscott, NY; Coco Pazzo and Coco Pazzo Teatro, NYC; others, plus retail foods.

We've chosen a page from two different issues to show you how ideas and recommendations from both employees and customers can give creditability and added interest to editorial.

Travel issues are extremely popular. For good reason: They take the reader on an adventure, through the eyes of the staff. This gives the places mentioned, restaurants hotels visited, historic sites seen, people met. This concept also fosters good employee relations through recognition and association

Luongo and his staff believe that the

le Madri

THE WINE LIST AT LE MADRI AND COCO PAZZO

Le Madri and Coco Pazzo only carry Italian wines, because they best compliment Italian regional cuisines. Because of this focus and the high volume of wine we sell, we are able offer a larger array of specific varieties including ten pinot grigios and twenty chianti classicos. We have room on the list for obscure and difficult to obtain wines such as Ribolla Gialla, Schioppettino, Grosso Sanese. Our limited focus on Italian wines also affords us the ability to carry a special list of fifteen "Super Tuscans". A Super Tuscan is a proprietary wine, usually a Sangiovese or a blend of Sangiovese with

Cabernet or Merlot. The key to this new style of wine is aging in small French oak casks, or "barriques", holding approximately 60 gallons. The new generation of Italian winemakers began creating these special, non-traditional blends in the mid 70's, hoping to create an "International" style of wine. Proprietary wines have become the fashion, so some are no more than a catchy name and an artistic label. Our fifteen Super Tuscans are the best examples of this new style, which defines Tuscany as the world class wine region of Italy.

In addition to the wine by the bottle list, we also offer 10 to 12 wines by the glass every day. Wine buyer Tim Wilson, has created an "Insider Selections" list for Le Madri and Coco Pazzo, which are lesser known, high quality wines that offer great value for the price.

CHEFS PICK: *Castelcosa "Refosco"*
Gianni Scappin, Executive Chef, Le Madri
Gianni is from the Veneto region, so he has a fondness for the "home". He likes Castelcosa Refosco "because it's a traditional wine in the rustic style, but with character and a little spice".

Current Top Selling Wines at Le Madri And Coco Pazzo

White
Teruzzi & Puthod - "Terre di Tufi" 1993
Felluga- Pinot Grigio 1993
Romans - Chardonnay 1993
Broglia - Gavi "La Fasciola" 1993

Red
Fontodi Chianti Classico Riserva 1988
Antinori "Tignanello" 1990
Abbona "Barolo" 1990
Troglia "Gattinara" 1985
Caparzo "Rosso di Montalcino" 1991

Insider wine info makes guests more confident—everybody wins.

Le Madri and Coco Pazzo Insider Selections: White Wine

Anselmi Soave Classico 1993 $22
For great value, Tim Wilson suggests Anselmi Soave. Soave in general is often overlooked because of its history of overproduction and the mass marketing of inferior brands like Bolla that ruined it's reputation. Anselmi takes a quality over quantity approach, creating a world class wine. Ageing in the bottle for three months makes a clean, refreshingly crisp wine with elegant fruit. A truly great value at $22. Try it with spicy food, seafood and risotto.

Haas Pinot Grigio 1993 $22
If you insist on Pinot Grigio, don't overpay. Haas makes a wine that is every bit as good as the overvalued "name" Pinot Grigios.

Puiatti Sauvignon 1993 $39
For a special occasion, we suggest Puiatti Sauvignon 1993. 100% Sauvignon with concentrated flavors, it rivals any good French Sancerre. This wine proves that Italy is making world class white wines as well as red.

Also consider trying:

Lageder Pinot Bianco 1993 $36
Verdicchio di Matelica 1992 $34

Giving away recipes isn't a threat to business. The more thet know, the more they appreciate what you do.

Chef's Recipe

Cesare Casella puts herbs into almost everything he cooks! This recipe for fresh herb brushetta is from the menu at Il Toscanccio, where the appetizer list starts with a variety of bruschettas.

BRUSCHETTA ALLE ERBE MISTE
Serves 8

½ lb plum tomatoes, peeled and seeded
7 tbsp olive oil
1 tsp salt
3 scallions, cleaned and chopped
1 fresh chili pepper or
1 hot red pepper pepper, seeded and chopped
2 tbsp balsamic vinegar

1 tbsp red wine vinegar
18 fresh basil leaves, chopped
3 cloves of garlic
leaves from 2 sprigs of fresh marjoram
leaves from 2 sprigs fresh oregano
8 thick slices of day old Tuscan bread, toasted golden brown

In a food processor, combine all ingredients except for the bread. Pulse on and off until all ingredients are in small bite size pieces. They should not be too small, so be careful. Spoon mixture onto toasted bread or serve in a bowl as a dip.

---

more knowledgeable people are about foods, wines, cultural differences and traditions, and the more their experiences are shared, the more they will be willing to experience.

Our reaction: Pino Luongo's introduction sets tone for entire newsletter—personal, helpful. Generous with recipes. Wine tips emphasize new experiences and value. Graphics are simple, but distinctive and elegant. Recommendations from those who've "tried it" is still the best advertising a restaurant can have.

Philadelphia

130 seats

Modern American
cusine with ethnic
influences in a rustic
late-1800s setting

Chef Michael &
Terry McNally, Owners
Tina Breslow, Editor

(215) 978-4545

Special kids menu
combined with early
dining hours helps fill
up slow times.

SUMMER 93 **LONDON CALLING**

THE NEWSLETTER OF LONDON GRILL · 2301 FAIRMOUNT AVENUE · PHILADELPHIA, PA 19130 · 978.4545

Katerin' to kids

Summertime is family time, the season to go out to eat with the kids, and London is a family, neighborhood restaurant. Before 6:30 pm we have a separate kids' menu which includes traditional and haute pizzas, veggie dips, burgers and pastas. We also have new coloring mats and crayons as well as high chairs and booster seats. And, best of all, kids under three eat for free.

...and the livin' is easy!

LONDON GRILL
SUMMER 1993

London chef and proprietor Michael McNally has been cooking up a summer storm. All new menus (lunch, brunch, café and dinner) include great original dishes and old favorites brought back by popular demand. **For lunch**: try a grilled Southwestern chicken salad in a corn and black pepper biscuit. The **café-bar** menu now offers a summer special, baby back ribs with guava barbecue sauce and plantain chips. **Dinner** features our warm weather duck breast with sweet corn pudding, cilantro pesto and mole sauce. The summer season calls for ocean fare; try our grilled sea scallops... or a cool succulent salade nicoise.

Café-bar: Summertime is the time for long cool drinks. Stop by for herbal flavored beverages made with our fabulous fruit syrups. We have delectable iced coffees and iced teas, potent lemonades and sparkling slushies that fight off the summer sun and bring a breeze to the summer night.
 iced teas: sugar and spice and everything iced. They are herbal, floral, fruity (and *no* caffeine) teas.
 We especially recommend rhubarb tea! Puréed rhubarb from Mom's garden and raspberry and lime tea, tea laced with raspberry juice and brightened by lime.

Black ink on buff-colored
paper

8 1/2 x 11

4 pages

2 issues/year

5000 printed and mailed

Published since 1991

When the McNallys took over ownership of the financially troubled London Grill, they had to overcome a long and storied past. "We made lots of changes in creating a new image," says Michael McNally, owner. "Then it was important to tell people what we had done."

"Restaurateurs rarely take the time, or have the time, to think through their marketing strategy," believes Tina Breslow, a

marketing consultant and editor. "A newsletter gave me the chance to sit down with Michael and help him focus and to work in advance."

"It was through the newsletter that I came to realize the power of communicating regularly with your clientele," adds Breslow. "The reaction was consistent and amazingly loyal. The newsletter became a conversation opener and has created a

LIBATIONS

Happy Hour! Join us Monday through Friday and always on Sunday from 5 to 7 PM. Enjoy our café menu and selected drinks at half price. Or eat all the hard-shell crabs you can for $12 while they last.

Thursday night specials

Every other Thursday night will be especially special at London Grill. Try free samples of new products. We'll have giveaways, games and prizes, all courtesy of our beverage distributors. Here's a sampling of who will be doing what:

July 8: **English Ales** with Friedland Distributors

July 22: **Fris Vodka** with Pennsylvania Spirits

August 12: **Rum and Reggae** with Maroney

August 26: **Absolut!** Citron, Pepper, Kurant with Margolis

September 9: **Bonny Doon's** "Big House Red", Malvasia Bianca and Vin Gris with Sussex Wines

September 23: Napa Valley's **Girard Winery** with Majestic Wines.

Terry's cocktail corner

Mocktails: Enliven club soda, water and teas with Fabria French or Italian syrups. Among the flavors offered are: tamarind, coconut, almond, raspberry, cherry, pineapple, mint, mango and grenadine.

Then there is Terry's newest mad drink, *orange hibiscus*, hibiscus flowers and orange blossom water.

Spirited drinks: **beer** is back and it's refreshing for summer. We have a wide variety of beers and ales. Try bok or weizen. And don't forget about our own famous Willie Sutton Ale. Come in and cool out.

We have a huge selection of London's specially flavored vodka drinks. You'll love the orange lizard kamikazis, gingered tangerine and honey mint.

EVENTS

AUGUST 7, NOON
Kids' cooking Class. Sign up now for a fun filled cooking hour with your kids. The chef in charge, Andy Schloss, author of *50 Ways to Cook Practically Anything*, will do a hands-on class on how to cook easy living summer dishes so simple that even your child can make them. Lemonade, Chocolate Dipped Strawberries and Fantasy Tortillas are on the menu.

SEPTEMBER 9
Brought back by popular demand the **cigar smoker dinner** sponsored by Macanudo and Partegas. The perfect ending to the perfect summer supper. Don't get locked out of this smoke-filled room. Call 978-4545 for reservations. Extra smoke eaters have been put in for a cigar friendly room.

SEPTEMBER 30
Join us for a very special double-header celebration. It is two years since Terry and Michael McNally took over the London Grill. In addition, it is their five year wedding anniversary. We think that calls for a celebration. Join us for a very **special open house** at the bar. There will be complimentary signature London dishes and a champagne toast on the house. Award winning local singer songwriter Karen Farr will perform. Karen who has been featured on WMMR and WXPN has just signed a record contract. She will sing the song she wrote for the McNally's wedding, *Linda's Song*. Terry, in case you were wondering, is short for Linda.

WEDNESDAY & THURSDAY, SEPTEMBER 15 & 16
Happy Rosh Hashanah! Usher in the Jewish New Year with us. London is the perfect place for an after service dinner or lunch.

Stop under our umbrellas for an iced cappuccino while we wait for our sidewalk café license.

As you can see, these tastings don't have to be elaborate affairs.

---

dialogue and rapport that didn't exist before."

In addition to regular features like "Tastes," "Libations" and a calendar of events, each issue spotlights a trouble spot or weakness in the restaurant's business. "If we want to book more banquets," says McNally, "we'll talk about the size and scope of our facilities, how flexible we are and how we are different from other restaurants. To build bar business we held a contest to name our house brew. Now it's so crowded most nights you can barely reach the bar."

Our reaction: This attractive three-column format allows flexibility and enhances readability. Attractive graphics lead the reader into each section or story.

If the president visited you, wouldn't you put him on page 1?.

Toasts

A Quarterly Newsletter of the Maisonette Group Volume 5 Issue 1

Friends and Famous Frequent Our Fine Eateries

It's been a busy few months at The Maisonette family of restaurants...

Several members of the cast of **Miss Saigon** took a much deserved break to enjoy a good meal away from the bright lights of the Aronoff Center at the center's next door neighbor —The Maisonette.

Ohio **Governor Voinovich** and former **Governor Gilligan** also enjoyed meals with us recently.

Downstairs in LaNormandie, **Boomer Esiason** was in town promoting "Boomer Esiason's Heroes Barbecue Sauce." Proceeds benefit the Cystic Fibrosis Foundation.

Members of the media mingled at **Chester's** recently. News anchor **Rob Braun** and his father, **Bob Braun**, took care of business at our tables on separate occasions. Another night, another table welcomed troubleshooter **Howard Ain**.

Tennis Anyone? Not just one, but four tennis greats — **Pete Sampras, Jim Courier, Stephan Edberg**, and **Todd Martin**, spent some of their free time enjoying a memorable meal.

Funny man **Gabriel Kaplan**, went bananas and then stopped in at Chester's for a quiet meal. He was appearing down the road at "Go Bananas."

Players and politicians were present as well. Former Reds **Johnny Bench, Dave Parker** and **Bill Doran**, a faithful fan of Chester's fare, all stepped up to the plate. And, our man in Washington, U.S. Congressman **Rob Portman** voted to enjoy a meal with us.

One guest who wasn't able to slip in unnoticed was **President Bill Clinton** who attended a luncheon at The Maisonette.

...And then there were our local stars, each and every one of you. ★

President Bill Clinton is welcomed to The Maisonette by Michael J. Comisar, Senior Vice President of The Maisonette Group.

The flagship Maisonette restaurant has been the toast of Cincinnati and a Mobil 5-star honoree for 32 years. But the rest of the group didn't enjoy equal billing. "Toasts" was conceived to heighten an awareness of all of the Maisonette restaurants among both consumers and media. Has it lived up to expectations? "We have a valued base of wonderful customers," says an appreciative Nat Comisar, co-owner and editor.

During the early years, the Comisars did everything themselves. But success has changed things somewhat. Nat Comisar no longer has the time to do it all himself. "I think a restaurateur's time is better spent being a restaurateur," he says. But that only means in the design and production end of things. He still writes and edits each issue.

Black type turquoise accent color on white coated stock

8 1/2 x 11, self mailer

4 to 6 pages

4 issues/year

6000 printed/4000 mailed

Published since 1991

Save on Sips at the Tavern

Take advantage of reduced prices on cocktails with dinner Monday through Thursday in the Black Horse Tavern at The Golden Lamb.

Reduced prices run from 5:30 to 9:30 p.m. with a different cocktail, wine or beverage featured.

On Tuesdays, enjoy dollar draft beers and reduced prices on domestic and imported bottled beers. On Wednesdays, sip any house wine for only $2 per glass (including chardonnays and merlots). On Thursday, experience almost half off on all house brand cocktails. And on Mondays...pick any price above!

The Black Horse Tavern features a lighter, more casual menu Monday through Friday evenings. On Tuesdays and Wednesdays, enjoy live entertainment with Jay Mills at the keyboard. ★

Exhibition Features Maisonette Artist

If you've ever admired the small painting titled "Windmill" which hangs on the western wall of the Maisonette, then you'll be glad to know that you have the chance to see 50 more paintings done by this same artist.

A traveling exhibition of Henry Mosler (1841-1920) paintings will be featured at the Cincinnati Art Museum from June 30 through September 2.

Born of German immigrant parents in New York, Mosler moved to Cincinnati in 1851 with his family.

Representative of American Impressionism, Mosler gained an international reputation for his scenes of peasant life which were awarded a number of medals in Europe and America. ★

It's Time to Eat Like the Dickens

April 16 through 28, The Golden Lamb will once again honor our most favorite guest with our annual salute to Charles Dickens.

Now in its 12th year, our two-week salute to our famous English visitor will feature a meal taken directly from his writings, a varied selection of English lunches daily and our soon to be famous (and Dickens own favorite) George and Vulture Punch.

Charles Dickens stopped at The Golden Lamb, then called The Bradley House, during his lecture tour of the United States in 1842. Despite his rater uncomplimentary opinion of our hotel in his book *American Notes* (Dickens was angry because he couldn't get a drink) The Golden Lamb has not one but two rooms named in his honor.

Guests for our Dickens meal can eat in the dining room named in his honor or even spend the night in the Dickens bedroom which features Victorian furnishings at their finest.

In our lobby, we'll display our collection of Dickens memorabilia including a complete 19th century collection of his works, and a unique set of Royal Doulton china dedicated to Dickens characters.

Our special Dickens dinner is one of our few featured meals that is available on the weekends. So make your reservations now. Spend an evening where Dickens did at The Golden Lamb, Ohio's Oldest Inn. ★

Building off-peak business.

We've Made Room for Christmas

The Golden Lamb Gift Shop has recently expanded to now feature an extensive line of Christmas merchandise twelve months a year.

The Gift Shop always began featuring their unique Christmas items in July of each year in their traditional Christmas Corner. Now, with the additional floor space, guests of the inn don't have to wait until mid-summer to begin their Christmas shopping.

The Golden Lamb Gift Shop has been a favorite destination for holiday shoppers for Christmas gifts and decorations which just can't be found anywhere else. What used to be the Inn's wine room now displays a colorful array of holiday ornaments, decorations, and tree trims.

Christmas comes but once a year, but now you can shop for the holidays all year round. Plan a trip to the country now and browse leisurely either before or after your meal. The merchandise constantly changes. So plan to stop often. The Gift Shop at The Golden Lamb opens daily at 10:00 a.m. and is closed only on Christmas Day.

Shake off the winter doldrums with a pleasant drive through some of Ohio's most scenic countryside and experience almost two centuries of tradition at The Golden Lamb, Ohio's Oldest Inn. ★

The mailing list has grown substantially, but carefully, through in-house charge accounts and special requests for the newsletter.

The length of each edition changes based on what Comisar has to say and what's going on in the restaurants. However, regular features include: Announcements of special dinners, celebrity sightings, seasonal menu changes, third-party accolades, local history and easy access to descriptions and phone numbers for all four Maisonette restaurants.

Our reaction: Nice to look at, easy-going style, but could contain more food and wine education given the restaurant group's prestige and cumulative knowledge.

West Orange, NJ

175 seats a la carte/
175 seats buffet

Relaxed, refined
elegance, American
Continental cuisine

Mary Jane Frankel,
editor

(201) 731-2369

Are you aware of
the special need of
your guests?

Editor: Mary Jane Frankel

WINTER/SPRING 1996

Manorisms *The Manor*

THE BEGINNING OF OUR 40TH ANNIVERSARY YEAR seems a good time to bring back *Manorisms*. Our switchboard personnel told us that many of you called to say you missed our newsletter. You indicated that the information contained in it was important to you. We thank you for your calls and we are happy to comply with your requests.

As always, The Manor has continued to apply progressive techniques to all aspects of its operation. As an example, we are taking our award-winning and precedent-setting recycling program one step further. As with the grinding of all seafood shells used at The Manor, we are now processing all egg shells and coffee grounds into our composter for use in our vegetable and flower gardens. Many of you have seen **Alfred Mayer**, our Executive Chef, walk into the greenhouse with scissors in hand to cut grapes off the vine for the preparation of your dessert. You may not have seen his herb and vegetable garden, but we can assure you that it makes any green thumber green with envy!

Did you know that we have just placed a brand-new menu in The Terrace Lounge? When we say new, we don't mean that we will have our waiters deliver these menus on roller skates, that we're going to hand you crayons to scribble your selections on the tablecloth, or that we'll have a sound-and-light circus herald this event. What we mean is that **Wade Knowles** has not only painted and designed a beautiful new cover, but **Freddy** (Alfred Mayer) has incorporated some beautifully executed new dishes for each season. We hope you'll try some of our wonderful spring selections in March, but until then we invite you to sample our Caribbean Food Fest, which begins February 15th.

Alfred Mayer, prior to settling at The Manor in 1972, and after completing his classical training in Europe, served as Executive Chef for five years at an upscale resort on the tiny Isle of Cat Cay in the Bahamas. To provide a delicious and very local Winter Getaway, Freddy will prepare recipes from his personal favorites collection, such as Conch Fritters Cat Cay, Bahamian Fish Chowder with Peppered Pastry Dome, Grouper Fingers with Rice and Tropical Fruit Compote, Grilled Wahoo with Spices of Grenada, St. James Chicken Breast, and Marinated Mangoes and Papayas with Coconut Sorbet.

Of course, you'll always find our most popular selections on the menu. (We've been threatened with bodily harm if we ever remove our Rack of Lamb or our Dover Sole!)

Incidentally, our menu is also available in braille for those of you who may be entertaining blind guests.

Harry Knowles, proprietor of The Manor, receiving the DiRoNA Award.

AWARDS

ONCE AGAIN, the Knowles family restaurants scored really high in all areas of recognition.

The Manor, Highlawn Pavilion and **Ram's Head Inn** all were awarded the DiRoNA, an award which recognizes those restaurants in the United States, Mexico and Canada which exemplify the highest standards in all aspects of the dining experience. The DiRoNA award was established in 1992 by Distinguished Restaurants of North America (DRNA), a nonprofit organization which seeks to promote dining excellence. It is the dining award in North America with standards comparable to Western Europe award programs.

All three of our restaurants were honored by *New Jersey Monthly* readers as well. **The Manor** was voted **"Best of the Best"** North and given the **"Best Service"** award. *New Jersey Monthly* readers voted **Highlawn Pavilion** among the five **"Best of the Best"** North and acknowledged that it has **"Best Atmosphere"** and **"Best Romantic Dining."** Finally, **Ram's Head Inn** was voted among the **"Best of the Best"** South. **Ram's Head Inn** was recognized also by *Atlantic City Magazine*, which voted it **"Best of the Shore"** for **"Best Restaurant Service"** and by *Delaware Today Magazine*, which named it **"Best Restaurant in New Jersey."**

All in all, it looks as though our efforts to give superior quality food, service and ambiance have not gone unnoticed!

Black copy plus color accent
on light-colored paper

8 1/2 x 11, self-mailer

8+ pages

4 issues/year

4500 printed/2500
mailed

Published since 1988

When customers started asking about "Manorisms" during a brief publishing hiatus, Editor Mary Jane Frankel knew she had a hit on her hands. And that she had to find the time to resume publishing— no matter how busy she was. Well, the newsletter is back, playing host to photos of beaming guests throughout its 8 pages. "Customers love to see themselves in print," enthuses Frankel. A veteran jour-

nalist, her theory is that the photos grab the reader's attention, and the captions tell them if they want to read the article that follows.

"The newsletter is an indispensible part of our cross-marketing," she says. People attending special events pick up the newsletter to learn that The Manor is a DiRoNA-winning white-tablecloth restaurant and dining customers discover

Dinner For One, Please

YOU'RE AN overworked executive. You commute or you're on the road constantly. You end your day with a mind full of projects. You're hungry. You have choices: stop for a quick hamburger and eat it on the run (not healthy, not wise); stop at a local take-out shop, buy the evening's meal, and hope it stays warm till you get home (not cheap, not guaranteed to keep its flavor); take a frozen entrée out of your freezer when you get home, pop it into the microwave, eat it in front of the TV (not nutritious, not healthy, not fun!).

There is a better choice: The Manor restaurant, long renowned for fine and relaxed dining, introduces the **Dining for One** program. A certain number of tables will be earmarked for the aforementioned overworked executives who need to dine alone for any number of reasons. No special menu, no special prices, no need to rush, no need to linger. It's simple really. You decide whether you want a quick, tasty meal or a leisurely tasty meal in one of the country's top restaurants which will cater to your personal needs after a full day's work. In other words, you pace the meal to your needs by giving the waiter your personal time frame.

The Manor will provide complimentary copies of *New Jersey Business*, the state's premier business publication, for your reading pleasure. If you need a copy of an article that might interest a colleague, we'll make all the FYI copies you want. If you need to have something faxed, we'll fax it. We aim to pamper you while you unwind. Now, if you don't like a little pampering, maybe you should opt for that TV dinner. But wouldn't it be preferable by far to walk into a friendly atmosphere and have one of our staff greet you with a "Good evening, Sir. Good evening, Madam. Dinner for one?"

Rev. Wilbert and Mrs. Svea Graffam

This group is too often overlooked. Good for hotel concierges and taxi drivers to know about.

CUSTOMERS OF THE YEAR

VISIT The Manor's luncheon buffet on any Wednesday and you will see the familiar faces of Cedar Grove residents **Reverend Doctor Wilbert Graffam** and his lovely wife **Svea**.

An ordained clergyman, Rev. Graffam performs many wedding ceremonies here. Considering they have been Manor patrons since 1961, we were curious to know what keeps the Graffams coming back on such a regular basis, given the fact that a good part of Rev. Graffam's professional life is spent here. The answer was very basic: "We always have a festive, relaxing and pleasant time here. Sometimes we come in and say that the buffet couldn't possibly be improved and a month later we have to eat our words. It just keeps getting better and better. Mr. Knowles is a genius at his profession."

Rev. Graffam and Mr. Knowles' father, Montclair Police Chief Harry Knowles Sr., were warm friends. Rev. Graffam recalls with affection the pleasant effect he had on the waiters and with sadness the passing of a gentleman he called "outstanding."

The Graffams celebrate many holidays and special occasions at The Manor, especially birthdays and anniversaries. They enjoy receiving yearly birthday cards from The Manor and want to express how much these cards are appreciated.

From time to time, they switch loyalties and dine elsewhere . . . in our à la carte dining room, The Terrace Lounge! But most of the time, they are drawn to the strawberries with cream.

The Graffams were quite sure that they had passed on their preferences for certain of the buffet items to the following generations when their grandson took them by surprise on his first visit to the buffet. After giving him a tour around the buffet table and pointing out and describing every delectable choice, they asked him what he would like to eat. He requested a mayonnaise sandwich, which the waiter promptly put together in the kitchen. The Manor aims to please its customers — no matter how young!

---

that The Manor is perfect for special events.

Frankel writes the newsletter herself, then submits the photos along with copy on a computer disk to a production house which designs each issue. Then it's mailed out bulk rate—except for one issue each year mailed first-class to clean up the list.

"One thing that always startles me," says Frankel, "is that the newsletter stimulates more interest from the consumer media than any press release we send out."

Our reaction: The Manor's customers are glad to have their newsletter back. We hope they've noticed the improvements, like additional white space, bolder headlines, new line art and fewer pages. It's more readable; friendlier too.

Appealing to business
community, showing
flexibility, desire to please.

Club members "tune in"
to find out about new
benefits.

WHAT'S HAPPENING AT MCGUIGAN'S
THIRD ANNIVERSARY ISSUE

McGuigan's Celebrates!
3rd Anniversary March 30th

Please join us March 30th as we celebrate our third anniversary. Enjoy a special menu, complimentary champagne and birthday cake as tokens of thanks for three wonderful years to our valued customers.

Lunch By Fax Program

In case you haven't already heard! McGuigan's now offers a "Lunch By Fax" program, with serious discounts!

Fax in your lunch order (our FAX number is 221-8094) and receive one of the following:

- 10% off lunch at McGuigan's, which will be ready for you at the time you request.
- 15% off your lunch order delivered (downtown Cambridge and orders of $15 or more only).
- 15% off your lunch order ready to go.

To participate, ask your server for details or just fax us your number.

Wedding Anniversary Discounts

Celebrate your wedding anniversary at McGuigan'sand receive a 1% discount for each year of happy marriage. Please call us in advance to make a reservation. This offer is also good for Gift Certificates purchased for that special occasion.

Murder Mystery Nights
Saturday, 9 & 23 March

WANTED — Amateur Sleuths to solve murder mystery. The plot unfolds over brunch at the Cambridge Country Club & continues with a search for clues throughout Dorchester County. Find out "who–dun–it" & win prizes while enjoying a full course dinner at McGuigan's that evening. Prices start at $40 and tickets are limited.

For more information call 1 (800) 636-7522.

Skipjack Cruises

McGuigan's is delighted to announce the return of our popular Skipjack Cruises onboard the *Nathan of Dorchester*. This year we will be offering a choice of Sunday afternoon sailings with lunch onboard or Thursday evening "Sunset/Steamed Crab" cruises. Complimentary cocktails at McGuigan's are part of both packages. Ask for our descriptive brochure which contains dates and sailing times. We will also be happy to organize private cruises for your office, family or organization at very competitive prices.

Frequent Diners Club

Since our first card was issued in June of 1995, the membership list has grown by leaps and bounds. We recently sent out card #700 and are pleased to report that every day 15-20 Frequent Diners' Club Members use their cards to receive McGuigan's discounts. Thank you, and keep using them.

Watch the next issue of *What's Happening* for details about a new benefit for members. We're instituting a system awarding points (based on dollars spent) which can be redeemed for prizes and meals at McGuigan's.

Entertainment
Saturday 16 March

St Patrick's Day party – (we know it should be the 17th, but that's a Sunday). All the fun of the Irish - Green Beer, Irish Menu, and plenty of genuine Irish (recorded) music. The music may not be live, but the other goings–on are sure to be lively!

Saturday 23 March and Friday 19 April
Rick Wright

McGuigan's Frequent Diner's Club is the source of names for their "What's Happening" newsletter and together they have fueled the restaurant's growth. "We think it's the most effective form of advertising we can do," says Gerry Boyle, owner. "It's personal. It lets customers know that something is going on at McGuigan's and makes them feel like they are a part of that."

Another benefit according to Boyle: "A newsletter allows us to be very targeted. We can talk to families in one section, bar patrons in another or announce special dinners elsewhere. Our beer dinner was a sell-out within a week of mailing the newsletter and with no other advertising."

Boyle reaches his 1000 frequent-diner customers quarterly for around 52¢ each including postage, printing and design. In

Catering

We are pleased to announce that McGuigan's has expanded our "off premises" catering capabilities. Although space in our second floor dining room is limited to 65, we will be happy to talk to you about catering larger groups (up to 250) at your site.

Help Us To Be Good Neighbors!

Please support our good neighbor policy by not parking in CreStar Bank's lot during normal banking hours, or in the drive–thru land at any time. Thank you.

They Said It...

Ex-Marriages – It's relaxing to go out with my ex-wife because she already knows I'm an idiot.
—Warren Thomas

Kids – Never lend your car to anyone to whom you have given birth.
—Erma Bombeck

Health – I know a man who gave up smoking, drinking, sex, and rich food. He was healthy right up to the time he killed himself.
—Johnny Carson

McGuigan's Pub and Restaurant
411 Muse Street
Cambridge, MD 21613

Address Correction Requested

Special Nights

Looking for something different to do on those long winter weekend nights? McGuigan's invites you to two extra special evenings coming up in March.

Microbrewery Dinner Night
Friday 15 March 1996

An evening for lovers of microbrew beer. Sample a different beer with each course during a dinner where the menu will reflect the theme of the evening - beer! Hear from the brewmasters the secrets of their trade and learn about the growing popularity of microbrew beers.

$25.00 per person inclusive. Advance ticket only.

Californian Dreaming
Saturday 30 March 1996

Diary Dates

So much is happening at McGuigan's in the coming months, you might want to keep this Newsletter very handy.

- Saturday 9 March - Murder Mystery Night
- Friday 15 March - Beer Lover's Dinner
- Saturday 16 March - St Patrick's Day Party
- Saturday 23 March - Murder Mystery Night
- Saturday 23 march - Live entertainment with *Rick Wright*
- Saturday 30 March - California Dreaming Dinner
- Saturday 30 March - McGuigan's 3rd Anniversary Party
- Thursday 4 April - Special appearance from Scotland, singer *Ian Bruce*

This looks impressive—something for everybody.

the three years of its existence the newsletter has been mailed first class, but Boyle anticipates changing over to bulk very soon as his list grows at the rate of 100 per month. He supplements the frequent-diner list with names from the area Chamber of Commerce and past private-party bookings. Once every three issues "Address correction requested" is added to clean up the list.

Our reaction: Here's a good example of a basic concept reaping big rewards. You can get started with a typewriter and a copy machine if you have to. We wouldn't mind seeing more of the owner's personality come through or even a wee bit o' Irish folklore.

Despite the Palm restaurant's size and far-reaching locations, Loren Bosies says, "Through the newsletter we try to preserve a family feeling, to convey through the newsletter what we're all about. We help our guests keep in touch."

The Palm Reader always opens with a message from owners Wally Ganzi and Bruce Bozzi. "They'll pick a subject that's on the front burner for us and discuss it,"

Bosies remarks. Other regular articles include "Family Tree": a column that profiles outstanding employees; "Palm-Pourri" news specific to each Palm restaurant and its clientele and "The Wine Cellar": general wine education.

"There's a lot of editing and such," comments Bosies. "We all put a lot of time into it." She solicits contributions from staff and may, on occasion, contract

TABLE HOPPING

CITY SPOTLIGHT

THE PALM RESTAURANT CELEBRATES 20 YEARS IN "LA LA LAND"

(Continued from page 1)

said the Palm's food was in a league of its own. Don Johnson admitted he was guilty as sin of finishing every bite on his plate, while Matt Dillon "singled" out his favorite Palm entrees — steak and lobster. Mariah Carey thought her dinner hit a high note, Lorraine Bracco found Palm meals to be the best medicine yet, and local favorite Governor Pataki was caught eating only from the right side of his plate.

WASHINGTON, D.C.: Redskins coach Norv, and wife Nancy Turner, along with Dallas Cowboys' Troy Aikman stopped by for some pre-season steak and lobster, Secretary of State Donna Shalala was seen taking a break from official duties and enjoying the swordfish chop, and there's nothing Connie Chung would rather be doing than dining at the Palm with hubby Maury Povich. New bride Nancy Kerrigan recently said "I do" when asked if she loved the Palm's food.

LOS ANGELES: Michael Jordan was spotted hoopin' it up recently at the L.A. Palm, and Paul Reiser said he was just mad about the steaks and lobster. Tony Bennett may have left his heart in San Francisco, but his appetite was definitely at the Palm. Comedians Dennis Leary and Andrew Clay ate so much it wasn't funny. No objections were heard from the O.J. Simpson Defense

(Continued on page 3)

The year was 1975. Billy Jean King and Arthur Ashe won Wimbledon, the Ford Pinto was introduced, "Jaws" was the top grossing movie, the Bee Gees topped the charts with "Jive Talkin" and The Palm opened in Los Angeles. In the 20 years following, 730,000 jumbo lobsters and 365,000 prime New York steaks have been served at the Los Angeles Palm and the restaurant remains the second home to some of the entertainment industry's hottest actors, producers and directors. In this same 20 years, thank goodness, the width of lapels has shrunk and disco has become but a retro fad.

Louis "Gigi" Delmaestro, maitre d' extraordinaire, opened the restaurant in 1975 and has rubbed elbows with some of the biggest stars in Tinseltown. From such Hollywood greats as Cary Grant, Frank Sinatra, Lana Turner, Faye Dunaway, Sidney Poitier and Johnny Carson — to more recent superstars such as Cindy Crawford, Julia Roberts, Al Pacino, Sylvester Stallone, Kevin Costner, Billy Crystal and Gary Shandling, the list goes

"Like all the Palm's servers I've seen, our waiter combined no-nonsense briskness with an almost paternal sensitivity to our need. I found his manner as refreshing as everything else about this restaurant."

— *Dallas Magazine*

"Proudly plain and utterly confident, the Palm symbolizes the consumable realities of the good life. If you appreciate caviar, cigars and powerfully flavored Cote Rotie, you know how well this place is run."

— *Philadelphia Magazine*

on and on. In addition, key executives from CAA, William Morris, ICM, NBC and Castle Rock regularly dine at the Palm and many famous deals have been negotiated over a sumptuous Nova Scotia lobster.

What many may not know is that for the first 15 years, the L.A. Palm did not even have a printed menu — the ultimate sign of a clubby, insider's kind of place. This novelty has since changed and with the exception of a few devoted patrons, the response has been positive. "Now regulars look at the menu and say, 'How long have you had linguine and clam sauce?' And we've had it for 17 years. It's just that the waiters never told them," explained Delmaestro.

The L.A. Palm's recipe for success is simple according to Delmaestro. "We make every effort to ensure that each and every one of our customers feel comfortable — as if they are dining in their own home. It does not matter if you are a celebrity or a banker. People continue to come back because we offer the best aged prime beef and lobster, personalized service, and a lively atmosphere that's been drawing people to the L.A. Palm for the past 20 years."

> A succinct expression of any restaurant's mission.

LOBSTER FACTS
THE ULTIMATE WHITE MEAT

The exceptional flavor of lobster has been enjoyed in this country for centuries. In fact, evidence shows that residents of North America savored lobster for several hundred years before the first European explorers settled in the region now consisting of Nova Scotia and Maine in 1605.

The first official lobster landings were reported by James Rosier, a member of Captain George Weymouth's crew. In an account of their 1605 arrival, Rosier wrote, "And towards night we drew with a small net twenty fathoms very nigh the shore, we got about thirty very good and great lobsters...which I omit to report because it showeth how great a profit fishing would be..."

The 12 Palms around the nation sell an average of 15,000 pounds of jumbo crustaceans each week.

> Helps affirm your guests' experiences.

FAMILY TREE

GIGI DELMAESTRO, GENERAL MANAGER
ROOTS FIRMLY PLANTED WITH THE L.A. PALM

Gigi Delmaestro is as much a part of Palm history as its gargantuan steak and lobster entrees and celebrity caricatures. He entered the restaurant industry 41 years ago with his own restaurant, Mario's Front Page, in New York City. Eighteen years later he began his career with the Palm at Palm Too for three years before making the move to sunny California where he opened the Los Angeles Palm on October 25, 1975.

Twenty years later, Gigi has become a legend among the Palm family. He is forever immortalized on the Palm menu for his self-inspired signature item, the "Gigi Salad", consisting of shrimp, string beans, tomato and bacon with seasonings — known across the country by critics and customers alike.

Palm patrons who know and love Gigi frequently see him having breakfast with his good friend Larry King or hanging out with his buddy Brian Dennehy. Gigi also enjoys dining with his long-time friend David Hopp, an LA plastic surgeon, and hasn't missed dinner with him on Thursday nights for the past 15 years. Could he know any celebrity nip and tuck secrets???

Palm Management's COO Fred Thimm describes Gigi as, "The heart and soul of the L.A. Palm. This restaurant is Gigi's baby. For 20 years, he has nurtured it and his customers like they were part of his family. We're all extremely proud of his two successful decades and we expect at least two more."

In his spare time Gigi enjoys going to the races and spending weekends in Palm Springs. He also spends a great deal of time with his two daughters, Madeline and Elizabeth and two granddaughters, four-year old Michelle and one-year old Allison who live in New Jersey.

---

out to freelance writers.

The Palm mails about 100,000 copies and overprints an extra 1000 or so for distribution in each restaurant. At 40¢ per copy, the promotion is expensive, but one that Bosies says she won't do without.

While certainly not for everybody, Bosies believes the Palm Reader's tabloid size and multicolor printing is eye-catching and memorable— especially among the other pieces of mail her upscale patrons receive.

Our reaction: With its tabloid size and three colors, the "Palm Reader" is one of the most elaborate newsletters in this book. As such, it holds sway with a largely upscale clientele who look forward to its ramblings and large sections of celebrity sightings.

Denver

80 seats inside/45 outside

American grill in neighborhood English pub setting

Richard Director, Owner

(303) 778-6475

Pearl Street Grill
April 1996 Newsletter

April is my favorite month of the year. April reminds me of baseball, warm weather, The Masters and birthdays!!! To celebrate the coming of April, we introduce to you our "Birthday Bucks" promo. If you are on our mailing list and we know your birthday, you will receive a $5.00 certificate good only at The Pearl Street Grill in your newsletter. (during the month of your birthday obviously). If we don't have yours on our calendar, fax us at 778-0565 or E-mail us at finishstrong@msn.com, ASAP!

The food news for the month takes place on our kids menu. Due to lagging sales and recommendations from our recent survey, the PBJ, the Macaroni and Cheese and the Kids Fish & Chips will no longer be available. New items will include a kids hamburger and a PSG version of spaghettio's!! Let us know what your children think.

The beer specials for April are excellent! Brand new from the Tabernash Brewery we will pour their Amber Steam Lager. From Phantom Canyon in Colorado Springs, we bring you their award winning I.P.A. Also from Colorado Springs we will feature Bristol's Beehive Honey Wheat. Our fruit beer for the month will be Great Divide's Wild Raspberry Ale and our blast from the past is the original micro, San Francisco's Anchor Steam! Rounding out the list will be Red Hooks new offering: Double Black Stout and lastly we reintroduce New Belgium's Fat Tire Amber Ale!! Enjoy!!!

Pearl Street News:

The Vogue Theatre is alive and well! The 60's musical "Suds" is the main event with shows on Thursday, Friday and Saturday nights. They also have plans for a film series and other live entertainment as well! Stop by and check out their full schedule.

Reminders:

1) PSG 3rd annual golf tournament will be held Monday August 5th.
2) Monday is Philly Cheese Steak night.
3) Professional Secretaries Day is Wednesday, April 24th.

Vino Vino!!

We will feature a chardonnay and a pinot noir from Hinman Cellars in April. Salut!!

Free Drink or Free Dessert Coupon

The Pearl Street Grill, 1477 S. Pearl St. Denver, CO 80210
This coupon entitles the bearer to one free drink or one free dessert of their choice at the PSG.   Expiration Date: July 1, 1996
Bearers Name: _____

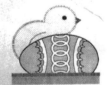

> If you want to know what your guests think, ask them.

> When you bring people into the neighborhood, everyone benefits.

Black copy on seasonal-themed paper

8 1/2 x 11

2 pages

12 issues/year

400 printed and mailed in business-sized envelope

Published since Jan 1994

"There are about 75 other restaurants in town that do exactly what I do, so I wanted to set myself apart," explains Owner Richard Director. "My goal was to turn infrequent customers into regular customers and regular customers into frequent customers."

Considering Pearl Street Grill prides itself on its progressive beer menu, what better way than the newsletter to announce the rotating selection of beers? Other "news" includes cross-promotions with local businesses and menu changes. A handy calendar of events now goes out with the one-page letter. And every month, diners are treated to a coupon for a free drink or free dessert, certainly defining this newsletter as a "must read." Director says about 30% of the 400 coupons are redeemed each month.

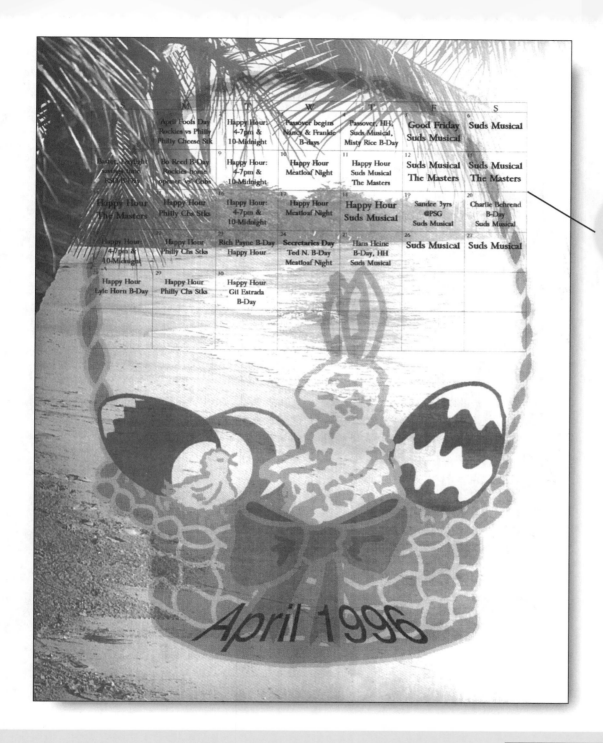

This doesn't have to include only events happening in your restaurant. Open it up to your community… or whimsy.

April 1996

Director estimates his outlay every month to be just $200, including postage, but not his time. The newsletter is written on a Gateway 2000 computer using Print Shop Deluxe software, printed out on a laser printer and even duplicated in-house.

"Things didn't come easy at first," says Director. "In the beginning my content wasn't very good and neither was the response from my customers, but you have to listen to what they're telling you and persevere."

Our reaction: Functional, basic design gets the job done. But why not talk more about the beers themselves? Helping guests understand differences, appreciate flavors; an ongoing beer education.

 A couple of words from David Melincoff....

THINK SNOW!

What Our Loyal Guests Say

(From a recent Perry Restaurant Group focus group conducted by Champlain College Hospitality Management School and published in their newsletter.)

A recent focus group study of "loyal" restaurant guests in the Burlington area revealed a number of consistent themes, as described by the guests themselves:

Trust in the Basics. Without the essentials like good food or a clean and comfortable room, guests will not develop the trust that is necessary to begin a lasting bond with your restaurant. All of the focus group participants expressed confidence that they would consistently be satisfied at their chosen restaurant--and if there were occasional mishaps, they felt sure that problems would be corrected quickly.

Recognition. This was the most common theme in the discussion. Many of the guests made specific references to the fact that the staff consistently recognized them and called them by name, and that they know some staff members' names, as well. Most of all, they were made to feel like they belonged and that people were happy to see them again.

Individualized Service. This group told of a variety of incidents in which employees had included personalized touches like offering that guest's regular drink, saving some of a special menu item for them, or even rigging up a coffee pot warmer at the table of a couple who were known for drinking lots of coffee. In all of these cases, the guests expressed appreciation for being treated like valued individuals.

Overall, these loyal guests expressed a surprising degree of comfort in their chosen restaurant, with some even noting that they felt like "part of the family". Obviously they were receiving a lot more than just competent foodservice.

Perry Restaurant Group History!!

The start of a restaurant empire....

In 1962, Tony Perry saw an opportunity to enliven Manchester's nightlife. He came to his home town with $1,000 saved and an idea to create a nightlife for residents, skiers and tourists alike. To expand, he needed more capital, which led him to recruit local stockholders.

The young nightclub owner managed to sell $8000 in stock to local residents. Together with a $6000 loan his father took out, Tony bought the property and lumber storage building on Route 11-30 that today is the Manchester Sirloin Saloon. There was no zoning at the time, so Tony had his own ideas on how to renovate the building to attract patrons.

"I put up this enormous sign with a huge fly on it that took up half the side of the building. On the other side, I put up these huge circus letters that read 'Dancing and Entertainment,'" Tony remembered. "The whole thing would have given the zoning administrator a hemorrhage."

Tony renovated the two-floor building to offer a dance floor, band stage, five bars and seating area downstairs, while the upstairs housed the kitchen and 32-seat restaurant area. He hired three staff and went on a one-man advertising campaign around town to entice residents to the new hot spot. On Dec. 18, 1963 the Manchester Five Flies opened up to rave reviews. (Continued on page 2.)

October, 1996
Volume 4, Issue 2

> **"The secret of happiness is not in doing what one likes,
> but in liking what one does."**

"We really hadn't planned to distribute our newsletter to guests, until they started asking for it," says Linda Gilbert, marketing director. "Perry"odical—named by a staff member of the Perry Restaurant Group in an employee "name the newsletter" contest—started as a company newsletter. The newsletter was also used as a "recruiting tool" when sending company information to potential employees. But after patrons began gobbling up issues left at a hostess stand, Gilbert reconsidered.

Last May she allowed guests of one restaurant to sign up to receive the newsletter by indicating their interest on comment cards. Her suspicions now confirmed, all comment cards offer guests the opportunity to receive "Perry"odical.

"The new mix of readers will give us a chance to do more guest and employee

DONATIONS

Summer traditionally seems to be a slower time for the Donation Committee. However, the advent of Fall will see an increase in donation requests. We provide donations in a variety of ways, over the past few months: Sweetwaters donated 2 nights of dinners to the Burlington Emergency Shelter. Chittenden County churches provide many of the Shelter's dinners but during the summer, when many parishioners are away, the Shelter asks local restaurants for assistance. Sweetwaters prepared dinners for approximately 20 people at the Shelter. In late June, the Sirloin Saloon provided brownies to the Burlington 24 Hour Relay. This event raises money for teen activities throughout the year. Earlier this spring, Sweetwaters also provided dinner for the YMCA Nurturing Program to Prevent Child Abuse. An entirely different avenue are the "Bears". Linda Gilbert cleverly "dresses" the Bears catching the attention of the passersby. One of the organizations the Bears supported this summer was the Alzheimer's Association. The Bears have also brought awareness to the Shelburne Farms' Harvest Festival, the Lyric Theatre, Ronald McDonald House, and the Visiting Nurses Association, to mention a few.

★ ★ ★ ★ ★
Anniversary Employees

5th anniversary
★Adam Croshier, Salad Bar/Day Prep, Pittsfield
★Sharon Stone, Bookkeeper, Manchester
★Horace Churchill, Day Prep, Rutland
★Cortney Cahill, Server, Shelburne
★Deb Rackliff, Server, Perry's
★Bradley Carleton, Host, Perry's

10th anniversary
★Peter Kapusta, GM, Rutland
★Rick Perry, Server, Rutland
★Sue Murphy, Bookkeeper, Rutland
★Martha Meister, Manager, Perry's
★Jason Bell, Maintenance, Corp.

Way to go! Your hard work and years of service are much appreciated!

Great Comments

Sweetwaters - Sarah was the best waitress we have had in the whole Burlington area in 5 years! She was awesome. Thanks a lot! (Sarah O'Brien)

Perry's Fish House - Had Lobster and Filet o' Beef. Couldn't ask for a better meal. Treated 3 relatives and all agree. Fine food, excellent service. (Cathy)

Sirloin Saloon of Shelburne - Salad bar is key - best around! It draws us sometimes more than the steak and the brownie pie - excellent.

Sirloin Saloon of Rutland - This was the best dinner out I can ever remember. Our server made the evening very special. (Ted)

Sirloin Saloon of Manchester - We enjoy coming to Vermont and especially the hospitality and quality of food at Sirloin Saloon. (Deb D.)

Dakota of Latham - On our first trip, we did not enjoy ourselves, but this time it was much different. The food was excellent. Again the service was great. I asked the waitress for tarter sauce, but Dakota did not have it. She suggested Dill sauce which was better and more delicious. Thank you very much for the experience. Keep up the good work. Your staff is incredible! Thanks again. (Darcelle)

Dakota of Pittsfield - We came from out of state, you were recommended by locals and now highly recommended by us! Great! Our waitress was more than efficient. Wonderful! Accommodating! (Kim)

Dakota of Avon - Enjoyed the courteous waitress Sarah who was so pleasant and sweet. Wish her the best. I have waitressed and worked banquets. Service is great!

> **#1**
> **Kitchen Contest Results**
> **June - Rutland**
> **July - Shelburne**
> **August - Avon**
> **September - Rutland**

Guest Profile
Marjorie & Larry Malitz
Dakota of Avon

Nice way of recognizing good service.

Two very loyal members of the Dakota guest family are Marjorie and Larry Malitz. They have been coming to Avon since day one and have a standing 7:30 reservation *every* Friday night. Larry is a Regional Master General Agent for the American Income Life Insurance Co. A 20 year employee with his company, last year he was the #4 top selling agent of 2000 agents across the country! He attended Trinity College and the University of Hartford. Marjorie went to Wellesley College and has a great sense of humor. She has enjoyed raising their two children, Leslie married to Dr. Steven Kaim, and Steven (35) a handsome, single and eligible gentlemen who is a partner in a prestigious law firm. The Malitz' reside in West Hartford and make the arduous journey over Avon mountain to join us for dinner. Some of their comments about us: "The best thing that ever happened to Connecticut", "Coming to Dakota is like coming home to eat!" and "The help is always so friendly!!". Now that we have changed our dressings at the salad bar, Marjorie says that she is "Done with the Russians and into the French and the Italians!!!". They love the theater and are avid Yankee fans. Go Yankees!!!

Their Favorite Entrees:
NY Sirloin and Ron's Baked Stuffed Shrimp.

---

profiles," says Gilbert. "I've been doing research on guest loyalty and wanted our employees to learn from that. Guests will learn about us and we'll learn about them." In addition, a typical issue might report on guests' comments, employee anniversaries, community involvement, recipes and even food history lessons.

Gilbert spends about 39¢ per letter for printing, and mails first class, which keeps her list clean. Maintaining the growing list in house is old hat to Perry Restaurant Group; its birthday club numbers more than 40,000 names.

Our reaction: This company has been diligent about keeping employees in the know about every aspect of its business and their place in it. The newsletter has been instrumental in that. Now it does double duty, and very soon according to Gilbert, may involve vendors as well.

PENULTIMATE

University City, MO

145 seats indoor,
40 outdoor

American eclectic
cuisine/Historical,
informal setting

Andy Ayers,
Owner

(314) 725-6985

You don't have to be
so serious.

Provocative teasers
build interest.

Riddles Penultimate

6307 Delmar - In The Loop   725-6985

NEWSLETTER

"It may come bulk rate, but it ain't junk mail!"   #33 - Winter, 1996

10th ANNUAL RIDDLE'S/
WINE CELLAR BEER DINNER

MONDAY, MARCH 4th - 6:30 P.M.
Advance reservations required - $45 per

CALL NOW - 725-6985
(But don't bug me about the menu - I'm working on it)

ALSO IN THIS ACTION-PACKED ISSUE:

- **ENJOY FRENCH WINE, STOP FRENCH BOMB TESTS**
  "The only reason I could think of to test nuclear weapons
  would be to build more of them, plainly a bad idea."

- **ELEPHANTS, INSECTS & BEER, OH MY!**
  "The idea that anything about a business enterprise might be thought of reverentially as
  'the family silver' is totally alien to the present-day corporate elite at Anheuser-Busch,
  whether in regard to a 900 year old brewing tradition or a 100 year old baseball club."

- **REPRINTED BY POPULAR DEMAND**
  "Just as I began to feel a great wellspring of resentment toward this rude and bombastic
  individual, I was struck, like Saul on the road to Damascus, by a realization....."

- **RIDDLE'S ZUCCHINI BREAD**
  "Gradually add the dry ingredients, blending well."

Black on light-colored
paper

8 1/2 x 11, self-mailer

8 pages

Published 4x/year

5700 printed/5500
mailed

Published since early 1986

92

The nameplate says, "It may come bulk rate, but it ain't junk mail!" That couldn't be more true. This newsletter doesn't contain special offers or bold splashy headlines. Owner Andy Ayers wins over fans with intelligent editorial. But you'll also find news about special tasting dinners, charitable fundraising and favorite recipes. Some of his best ideas for stories have come from customers. "If I find myself

having the same conversations with customers, there's probably general interest in the topic," he says.

Ayers doesn't cower from controversial subjects which can sometimes occupy a significant portion of his eight pages. "I've never taken the approach that I've had to keep my politics under wraps. It's what gets the newsletter read, gets customers talking and why they pass it along to friends. It's

ENJOY FRENCH WINE, STOP FRENCH BOMB TESTS

The recently completed series of nuclear bomb tests conducted by the French government in the South Pacific didn't make much sense to me because it came at the precise time when it seemed that almost all of the world's nuclear nations were prepared to sign a comprehensive ban on even small nuclear tests. The French government indicated that it would sign the new treaty, but not until it finished this one last series of tests. The only reason I could think of to test nuclear weapons would be in anticipation of building more of them, plainly a bad idea.

The announcement of the tests was met with an immediate response from Greenpeace, an organization for which I have a great deal of respect because of their emphasis on creative, direct, non-violent action to protect the environment. There was an added irony because the new French tests were to commence almost 10 years to the day after an earlier series at the same site that had resulted in a Greenpeace protest and, incredibly, the destruction of their ship, *The Rainbow Warrior*, when French navy commandos bombed and sank it in the harbor of Auckland, New Zealand, killing a crew-member.

The dearth of news coverage in St. Louis of the world-wide opposition to the French decision was especially obvious to me because I had just begun to access the Internet and I picked up on protests across the globe that I didn't read much about in the Post Dispatch. There were protests in Australia, New Zealand, Fiji, South Africa, Germany and Japan and riots in French Tahiti. I even found a Greenpeace home page that posted real time reports on the 'net via sattelite telephone from the deck of the *Rainbow Warrior II* as it sailed into the restricted zone around the test site only to be boarded and impounded by the same French navy that had illegally destroyed its predecessor.

There were widespread boycotts of French wine around the world because wine is a product so closely identified with its point of origin. I considered joining in that action, but decided against it. Rather than discourage French wine sales, we decided to promote them for the duration of the nuclear tests by donating 10% of each sale to .... Greenpeace!

President Chirac began by insisting that a series of eight explosions from September through May was absolutely necessary, that nothing anyone could do would affect his timetable and that he would remain completely oblivious to the mounting protests. After he had been burned in effigy all across the globe, his domestic approval rating had plummeted, 95 nations of the UN voted to condemn the tests and he had to repeatedly impound Greenpeace protest ships, he saw his way clear to canceling the last two tests and wrapping up the series in January.

This may seem like a small victory, but the initial Greenpeace argument was that any testing is bad but repeated testing would degrade the integrity of the test site, calling into question the French claims that the geology of the site would contain the radiation. In effect, each successive test was more and more dangerous to the environment of the South Pacific, so the cancellation of the final two tests was, indeed, a significant achievement. I feel certain that if there had been no protests there would have been no fewer than the originally announced eight tests.

We had a lot of fun with the promotion, sold a lot of French wine and collected more than $1,600 for Greenpeace. We did well by doing good and our little fund-raiser was covered in the Riverfront Times, the Wine Spectator, Restaurant Wine Magaine and Jerry Mead's syndicated newspaper wine column. It's only February and the tests are already over. Hooray!

The Greenpeace effort to stop the French nuclear tests cost the organization a lot more than we raised. You can help by sending a check to: **Green peace, 1436 U St. NW, Washington, DC 20009**. And check out that home page: **http:\\www.green peace.org.**

A pet project or cause and a little creativity equals good business.

---

also what elevates it above junk mail in my customers' minds."

Ayers times his newsletter to coincide with special events, or as was the case recently, to reintroduce lunch service. "It's by far the single most effective advertising I use," admits Ayers, generally an advertising and media skeptic. "Whenever I print an issue, I have to add an extra person to handle the additional bookings. The same goes for any recipe we print; sales of that item skyrocket."

Our reaction: When you tackle nuclear testing, corporate bullying and zucchini bread in the same issue, you've bitten off quite a mouthful. The seriously written content that doesn't take itself too seriously is refreshing.

TRATTORIA &
WINE BAR

New Haven, CT

100 seats

Northern Italian
and Mediterranean
cuisine

Susan McQuade,
editor & general
manager, Stephen
Phillips, graphic
designer

(203) 776-8268

Bold Illustration in pink
enlivens page 1, but doesn't
interfere with readability.

Scoozzi

TRATTORIA & WINE BAR
April-May 1996 Issue One

Dear Friends of Scoozzi
Trattoria and Wine Bar,
    Welcome to the first
edition of the Scoozzi Newsletter!
We will be bringing you this newsletter quarterly to keep you informed of
all Scoozzi happenings involving food,
wine, special events and anything else
we think you would be interested in.
We hope you enjoy it and your
comments and suggestions are always
welcome.
    First we would like to
thank you, our loyal guests, for
making 1995 a tremendous success.
We experienced one of our busiest
years ever and could not have done it
without those of you who returned
week after week to show us your
support and loyalty. Thank you!

    It is hard to believe
that 1996 is already here and Spring is
right aroud the corner. Before we
know it summer will be here and the
Patio will be in full bloom.

1995 IN REVIEW
    As we mentioned,
1995 was an excellent year. Here is
what Connecticut was saying about
us:
    In April, the Hartford
Courant gave us three stars, *"Scoozzi
is not to be missed."*
    In June, Connecticut
Magazine wrote, *"New Haven does
need a place like Scoozzi."*
    And in September, the
New Haven Advocate stated, *"Thank
heavens we still have Scoozzi."*
    Again, this is a tribute
to each and every one of our guests
who inspire us to provide the freshest,
most innovative, Northern Italian
cuisine, the most value priced wines,
the most intensely personal service
and an overall dining experience not
to be missed.

Here is what our guests are saying
about us:
*"We can't remember the last time we
were so impressed with a restaurant!
Both the food and service exceeded our
wildest expectations!! Thanks for a
great experience."*
    -Rob Pedersen, Hamden
*"Everything was fantastic! Food and
service, atmosphere is great.
No changes necessary!"*
    -Vincent Bicello, Hamden
*"We'll be back again & again &
again..."*
    -Dee W. Murdock, Wallingford

And, speaking of our guests, there are
some that we would like to specifically
mention by name, for they truly are
appreciated by all of us here for their
dedication and loyalty to us. We
would like to thank: Guy Jaconelli, C.C.
Clements, Janet Dickson, Dr. Flamm,
Dr. & Mrs. Blum, Mr. Robert Thompson, Mr & Mrs. David Canandine, Mr.
& Mrs. Ken Gammerman, Dr. & Mrs.
Melchinger and Cybil Houlding, just to
mention a few. These guests join us
weekly and even daily and are our
lifeline to our guests' satisfaction.
Thank you again for helping to make
this year so spectacular!

A MESSAGE FROM OUR CHEF
    We have rounded the
corner of winter and the spring season
is shortly upon us. With the spring will
come the first menu change of 1996. I
like to take advantage of the spring
produce selections and the warmer
weather to accent our dishes with the
celebration of spring freshness. Look
for the return of asparagus as the first
sign. I expect the first change to occur
in the first weeks of April, followed by
another in mid-June which will take
advantage of garden ripening beefsteak
tomatoes and the very special golden
yellow beefsteak tomato.

Our celebration will
continue with each passing season by
taking advantage of the marriage of
seasonal food and wine through
special dinners offered to the friends
of Scoozzi.

    I look forward to
seeing you all soon and receiving your
comments.

Timothy Scott, Executive Chef

LOOKING FORWARD TO 1996
    We are currently in
high gear planning for the 1996
season. Here are some of the events
we have scheduled so far:

CIGARS, CIGARS, CIGARS
    For centuries great
historical figures such as Thomas
Edison, Sir Winston Churchill and
Samuel Clemens have indulged in the
soothing act of cigar smoking. Even
with all the recent downplay of
smoking, interest in smoking cigars
has risen like the Phoenix to become
one of todays favorite pleasures
among the famous, and everyday men
and women alike. Yes, even women
are enjoying a good Macanudo now
and then.
    Doctors, lawyers,
truckdrivers; fine men and women
everywhere, are looking for a comfortable relaxed atmosphere in which to
enjoy their recently acquired hand
wrapped gems. Picture this...An
evening under the stars, wisteria
gently swaying overhead, a single
malt scotch in one hand and a Monte
Cristo between your fingers. What
could be better than that? Yes, it's the
Scoozzi Patio this summer!
    The Scoozzi Patio will
be cigar friendly any time of the day
or night as soon as the weather
permits. We will be hosting **Cigar
Happy Hours** Monday through Friday
from 4-7 P.M.

Black on heavy white
stock, red and screened
red second color

8 1/2 x 11, self-mailer

4 pages

6,000 printed/3,200
mailed

Published since 4/96

Ten months after founding their newsletter, general manager Susan McQuade
says her biggest surprise about publishing
is that "it has taken way longer than I
have or planned on having." But it's
worth it. "We're the only ones in New
Haven that I know of that have a restaurant newsletter. And customers tell us that
they like the recipes, as well as the design
and flow of the newsletter."

What about that time element in producing the newsletter? "I plan on mostly
administrative and editorial changes—to
spread the work load around," McQuade
says. She produces the newsletter in-house
on a Windows software program and has
an outside service print it—at a total cost
of about 50 cents per copy.

The approximately 2,800 copies not
mailed are distributed on tabletops. They

1. Preheat the oven to 350 . Melt butter in a large heavy skillet. Stir in the leeks and cook over moderate heat, stirring occasionally, until just tender, about 5 minutes. Add the mushrooms and cook, stirring, until softened, about 6 minutes. Transfer to a large bowl and add the garlic and parsley.

2. Wipe out the skillet. Add the spinach and toss over moderately high heat until wilted, about 2 minutes. Stir the spinach into the mushrooms and season with coarse salt. In a small bowl, combine the clam juice, cream, tarragon and 1 teaspoon coarse salt.

3. In a large bowl, rinse the potato slices in cold running water until water runs clear. Drain the potato slices and pat dry. In a 9-by-13 inch nonreactive baking dish, arrange one-third of the potatoes, overlaping the slices.
Spread half the spinach-mushroom mixture over the potatoes and sprinkle with half of the smoked salmon. Repeat the process with another third of the potato slices and the remaining spinach-mushroom mixture and smoked salmon. Cover with the remaining potatoes and pour the cream mixture evenly over the top

4. Cover the lasagna with foil and bake for 1 hour. Uncover and bake for about 30 mintues longer, or until the potatoes are tender and golden. (The lasagna can be made 1 day ahead; cover and refrigerate. Let return to room temperature, then warm in a 350 degree oven for about 30 minutes.)

5. Preheat the broiler. Broil the lasagna for about one minute, until the potatoes are crisp. Let cool slightly before serving.

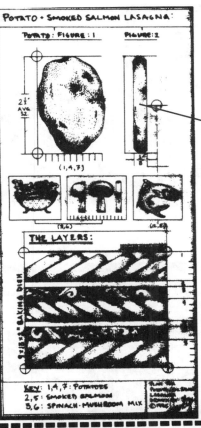

The ingredients in this dish all point to a rich, deep flavored Chardonnay. Consider the 1994 Lindemans Bin 65 from Australia or the 1993 Arrowood Reserve Cuvee Michel Berthoud from California.

Again, many thanks for making our seventh year another gratifying one. As always it is our pleasure to welcome you with unforgettable cooking, wonderful wine and intensely personal service.

Susan McQuade,
and the Management and Staff of Scoozzi Trattoria and Wine Bar

ALERT!! We are in the process of purging and updating our current data base in hopes of saving on postage and paper waste. If you are interested in receiving future editions of the Scoozzi Newsletter or any other information please fill out this short questionnaire and mail it back to us (postage paid). We would really love to hear from you. Thanks! (If you would like to fax it back, our fax# is 203 772 2124)

Eye-catching illustration accompanies recipe for potato and smoked salmon lasagna.

Customer reply coupon resulted in the staging of special-interest events—for cigar lovers, beer lovers, etc. Back is BRC.

By checking the categories below please tell us what you are interested in hearing about and/or attending:

❑ CIGAR EVENTS   ❑ RECIPES
❑ WINE TASTINGS   ❑ CULINARY CLASSES
❑ WINE INFO/EDUCATION   ❑ CULINARY EVENTS
❑ BEER TASTINGS   ❑ SPIRIT TASTINGS
❑ BEER INFO/EDUCATION   ❑ OTHER
❑ NETWORKING/MEETING PEOPLE

We would also love to hear your comments, suggestions and/or ideas for making Scoozzi Trattoria and Wine Bar a better restaurant and gathering place

NAME
ADDRESS
PHONE
FAX and or E-MAIL

acquire names by having customers fill out data cards. "But, because we're in the heart of Yale University," McQuade says, "we purge students' names once a year. They have to mail back the coupon in the newsletter to stay on the mailing list."

To other would-be restaurant newsletter editors, McQuade advises, "Look at as many other restaurant newsletters as possible."

Our reaction: Bold art work reflects the celebratory atmosphere of Scoozzi! And, set against the art, fairly conservative page layout and serif body type make the newsletter easy to read

Jenkintown. PA

180 seats

Upbeat contemporary setting

Anthony DiMarco. Owner

(215)885-9000

ISSUE VIII

Press·to

Stazi People

PROFILE: NICK OSWALD

Former Sous Chef, Nick Oswald has recently been appointed Executive Chef at Stazi Milano. Nick has been a Stazi anchor for several years now, and his contribution to the operation doesn't stop in the kitchen. Day after day, Nick has been the first one in each morning to open and begin the Stazi day. He oversees scheduling concerns, plumbing, heating and equipment maintenance, even electrical blackouts – and we haven't gotten to Nick's real talent!

Over the years his input has been invaluable when it comes to our seasonal menu changes. There's a sense of pride in all his creations and you can see it with each presentation. The responsibility for controlling every ounce of food product that is delivered to our back door is immense and it takes a true professional to handle those volumes. Nick takes on these challenges and performs his job with a passion that most would envy.

A face-to-face encounter with your chef.

As a graduate of the Philadelphia Restaurant School, Nick likes the idea of continuing education for aspiring chefs and goes out of his way to keep his "extern" program active and productive. At any given time you will find several students "working in the field" at Stazi. Nick is a mentor, advisor and friend to these students while grooming and fine tuning their skills and proudly directs them toward culinary careers.

Our Executive Chef, as all great chefs, loves good food and travels far and wide to taste the best (he leans toward California style cuisine). With companion Susan Weisman, a very talented Chef in her own rite, they share savory memories of trips to the West Coast and have returned energized with new ideas.

We like to think Nick's learned a lot at Stazi and we know that Stazi has learned a lot from him. Thanks for sharing your talent and determination with us. Best of Luck in your new position!

Black type plus red on white coated stock

8 1/2 x 11, self mailer

4 pages

Published 2 times/year

5000 printed and mailed

Published since Spring 1994

"Next to our menu, the newsletter is our most important means of communicating with our customers," believes Anthony DiMarco, owner. "75% of our clientele lives within a 3-5 mile radius," says Chris Donovan, editor,"and the newsletter is a great way of keeping our customers informed about what's going on at their restaurant. We can cook a great salmon but so can the guy up the street. This is what sets us apart."

"Press-To" includes not only recipes, industry news, special events, staff profiles and directional maps, it also educates customers about restaurant policies and creates a bridge between the customer and the restaurant. "In a sense, the newsletter serves as well-rounded form of advertising," affirms DiMarco. "The beauty is that you maintain complete editorial con-

A COMMENT ON YOUR COMMENTS

OUR PATRONS REGULARLY COMMENT (BY WAY OF THE CARDS WE KEEP IN OUR FOYER AND REGULARLY SEND OUT TO GUESTS WHO HAVE HELD PRIVATE FUNCTIONS HERE) ON OUR FOOD AND SERVICE, OUR ATMOSPHERE AND ARCHITECTURE, THE GREETING FROM THE HOSTESS ETC. ETC. WE CAN PLEASANTLY BOAST THAT A VAST MAJORITY OF THE COMMENTS ARE "GOOD TO EXCELLENT" IN ALMOST EVERY CATEGORY. I WANT TO SHARE SOME OF THESE GENEROUS, WITTY, KIND AND CRAZY REMARKS WITH YOU: HERE'S WHAT SOME OF YOU SAID:

"OUR WAITER WAS EXCELLENT-TOO BAD I CAN'T REMEMBER HIS NAME"

"GOOD JOB ! HOT FOOD WAS HOT AND COLD FOOD WAS COLD"

"OUR WAITER DID A GREAT JOB DISCIPLINING OUR NOISY AND ROWDY GROUP"

"I'VE HAD POLENTA IN ITALY THAT WASN'T AS GOOD AS STAZI'S"

"I CIRCLED ALL 5'S (EXCELLENT) BECAUSE THERE WERE NO 6"S ON THE CARD"

"I'M A VEGETARIAN-MORE SPECIALS FOR ME"

"PAUL WAS EXCELLENT BEYOND BELIEF. THIS IS NOT FROM PAUL'S MOTHER"

"I LOVE YOUR RESTAURANT BUT NOT WHEN THERE'S PEOPLE IN IT"

"MY ENTREE DIDN'T TASTE ITALIAN"

"I NEED AN EXPLANATION FOR THE TARDINESS OF MY SHRIMP"

"YOUR BUSBOYS ARE AMAZING-ESPECIALLY THE CUTE BLONDE ONE"

THANKS FOR THE REVIEWS-KEEP THEM COMING!

Chris Donovan

STAZI ——— STAZI

You Can Purchase

Stazi's Olive Oil with Peppers
$7.50 per Bottle Plus Tax
Stazi Bread $2.50 Plus Tax
Stazi Sweatshirt $30.00 (Grey or Black)
Stazi Baseball Hat $12.00

**Stazi Gift Certificates are available in any denomination
Great Gift Ideas**

Give us a call at 215.885.9000 and we'll mail order your item at no charge.
We will gladly prepare any of our menu items "to go".
Just give us a call (885.9000) and let us know what you would like and when you'd like us to have it ready.

STAZI MILANO INVITES YOU TO ENJOY

ONE FREE ENTREE
UP TO A $10.00 VALUE

when another entree of equal or greater value is purchased

**Bring this card in any Sunday through Thursday
from now until September 30, 1996**

limit one per couple, three per table, not valid with any other discount promotion or coupon

PASTA   PESTO   PIZZA   PRESTO

PRESENTING
STAZI MILANO'S NEW SPRING AND SUMMER MENU

Here are some suggestions from Chef Nick Oswald's latest menu to tease your tastebuds

ROTOLLO ORIENTALE
Shrimp, scallop and vegetable filled pasta spring roll with a sweet and sour balsamic glaze

VITELLO GENOVESE
Sauteed bundles of tender veal cutlet, filled with spinach, proscuitto, and bel paese cheese, served with marsala wine sauce, whipped potatoes and rattatouille

AGNELLO PIZA
grilled marinated medallions of lamb, roasted eggplant, sweet carmelized onion, oven dried tomato, herb olive oil and garlic chic pea mash topped with shoestring potatoes

These are just a few selections.

YOU WON'T WANT TO MISS THE ENTIRE COLLECTION OF EXCITING AND NEW MENU ITEMS ON STAGE, LIVE AT STAZI MILANO

MAMA'S KITCHEN

Chilled Tuna-Pasta Salad
SERVES 4 TO 6

1 #	PASTA OF CHOICE
1 #	CANNED TUNA
4 CUP	FRESH DRIED PLUM TOMATOES
1/2 CUP	SUNDRIED TOMATOES, I.E. RE-HYDRATED AND SLICED THIN
1 TBL.	MINCED GARLIC
1/4 CUP	RED ONION, DICED
1 TBL.	SHREDDED BASIL
1 TBL.	CHOPPED PARSLEY
1/4 CUP	OLIVE OIL
2 TBL.	BALSAMIC VINEGAR
THE JUICE OF 1 LEMON	
1/2 TSP.	SALT
	PINCH SUGAR
	PINCH GROUND BLACK PEPPER

COOK AND REFRESH THE PASTA. DRAIN AND FLAKE THE TUNA. COMBINE WITH THE PASTA IN A MIXING BOWL.

ARRANGE THE REMAINING INGREDIENTS, COMBINE TOGETHER TO MAKE THE SALSA CRUDA.

TOSS THIS WITH THE COOKED PASTA AND TUNA MIXTURE, TASTE FOR SEASONING AND SERVE AS A REFRESHING LUNCHEON ENTREE.

TECH-NICK
HERE'S SOME BASIC INFORMATION ABOUT COOKING ANY TYPE OF PASTA: THERE ARE TWO KINDS.
1- FRESH OR "AL OUVA" MEANING MADE WITH EGG AND
2- DRIED OR "MACCHERONI" MEANING MADE WITH SEMOLINA FLOUR AND WATER. NEITHER IS BETTER THAN THE OTHER EXCEPT THAT SOME PEOPLE HAVE SPECIAL DIETARY NEEDS REGARDING EGG OR FLOUR INGREDIENTS. FRESH PASTA IS DELICATE AND COOKS QUICKLY (30 TO 45 SECONDS) DRIED PASTA TAKES LONGER (CHECK COOKING TIME INSTRUCTIONS ON THE PACKAGE REMEMBERING THAT ALL COOKING TIMES ARE APPROXIMATE.)

READY TO COOK?
WATER TO PASTA RATIO IS 4 QUARTS TO EVERY POUND OF PASTA. ONE POUND SERVES 4-6 EASILY
1- BRING THE WATER TO A ROLLING BOIL OVER HIGH HEAT ADDING SALT TO TASTE AND 1 TBL. OLIVE OIL (BOTH WILL ADD FLAVOR)
2- ADD THE PASTA AND STIR TO SEPARATE THE STRANDS
3- COOK FOR APPROPRIATE TIME UNTIL IT IS "AL DENTE" OR TENDER BUT FIRM WITH A DEFINITE BITE
4- IF YOU ARE NOT PLANNING TO SERVE IMMEDIATELY YOU WILL NEED TO "REFRESH" YOUR PASTA. COOL IT DOWN IN ICE COLD WATER. TOSS WITH A LITTLE SALAD OIL TO KEEP THE STRANDS FROM CLUMPING. TO REHEAT, PLACE IT IN A WIRE BASKET AND DROP IN SIMMERING WATER FOR A FEW SECONDS. DRAIN AND SERVE.
HAPPY COOKING !

Freedom of expression— guests won't leave mad.

---

trol over what messages are being conveyed. The design of the newsletter reflects the philosophy, decor and feeling of the restaurant and its community."

"It's definitely a two-way communication," emphasizes Donovan. "Articles often report, 'This is what you told us' on any number of issues."

And the ultimate compliment? DiMarco has been getting calls from fellow restaurant owners asking how to create a newsletter like his. "I'm careful to remind them [as are we in this book] that the newsletter must mirror their restaurant in both look and tone."

Our reaction: Mr. DiMarco is a man of his word. Stazi Milano calls itself a "pop" Italian restaurant, reflected in design, food and attitude. That's exactly how the newsletter comes across with its bold, splashy graphics and coated paper.

TAVERN ON TOWN SQUARE

Spartanburg, SC

130 dining room seats/240 including bar dining and deck

Casual dining atmosphere, eclectic menu

Pano Stathakis and Jim Hartell, Co-owners

(864) 948-0052

Subheads help readers scan.

THE TAVERN TIMES

Volume 1, Number 1   SERVING SPARTANBURG SINCE 1994   Summer 1996

◆ Weather

Sunny and beautiful
No chance of rain
High 78. **Low** 68
Perfect Day for enjoying The Tavern's Deck!

◆ In Brief

The Tavern re-opens with great success

After being partially destroyed by a fire in late March of 95, The Tavern on Town Square was officially reopened October 16, 1995. After four months of steady business, patrons have named it one of their favorite restaurants in the upstate.

Unusual Concept

If you are looking to escape from the usual restaurant atmosphere, then The Tavern on Town Square is what you are trying to find. The Tavern offers a wide variety of your favorite foods, but we go the extra mile to add our unique flair to each dish we serve. There's the Chicken Salad Club Croissant, Hunter's Chicken, Grilled Chicken Haight-Ashbury, Spanakopita, Barbecue Chicken Pizza, and many more tantalizing dishes to chose from. Food is definitely happening at The Tavern.

The Tavern isn't just the wonderful restaurant you've hoped for, it's also a high-energy bar that offers a comfortable atmosphere and excitement for you and your friends. Every weekend there's free live entertainment and drink specials are offered each night.

During the warm spring and summer months, The Tavern opens its gigantic outdoor deck. The Tavern's deck is one-of-a-kind in Spartanburg, so don't get stuck on some boring sidewalk when you seek outside dining. Come to The Tavern and experience the deck's explosive atmosphere and our delicious foods.

A Theme for You

Each night in the bar features a different theme to bring you a variety of food and drink specials.

◆ Generation Xers show they care

The Tavern and Red Cross team up to raise money

Spartanburg's Piedmont Chapter of the American Red Cross and The Tavern on Town Square teamed-up to host their 1st Annual Celebrity Dash-for-Cash Luncheon on November 8, 1995. The luncheon provided an opportunity for Spartanburg's Generation X Professionals to donate their time to help raise money for their local Red Cross Chapter. Each volunteer worked at the Tavern as a waiter and all tips generated went to the Red Cross. The guest waitstaff represented various professional fields: Steve Jobe, Teacher-Dorman; Chuck Kayser, Teacher-SPTBG. Day School; James Drennan, Owner-Express Car Wash; Alan Richard, Reporter-Herald-Journal; Jay Brown, Sherman Chiropractor; Heather Smith, SRMC Nurse; Stacey Zabel, SRMC Nurse; Dr. Steve Winston; Nancy Owens, Interior Motives;

Top: *Members of The Tavern and Spartanburg's Piedmont Chapter of the American Red Cross along with volunteer "celebrities" mix to raise money for their local Red Cross Chapter.*

Bottom: *Pano Stathakis (left) and Jim Hartell (right) pose with the Carolina Panther Mascot at the 1st Annual Celebrity Dash-for-Cash Luncheon held at The Tavern on Town Square.*

Keith Alexander, BB&T Loan Officer, Rachel Smith, Jim Smith Realtor & Assoc. and Chris Schauble and Tricia Kean, WSPA-TV Anchors. There was also a special appearance made by the Carolina Panther Mascot that really added to the excitement.

Ranie Vernon, public support associate with the Red Cross, was extremely happy with the overall support of the community and she definitely felt the fund raiser was a huge success.

Jim Hartell and Pano Stathakis, owners of The Tavern, were also pleased with the crowd turnout and the number of young professionals who showed an interest in community service. ◆

The Second Annual Celebrity Dash-for-Cash Luncheon will be held on Tuesday, April 16, 1996. Please mark your calendar and plan to attend.

2-color on glossy buff-colored paper

8 1/2 x 11, self-mailer

4 pages

2 issues/year

5000 printed/3200 mailed

Published since Spring/Summer 1996

"We knew we couldn't afford traditional forms of advertising but still wanted an effective way to reach potential customers," says Jim Hartell, co-owner. "A newsletter does that and builds good will at the same time." Especially since The Tavern is very active in community affairs—hosting charity fundraisers and cooperating with a local museum to advance the work of area artists.

5000 pieces are printed and distributed twice a year at a cost of about $1200 including outside design services, printing and mailing. An initial list of 3200 names was obtained from a mail house chosen by carrier routes that matched the demograpics of existing customers. Additional copies are available at the restaurant. The mailing label is attached to an area of the newsletter that becomes

◆ Art & The Tavern

The Tavern Supports Local Artists

The Tavern on Town Square has recently joined the Spartanburg County Museum of Art to help promote local South Carolina artists. The Spartanburg Museum of Art is a community service and non-profit organization that provides exhibits, programs, educational trips, workshops and classes for adults and children in all areas of the visual arts. Local artists are being promoted by The Tavern and The Museum through the Outreach Program.

The Outreach program serves as a link between local artists and Corporate Spartanburg by offering local businesses the opportunity to exhibit works by South Carolina artists. Pano Stathakis and Jim Hartwell, owners of The Tavern, said they were proud to support local artists and were very pleased with the quality of work displayed in their restaurant. Other Spartanburg businesses contribute to the Outreach program

Spartanburg County Museum of Art

and there is also an exhibit at the Greenville/Spartanburg Airport called "Art of the Upstate."

All works displayed in The Tavern are painted by local artists and some of the pieces actually depict different aspects of Spartanburg. "Milliken's Green" by Doris Turner is a painting of the fountain outside the Milliken Research Plant and the mural located inside The Tavern, painted by Richard Conn, shows the scenery surrounding the old Converse Mill. There is also an outside mural, enclosing part of The Tavern's deck, that depicts historic downtown Spartanburg.

Patrons interested in purchasing any works displayed in The Tavern are welcome to call Theresa Mann at the Spartanburg County Museum of Art. Her number is (864) 583-2776. ◆

◆ Events at The Tavern

The Tavern Hosts Guest Chefs

Have you ever dreamed of being a chef at your favorite restaurant? Do you feel your home cooking skills are ready to satisfy the public's taste buds?

If you have dreamed of being a chef and you feel you have some cooking talent then call The Tavern between 3 p.m. and 5 p.m. to set up an appointment.

The Tavern will host a Guest Chef the first Monday night of each month starting May 6th.

Each Tavern Guest Chef will create their own recipe for an Evening Special and half of the proceeds generated by the special will be donated to a local community service group.

Look for the Taven Guest Chef announce-

ments on the What's Happening Board located at The Tavern. If you see a chef that excites you then gather a group of friends and call ahead for reservations. The Tavern's number is 948-0052. ◆

◆ Meet the Owners

Jim Hartell

When Jim Hartell left North Carolina for college, he knew his plans would include some unexpected opportunities, but forming a partnership with one of Spartanburg's most well-known restaurant families never crossed his mind.

Now, the son of George and Linda Hartell of Charlotte, NC, is working as an owner/operator with his partner, Pano Stathakis, at The Tavern on Town Square.

Owning a restaurant, Hartell says, has always been a wish and fortunately after meeting Pano in college it became a reality. Jim worked as Pano's assistant manager at the Carolina Coliseum and Koger Arts Center while he attended the University of South Carolina.

"I believe the offer to become partners with the Stathakis brothers was greatly influenced by the strong working relationship I developed with Pano at USC," says Jim.

At USC, Hartell also worked with Columbia volunteer agencies through his university scholarship. His main volunteer interest was in tutoring elementary students who were in danger of being expelled by the Richland County School System. Jim received the GM Volunteer Spirit Award in 1992 for his dedication to community service. ◆

◆ General Info about The Tavern

Phone
(864) 948-0052

Fax
(864) 948-0054

Hours of Operation
Mon. - Thur.
11 a.m. - 10 p.m.
Friday
11 a.m. - 11 p.m.
Saturday
4 p.m. - 11 p.m.

This works twice: it brightens up your dining room and makes you an arts supporter.

Not egotistical—it puts a face with the host.

an entry ticket for a giveaway.

Hartell advises owners and managers to keep as much of the newsletter in-house as possible. Not only to save money but because nobody has a feel for the mood of your restaurant like you do.

Response to the newsletter has been quick and positive. Customers have commented on its profession-

alism and a nearby competitor has attempted to mimic the publication: "Imitation is the sincerest form of flattery," quips Hartell.

Our reaction: Professional, well-organized design is somewhat corporate-looking, but thoughtful content will be a good community ambassador. The contest entry ticket is a clever way to track responses.

New York City

125 Seats

An enviable
balance of updated
American cuisine,
caring attitude,
comfortable
surroundings.

Danny Meyer,
Owner (also
Gramercy Tavern)

(212) 243-2010

Good "tease" concept.

Union Square Cafe

21 East 16th Street, New York NY 10003
(212) 243-4020

Autumn 1996

Dear Friend of Union Square Cafe,

The fresh excitement of autumn in New York always makes it feel like our city's true New Year, and we're ready to begin our twelfth fall season with an unbridled appetite for excellence, warm hospitality, steadfast reliability, and most of all, continued improvement. Since the day Union Square Cafe opened in 1985, we've always enjoyed the ongoing pursuit of refining our product for you. Thanks to another enthusiastic year of dedication from our entire team, 1996 has been a lively year of renewal for us, and as we celebrate our eleventh birthday, we hope you'll agree that the restaurant has never looked, felt or tasted better. According to unofficial reports from our plate-inspecting dishwashing team, you do! Thank you, as always, for being with us every bite of the way.

USC Unveils New User-Friendly Wine List Format

We'd love to have five French Francs for every guest who has raved about the dramatic culinary evolution in American restaurants, yet lamented over the laborious experience of ordering wine from a wine list. With a passionate commitment to seeing a bottle on every table, we've consistently strived to make it simple, fun and affordable to order wine at Union Square Cafe. Presented by vinously well-versed waiters, our list has always included accurate vintage, producer and appellation information, but to keep pace with a whirlwind of exciting change in today's wine world, we've decided that that's no longer enough.

To make it easier and more enjoyable to choose wine when you visit Union Square Cafe, we've scrapped our old format -- which listed wines according to the country in which they were made -- and reorganized our list so that wines are instead grouped by similar flavors and grapes. It now follows the same logic as a dinner menu which has separate sections for salads, soups, vegetables, pasta, seafood and meat -- allowing you to order according to the *flavors* you feel like tasting. (It's hard to imagine ordering dinner from a menu organized by the national origins of its various dishes -- Italian, French, Spanish, American, etc.).

So here's how to order wine next time you dine at USC. First, try to think of our wine list simply as a selection of 200 condiments to add further seasoning to the food you've ordered. Let's say you've decided to try our Roasted Lemon-Pepper Duck for dinner. Forgetting wine for a moment, imagine a flavor you think would complement the duck (for example: herbs, pepper, lemon, berries). Once you've made up your mind, you will have considerably narrowed your choices, and the fun of selecting can begin. Want something peppery? Our new "Spicy Wines" category includes comparably-styled wines like Australia's Mitchelton Shiraz, Martinelli Vineyards Zinfandel from Sonoma, and Chateau de Fonsalette "Syrah" from the Rhône Valley. How about something fruity? Turn to the "Floral" category and choose among diverse, yet stylistically similar wines such as Albert Boxler's Alsace Riesling, Domaine Huet's Vouvray Sec from the Loire Valley, or Renwood Winery's Viognier from Amador County, California. You'll find a category for "Rustic, Full-Flavored Red Wines," another for "Sweet Wines", as well as individual groupings for international wines made from Chardonnay, Sauvignon Blanc, Pinot Noir & Gamay, Merlot, Sangiovese and Nebbiolo & Barbera.

We're aware that certain social or business occasions warrant drinking a special wine, but don't lend themselves to spending lots of time pouring over the vast possibilities of a lengthy wine list. If that's ever the case for you, please ask us to fax you our current wine list *before* you come to the restaurant. You'll have a chance to peruse the list at your leisure, and if you need further assistance, you are welcome to seek the guidance of our wine director, Karen King, at (212) 989-3510 ext. 22. When your wine list arrives at the table, you'll be able to dispense with it quickly and get right down to business.

And here's a tip how to ask for advice effectively on a wine selection within your budget, without making an issue of price in front of your guests: after you've ordered your food and figured out what color wine you

---

Black on off-white, maroon headlines

Sparing use of black bold for emphasis

8 1/2 x 14

40,000 mailed twice each year

Published since restaurant opened in 1985

100

This simple newsletter design, with restaurant's logo as the only art, addressed to "Dear Friend of Union Square Cafe," and signed "Cheers! Danny Meyer and the staff," has attracted an enormous and loyal readership, with its visual appeal virtually the same for more than ten years.

Danny Meyer considers the newsletter as "important a part of USC's overall product as bread on the table. It's a great way of making your restaurant down to earth and accessible to the public."

It's also an extremely effective way to educate customers. Something Meyer feels strongly about: "If you're going to help people become more knowledgeable about wine, do it when they're at home, not in front of their guests at the restaurant table." An added advantage is the free advertising when articles are picked

...guests. Dinner will begin promptly at 7:30 PM so that we can ring in the New Year together.

Since space is extremely limited for the **Wine & Food Dinners**, we'll conduct a lottery to fill each event. Please fill out the attached request form, and make sure we receive it by **October 9**. We'll notify you by phone immediately if your name has been selected.

USC Side Dishes and Sound Bites

- **Overheard** of two professional women on a balmy August evening, bidding each other farewell after finishing a pre-theater dinner at Union Square Cafe. A true story:

  > Woman #1: "That was yummy!"
  > Woman #2: "Yes, but where's the New York arrogance I've come to expect?"

- Warmest congratulations to **Roger Straus** and all of our very good friends at **Farrar, Straus & Giroux** on the occasion of the legendary publisher's 50th Anniversary. FSG's acclaimed authors, editors and associates have enriched lunchtime conversation at Union Square Cafe on a daily basis since 1985, and thanks to them, we've had the thrilling opportunity to serve and cook for more than our share of Nobel Prize winners.

- We salute USC guests **Anne Minor** of Gary, Indiana, and **Cheryl Rehak** of Hoboken, New Jersey, co-winners of "The First and Last Great Scaffold Demolition Sweepstakes." Each of them correctly predicted the day our 15-month old scaffolding ("The Tower of Union Square") would finally be dismantled and carted away. Cheryl's strategy was simple: she picked her wedding day, May 18th!

- We're proud to recognize three Union Square Cafe employees for whom this fall marks a decade of dedication to our team: **Andres Herrera, Jose Cespedes,** and **Benijno Cabrera.** As USC's steward, butcher and night porter, respectively, these men have worked behind-the-scenes with tremendous devotion and have made an enormous contribution to our success.

- Please join us in welcoming two new members of the USC Class of '96, pastry chef **Stacie Pierce,** and dining room hospitality manager **Kelvin Kubo.** Stacie inherits the whisk from our pastry chef of 3 years, **Larry Hayden,** who is devoting full time to writing his highly awaited dessert cookbook. Next time you visit USC, you *must* save room to sample Stacie's new twist on the classic Baked Alaska!

- Notwithstanding how closely Union Square Cafe and Gramercy Tavern are situated to one another, it's no secret how challenging it is to effectively manage and operate two restaurants at the very high levels you've come to expect from us. To that end, we're thrilled to welcome **Richard Coraine** to our organization as director of operations for both of our restaurants. You may know Richard from San Francisco, where he was general manager of Postrio, and later a managing partner of Hawthorne Lane. We're glad he's on our team!

- In addition to nominating USC as Restaurant of the Year and Michael Romano as Best Chef in New York, **The James Beard Foundation** honored me with an induction into their **"Who's Who of Food and Beverage in America,"** and with their **1996 Humanitarian of the Year Award** for our work to fight hunger. I was equally gratified to receive the **IACP Award of Excellence as Restaurateur of the Year.**

- If you're stuck on ideas for holiday gifts for food-loving friends, we hope you'll consider sending them *The Union Square Cafe Cookbook* (autographed, $30), **USC Recipe Notecards** ($9.00), and **USC Dining Gift Certificates.** To order gifts please phone Karen Shain at (212) 989-3510, ext. 24.

As always, we thank you for your friendship and loyalty, and for allowing us to share our hospitality and cooking with you throughout this past year. We wish you a healthy and invigorating fall season, and hope that all your apples are crisp, juicy, and sweet. See you soon at Union Square Cafe!

Cheers,

Danny Meyer

Danny Meyer and
the Staff of Union Square Cafe

Variety of topics makes good reading.

---

up (as in the case of how to order wine) by *The New York Times, Daily News*, radio. Other general interest articles have concerned hunger relief, smoking, tipping.

Meyer uses the newsletter not only to praise his staff, but extends his definition of "staff" to include vendors and purveyors. Located near the Union Square Greenmarket,

Meyer conducts Wednesday "Morning Market Meeting," welcoming participants to a behind-the-scenes look at the restaurant, coffee, homemade muffins, and chat about any food-related subject they're interested in. $45 cost includes tour of market and USC cookbook.

Our reaction: Wide range of subjects, written in a concise but friendly tone, mirrors the restaurant and has readers asking for more.

LOBSTER TAILS
A NEWSLETTER WITH TALES OF WARREN'S

Volume 2 Issue 6   *December 1995*

▲▲▲▲▲▲▲▲▲▲▲▲▲▲▲▲▲

**All of us at Warren's wish you
and your family a joyous
Holiday Season!!**

Everyone gets so busy during the Holiday Season. All the shopping to do, fitting in visits to family and friends, decorating the house and cleaning the chimney in preparation for the arrival of Santa Claus! At Warren's the Holiday Season is a bit slower. So why not let us help you with some of these 'chores'? Make plans to meet your family and friends at Warren's for a special get together. We are always beautifully decorated for the holidays. Give us a call today and we'll reserve that special table for you! And if you pay the check, you'll be on your way to another gift certificate.

CHRISTMAS COOKIES

We all can make them, but who has time? We do at Warren's!! Our Head Baker, Dave Turner who retired last month is already bored. He will be returning for a couple of days a week at the beginning of November. He will team up with our new Baker, John Halka, to keep our pastry case filled and like the Keebler Elves, when the time comes they will work day and night to prepare a great selection of Christmas cookies. We will have an assortment of trays and tins of cookies available. If you would like something special or a quantity of trays for gifts, give us a call and we'll be glad to help you out!

GIFTS

The Captain's Treasure Chest, our unique Gift Shop features some great gifts for that hard to buy for person on your list. We are nearing the end of the season for the Gift Shop.(It will close after the Holidays til Spring) We are offering a 20% discount on everything in the shop (except postcards, candy and The Warren's Cookbook)

GIFT CERTIFICATES

A Warren's gift certificate makes a great holiday gift, and are available in any amount. Stop by anytime or give us a call at 207-439-1630 with your credit card number and we'll be happy to mail them for you!!

LOTS MORE INSIDE...
- FOOTPRINTS FOOD PANTRY
- HOLIDAY HOURS
- VALUABLE COUPON
- A GIFT FOR YOU

Clip art adds homey touch to down-home newsletters.

Black ink on white, green nameplate and second color

8 1/2 x 11. self-mailer

8 pages

6 issues/year

1200 printed and mailed

Published since early 1994

Lobster Tails is the communications vehicle for Warren's Lobster House's "Preferred Customer/Frequent Diner" program. As such, it's easy to keep the mailing list clean: if the customers don't eat at Warren's at least two times a year, they're no longer in the Frequent Diner program. Members get a card similar to a credit card, and expenditures are kept track of: each time the total reaches $100, they receive a Gift Certificate for $10. And, of course, members—and only members—receive the newsletter.

Dave Mickee writes and produces camera-ready copy, including clip art, which he delivers to the printer. For story ideas, "I just jot down ideas as they come to me. I read the trade publications and get ideas there. The kitchen manager provides recipes, and co-owner Scott Cunningham

LOBSTER TAILS ... A newsletter with Tales of Warren's

Boy, oh boy!! Warren's has kept me _real_ busy !!

"THINGS ALWAYS HAPPEN IN THREES"
(And sometimes fours)

Have you ever heard that saying? Well, in the past several weeks **three** babies have been born to **three** of our kitchen managers. All **three** of them are boys!!

Rick Provost and his wife Melissa became parents on August 7, 1995. Their son's name is Carter Hartley.

Brad Cunningham and his wife Vonda's son is named Matthew Scott. He was born on October 15,1995.

Darren Scott and his wife Sue will celebrate their son Trevin Darnell's Birthday every year on October24th.

Also,one of our servers, Becky Guy and her husband Leo had a bouncing baby girl, Brittany on August 11,1995.

We wish the best to all of the parents and babies!!

FREQUENT DINER
HOLIDAY GIFT

It's all the "regulars" like you that have made us successful. As a token of thanks for your patronage we have a little something waiting for you at Warren's. So on your next visit between now and Christmas we will give you your gift when you use your Frequent Diners Card.

FREQUENT DINER
SCHEDULE OF BENEFITS

As a Frequent Diner, be sure to present your Preferred Customer Card to your server when your check is presented to you. They will return a copy of the card slip to you for your records. We will keep track of your expenditures for food and drink. Each time your total reaches $100.00, we will send you a Complimentary Gift Certificate for $10.00. That's like saving 10%! (complimentary gift certificates, coupons, tax and tip do not count towards your total)

You have the privilege of making reservations any day of the year as long as you give us at least one hour notice. *This includes the summer time, and all holidays. If you call for a reservation and the person answering the phone says we are not taking reservations, simply tell them you are a Frequent diner and they will take your reservation.* (Occasionally, there may be a short wait when you arrive)

You will continue to receive LOBSTER TAILS... A Newsletter with Tales of Warren's. It's filled with inside information, upcoming events, special discount coupons and programs available only to Frequent Diners.

All you need to do to keep your account active is to use it a minimum of twice a year.

..As a Frequent Diner you'll save money and also help the economy! Thank you and Merry Christmas! *Bill*

Frequent Diner membership benefits are repeated in each issue.

6

---

writes an employee profile each issue. Although it's not an employee newsletter, the employees have a good time with it.

He says his only surprise as a newsletter editor-publisher is that there have been no surprises. "We've gotten a good response from the newsletter. People say they love it! I periodically do a reader survey and get good response from that, too. The newsletter does what it's supposed to—keeps 'em coming back." As many restaurateurs report, Mickee says, "Shortly after we produce an issue, we experience a surge in business."

Our reaction: The "Frequent Diner" program is an imaginative and uncomplicated way to build customer loyalty, and the newsletter is a value-added benefit which, six times a year, reminds them of their membership and its privileges.

THE WASHINGTON INN

Cape May, NJ

150 seats

American Continental cuisine/1841 plantation house

Dave Craig, Owner

(609) 884-5697

As the dining-out public becomes better educated, a chef's resume can pique their interest.

The Cherry Tree

NEWS PICKINGS FROM

The Official Newsletter of the Washington Inn

★★★ Mobile Guide · Victorian Cape May, New Jersey · ◆◆◆AAA

Volume 7, Number 1 · Winter 1996

Authentic Gas Lights Illuminates Inn

In 1976, in the height of the energy crisis, the majority of the towns gas lamps were dismantled and replaced with electric street lights. Recently, the city decided to replace a number of lights throughout the town. The Washington Inn sponsored a gas light for the 800 block of Washington Street, where one once stood. Look for it as you stroll past the Inn.

Mimi Wood Returns To Inn As Executive Chef

We are very proud to officially introduce Miriam Wood, the new executive chef at the Washington Inn. "Mimi" has been in our restaurant family for the past six years. Before coming to Cape May, her cooking experiences included work in Bucks County, Switzerland, and the Caribbean. For the past three years Mimi has been responsible for putting our country cousin, The Old Grange restaurant on the culinary map. Her creative & delicious food brought rave reviews from the Philadelphia Inquirer & the Atlantic City Press, as well as winning the 1995 New Jersey Monthlys' Award for the Best New Restaurant in southern New Jersey.

Chef Mimi will bring her experienced skills to create spectacular menus, continuing the tradition of Great Dining at the Washington Inn.

Our Winter Schedule
Re-opening
Valentines Day February 14

February & March
Friday-Sunday

April
Thursday-Sunday

May
7 Days a Week

Bulk Rate
US POSTAGE
PAID
PERMIT NO. 54
CAPE MAY, NJ 08204

801 WASHINGTON ST
CAPE MAY, NJ 08204

The Washington Inn, 801 Washington Street Cape May, New Jersey 08204. Any comments or questions, please call us at 609-884-5697, write, or fax (609) 884-1620. e-mail us WashInn@aol.com

---

2-color (varies issue to issue)

8 1/2 x 11, self mailer

4 pages

3 issues/year

4000 printed and mailed

Published since 1988

"There's no better way to talk up special events," believes Dave Craig, owner, "but just as importantly the newsletter sparks the interest of those who may have forgotten about us."

The entire design and layout of "News Pickings from the Cherry Tree" is done in-house on a Macintosh computer using Quark software, and is delivered "camera ready" to the printer. Print and paper col-

ors change seasonally. Topics range from notices of upcoming wine dinners to employee profiles to a carefully researched history of the Inn spotlighting its so-called ghost. Story ideas have come from brainstorming with staff and scanning other restaurant newsletters.

The mailing list has been built over the years from the inn's guest book, gift certificate sales and through the local cham-

FALL CIGAR DINNER LIGHTS UP THE JOINT
Spring Smoker Slated for March 28th

What do you get when you cross delicious food, savory cigars, a dynamic expert speaker, and great wine & cognac? No, not a large dry cleaning bill, you have a great evening during the Washington Inn's Cigar Classic Dinner. Dynamic Cigar Afficionado Manny Ferrero, of The Ashton Cigar Company romanced the crowd with his tireless enthusiasm for the cigar. A delicious menu was carefully created to match the characteristics of each cigar. The great cigars served were: the Ashton Magnum, The Ashton Madoro 20, the Ashton Cordial, the Ashton Prime Minister, and the Ashton Madoro 40.

Mike Laffey, whose table of 14 was one of the last to leave says, "Tonight was smashing. We haven't had this much fun since the last cigar dinner!" Bridget Fowler says of the event, " It was better than a Michael Jackson concert!" Finally owner Toby says, "It was worth stripping the restaurant down and giving it a bath." The next cigar dinner is scheduled for Thursday March 28th featuring the wines of Baron Phillipe Rothschild.

With stricter anti-smoking laws being enacted, devoted smokers may be looking for these events.

ber of commerce membership rolls.

Craig plans two substantive changes to his publication in the next few months: "We're going to hire an outside firm to handle our mail-list management and mailing functions. We're more concerned about adding names and just don't have the time to keep the list clean. The service will charge around 10¢ apiece but that will be offset by lower postage costs and of course free us up to do other things." In addition, Craig will eliminate all but a single type font to establish a cleaner look.

Our reaction: This letter's success is built on knowing and exploiting the restaurant's strengths. A little roll-up-your-sleeves research on the inn's history has yielded interesting copy and gives the restaurant an appealing character.

Philadelphia

200 seats

Contemporary
American cuisine
served in a country
inn in the city

Judy Wicks, Owner

(215) 386-9224

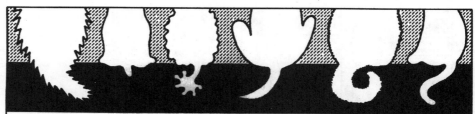

Tales from the White Dog Cafe

A Quarterly Newsletter 3420 Sansom St. Philadelphia Spring, 1996

Sharing Our Strength, Keeping Our Promise

This was my first seal party, and I hurried across the snow covered tundra in my mukluks to Maria's house where she would celebrate her husband's first catch of the spring. As the Eskimo women gathered outside her door, Maria dropped a large hunk of red seal meat along with a strip of blubber into each pail. When the seal had been evenly divided between the families, Maria handed out ribbon, buttons and pieces of fabric for sewing. Then the fun began as she tossed candy and bubble gum into the air. With glee the women held out the wide skirts of their fur lined tunics to catch the falling goodies. When root beer barrels, my favorite, were tossed, I overcame my shyness and stretched out my skirt to scoop them up.

My year in a remote Eskimo village in Alaska during my VISTA internship in 1969 helped form my sense of community in a way that has affected my whole life. The seal party demonstrated the Eskimo philosophy of sharing. In order to survive the harsh climate, individuals depended on the strength of the group and acted in ways which supported the whole rather than profiting at the expense of others. The seal party was a means for re-distributing wealth gained during the year, even when measured in buttons and bubble gum. Accumulating more than your neighbor was not valued. Envy did not exist; if you admired something an Eskimo had, they offered it to you. In contrast, I saw that our consumer economy is actually based on creating envy, rewarding greed, and admiring those who accumulate the most.

As the most unegalitarian country in the industrialized world with the largest and most rapidly growing division between rich and poor, America's promise of equal opportunity is far from reality. Poverty in America into which one in every four child is born, and the isolation and hopelessness it causes are a national disgrace. From Jonathan Kozol's compelling book *Amazing Grace*: "It is not like prison," says one 15 yr old about her life in an segregated ghetto, "It's more like being hidden. It's as if you have been put in a garage where, if they don't have room for something but aren't sure if they should throw it out, they put it there where they don't need to think of it again."

Serving in VISTA developed my sense of interconnectedness and my understanding that what helps one helps all, and what hurts one weakens everyone. Today VISTA is part of AmeriCorps which sends young adults to live and serve in low income urban and rural communities where they play a crucial role in developing community organizations struggling to meet the growing need for services during a time of diminishing funds. The participants are

not only compensated by college tuition assistance, but gain, as I did, a deep sense of community across the economic barriers that so vividly divide our society.

A favorite program of the Clinton administration, Americorps is targeted for elimination by a conservative Congress intent on cutting services for the most vulnerable, while cutting taxes for the wealthy. Join our bus to Washington on June 1 to "Stand Up for Children," or attend a breakfast with the Center on Budget and Policy Priorities analyzing the effects of the budget cuts followed by a tour of local children's services in jeopardy. Several Table Talks feature leaders in community service including Harris Wofford, CEO of our national service program, Bill Shore, founder and director of SOS (Share Our Strength)who will discuss his new book *Revolution of the Heart*, and Drs. Charlie Clements and Steve Larson, on the forefront of humanitarian medicine.

Although we do not have seal parties to re-distribute our stereos, cars, and designer clothing, we can volunteer our time and share our concern, and elect political leaders who will use our tax-dollars to provide every child in our country the basic necessities for becoming a successful and self-sufficient adult - a meaningful education, proper health care and nutrition, and decent housing. If we do, we will strengthen our whole society, and if we do not, we will be hurting ourselves, and breaking our country's promise that each of us be born into a land of justice and opportunity for all citizens.

Judy Wicks

White Dog Cafe Community Service Day

Saturday, May 25, 8am-4pm
"Sister to Sister All-Women's Build"
Habitat for Humanity - North Central Philadelphia
1829 N. 19th St. 765-6070

In the Sister to Sister Build project, all of the work is done by women who will contribute their time and energy to build the Habitat home along with a single mother in need of decent housing. We will work on a variety of construction jobs with supervision from the Habitat crew. No construction experience necessary. Women skilled in construction, or those who wish to volunteer on public relations or fundraising committees, or make a financial contribution should contact Habitat directly.

To join our volunteer group (teenage daugters welcome), call 386-9224. A Complimentary White Dog lunch will be served.. *We were pleased that 35 White Dog customers participated in our Martin Luther King community service day, on January 15.*

The commitment is real, and think of the goodwill this creates.

Black soy ink on white recycled stock

8 1/2 x 11, self mailer

8 pages

4 issues/year

16,000 printed and mailed

Published since 1990

"I enjoy my repeat clientele," says Judy Wicks, owner. "And a newsletter works well to build an atmosphere of belonging that brings people back."

Another job of the newsletter is to express the company's values. Social concerns are part and parcel of newsletter content. One of Wicks' many selfless gestures is recommending minority-owned Philadelphia restaurants. "It gets people

moving around to other neighborhoods and allows them to patronize wonderful restaurants they might not have known about otherwise." In a broader show of cultural understanding, Wicks organizes 20-person trips abroad to countries that have had a rocky past with the U.S., again, using food to bridge the gap. These international forays have all been sell-outs with no outside advertising.

Freedom Seder

Monday, April 1, 6pm

A Jewish Passover dinner with music and communal story-reading celebrating the message of renewal and of freedom from tyranny and oppression for all peoples. Conducted by **Rabbi Sanford H. Hahn** and **Rev. William B. Moore** co-chairs of The Black/Jewish Coalition of Greater Philadelphia, which was established eleven years ago by the Black Clergy of Phila. and the Jewish Community Relations Council with the belief that there are many positive aspects to the relationship between the African American & Jewish communities that must be nurtured. Rev. Moore has served as Senior Pastor of the Tenth Memorial Baptist Church in North Philadelphia for the past 20 years and is Chairman of the Board of Black Clergy. Rabbi Hahn is Rabbi Emeritus of the Germantown Jewish Center and serves as weekend Rabbi in Brigantine, N.J.

Members of **Atzilut: The Fourth World,**
will perform music of the pre-western Jewish Diaspora.
$30, including tax and gratuity. Reservations 386-9224.
Tuesday, April 2, Storytelling will be **"A Black-Jewish Dialogue."**
See Tails storytelling schedule for details.

New Visions for Business
A quarterly forum on making work meaningful
Tuesday, April 16, 8am

"Leading People:
Transforming Business from the Inside Out"
with **Robert H. Rosen,**

author of this recently published book, a nationally known speaker on leadership, consultant to Fortune 500 companies, governments and entrepreneurial businesses, and founder and president of **Healthy Companies Institute,** which studies high performance business. Rosen will address the need to restructure American businesses, universities and non-profits by developing a new kind of leadership utilizing the competence, creativity and commitment of employees. He will share his insights as well as the lessons of outstanding leaders featured in his book such as Alan Mulally, head of the Boeing 777 Project, Barry Alvarez, head football coach at the University of Wisconsin, and Shirley DeLibero of the New Jersey Public Transit Authority. Breakfast is $12, including tax & gratuity.
$10 for members of Business for Social Responsibility.
Reservations 386-9224

Leading People: Transforming Business from the Inside Out and other books in the **New Visions for Business book section** in The Black Cat, will be **15% off** for those attending.
For information on joining Business for Social Responsibility, contact John O'Connell at (610)696-2832

Child Watch Tour
"Budget Cuts and Children"
Monday, April 29, 8am
with **Philadelphia Citizens for Children and Youth**

Experience first hand Philadelphia children's services which will be lost or reduced by the impending state and federal budget cuts. The Child Watch concept was developed by Marian Wright Edelman of the Children's Defense Fund to provide an opportunity for citizens to experience the lives of inner city children. Locally, the program was initiated by the White Dog Cafe and Philadelphia Citizens for Children and Youth, who will lead the tour with discussion on state funding cuts.

The morning will begin with a breakfast discussion on the effects of the federal budget cuts on human lives with David Super of the Washington-based **Center on Budget and Policy Priorities** *(see Table Talk listing.)*

After breakfast, the tour will proceed by van at 9:30, returning to the cafe no later than noon. $12 / person for breakfast and discussion. Tour is free, but space is limited. Reservations 386-9224. For additional tour information, call Bill Madeira at PCCY, 563-5848.

CrossTalk at Noon
A Tuesday lunch series presenting
diverse perspectives on civic issues

"The American Dream in the 21st Century"

March 26: What is it now?
April 30: Does it need to change?
May 28: How would you change it?

with **Graham Finney,**
convener of The 21st Century League

Progress, Freedom and Responsibility. The Mission of America. Can common views about these terms hold Americans together in the years ahead? Join a diverse group to rethink the American Dream.

Noon a la carte lunch. (Entrees range $7-9.)
Reservations 386-9224

Transportation from Center City: Take the Subway Surface Car (any other than #10) and get off at 36th and Sansom. Starts at 13th & Market with stops at 15th, 19th, and 22nd; or take the Walnut St. bus #21 or 42 to 34th and Walnut, and back on the Chestnut St. bus from 34th and Chestnut St..

Something for everyone.

The White Dog's huge mailing list is costly to maintain even though "Address correction requested" helps keep things clean. Wicks is reluctant to pare it down since it is the primary means of announcing special events – and there are a lot of them. "People tell me that you're not 'with it' unless you're on the White Dog mailing list," she says.

Our reaction: This newsletter is a perfect vehicle for publicizing the unbelievably busy slate of special events and plate of social concerns.

Portland, OR

97 seats

Modern Mediterranean
cuisine in an intimate
bistro setting

Bruce Carey, Owner

(503) 226-3394

No.5 Zefiro

Black ink on white
stationery or reverse side
of recycled menus

8 1/2 x 11

1 page

4 issues/year

1000 printed and 900 mailed

Published since 8/90

Convinced that his newsletter's "chatti-ness" sets it apart, Bruce Carey writes every issue with the feeling that he's keeping friends up to date. "I do whatever I can to make it look and feel like a personal letter," he says. "Of course, not all 900 readers are personal friends of mine, but we can facilitate a family feeling. Portland is still a manageable-sized city where it's possible to make people feel like this is their place."

Carey used to print on office stationery, now, however he occasionally uses the back side of old menus, which change every two weeks anyway. "We don't eliminate the ones that have finger prints or wine stains on them," he insists. "Rather, we involve readers by suggesting that they may have actually contributed to the stains."

While Carey writes every issue himself, employees do get involved. He asks his

30 September 1995

Dear Friends of Zefiro:

The restaurant business is a trap! At some point, you have to decide to get out of it completely, or give in to it completely. For most, working in restaurants allows time for school, art, and sleeping in, but then you get used to the cash and the hours, and you get good at it. That's when it becomes a trap. Six years ago Chris and I were already good at it, having worked in top restaurants in San Francisco for years, so we decided to give into it, move to Portland and be our own bosses. We opened Zefiro and wow, now look what happened. We have been busy serving you all for years. Zero, the ice cream/bakery is already four months old and last month we quietly celebrated the five year anniversary of Zefiro's opening. The week before the anniversary, the Oregonian gave us a glowing review and a rare and coveted <u>four-star</u> rating. And as if we weren't embroiled enough in this business, that same week we opened our new cafe/bar downtown called Saucebox.

In a way, opening Saucebox is how we are celebrating our five successful years at Zefiro. Going there will be like an ongoing party; every day and night at Saucebox; a celebration of Portland and what we can do. Don't expect another Zefiro however. Jonathan Nicholas quoted me correctly summing it up in three words: "small, dark, loud". It's a DJ Cafe. It's the hang out we are missing in this town, a place not for everyone but for many. The chef at Sauce box, Emi Masumoto made over 40,000 caesar salads, among other things for you in the five years she was at Zefiro. Under Chris' direction, she is in charge of the kitchen at Saucebox, and the food is delicious. Try Saucebox for an inexpensive lunch or dinner, Tuesday through Saturday.

Things are going well at Zero too. Michelle Dennis, our pastry princess, is changing the way Portlanders think about ice cream. The nectarine and ginger 50/50 blew a few minds while it was in season, and this fall we can look forward to more reflections of the farm with her Autumn fruit tarts, pumpkin/pecan pies and new ice cream flavors, as well as whole pastries available to go with a days advance notice. If you are planning a family get-together around the holidays think of Zero for making it easier. To order call Zefiro and ask for the bakery. In November look for expanded hours at Zero for morning coffee, muffins and scones reminiscent of the "gone but not forgotten" Zefiro breakfast.

Another small way of celebrating the anniversary is to remember the original menu and the founding concept. Our compass logo and map motif hearkens to travel, and it's our travels that inspire what we do. It has always been the basis of the Zefiro concept. The most obvious influence is happening now as we enjoy Chris' new Asian flavors. The **"five year anniversary menu"** we are currently serving also revives favorites from years ago like the Moroccan chicken tagine, Ahi tuna with avocado and ginger-lime vinaigrette, and risotto with butternut squash and prosciutto. In September we skipped our regular menu change, which happens every two weeks, to allow Chris the opportunity to go to New York and cook for a bunch of food aficionados at the <u>James Beard House</u>. From there he will take a couple weeks to visit Paris and Spain, because after all, travel is what keeps Zefiro grounded, fresh, and on top.

Our reluctant bow to the onset of the colder season is the <u>Fall Festival of Pinot Gris</u> on October 15th which will be a diverting event we are planning in tandem with Cooper Mountain Vineyards, to benefit breast cancer research. This reception-style event will feature Thomas Lauderdale on piano, a special vertical tasting of seven Cooper Mountains award-winning Pinot Gris, and an extravagant seafood buffet with oysters, shellfish and regional European specialties suited for the delicious, crisp Pinot Gris. The event is on Sunday, the 15th of October, and tickets are available through Cooper Mountain, for $50.00 per person. Call Cooper Mountain at 649-0027 for a reservation.

The way you have consistently supported Zefiro through several years of business is very much appreciated by Chris and I and by the whole staff at the restaurant. It's a special place to work, because it is so well received, and you make a difference to us every time you return for more. We are all looking forward to serving you, learning about what you like, and exposing you occasionally to something new.

Thank you for being part of Zefiro.

Sincerely,

B. Carey

Bruce Carey

PS: You can buy a five year anniversary T-shirt with the design on the reverse of this page at Zero for $15

Talking about your staff gives your restaurant personality.

Don't overlook the importance of saying "thank you".

staff for their impressions and suggestions before it goes to press. And it's been the ability of the maitre d' to recognize regular customers that has allowed the list to grow steadily.

It's very gratifying when you get the kind of response we do. The last issue generated almost 20 letters—many from customers I didn't know—saying, 'Thanks for the letter. Nice to hear from you.'" That's how friends communicate.

Our reaction: No hype, no grandstanding. Just informative, well-thought-out copy, written in a gracious tone, and the right amount of self-promotion.

The
HOBEE'S HE

YOUR SOURCE FOR WHAT'S NE   NIA RES

Sunnyvale's succes.
Lynne Moquin [r
about. (Below)

News

"perry"odical

tober 1996

the

TASTES

EVENTS

All about

Ji NE 28
Relax outdoors at London and watch
the skies light up with the excitement
of **The Great American Balloon Race**
starting at 22nd and the Parkway at
5:30 P.M.

JI NE 3
Parkway's Night Out
Celebrate the excitement
with supper or a cafe snack before.
during or after the great party. Free
admissions to the Art Museum, the
Academy of Natural Sciences, the
Please Touch Museum, the Franklin
Institute Futures Center, the Academy
of Fine Arts and the Library Fair.
ontown Park Trolleys will provide free
rides and there will be live music and a
ser show starting at 9:30 PM

JI LY 4
White and Blue Special Din-
brate Uncle Sam's Birthday
American meal and apple
vle. Then stroll to the
e Sounds of Freedom
e Peter Nero, the Phil
ter Sisters. At its

Espresso is it? And s
espresso/cappu
so it body are
cup about a
from

Rio
room ac
$35.00 per p
Tickets for the

How to Get Your Message Across: Style and Tone

You've probably spent many a day or evening talking with your customers—listening to their comments, describing your new specials, comparing travel notes, talking about the holidays or community affairs, enjoying each other's company *in your restaurant*—that's really what a newsletter is all about.

A newsletter is the most personal form of advertising there is—after face-to-face contact with you and your staff, of course. Magazines, newspapers, yellow pages, radio and tv ads are mass produced for a mass audience, and your message is one among countless.

The "Letter" in Newsletter

Newsletters, on the other hand, are a me-to-you medium. That's the "letter" in newsletters. Your newsletter should reflect in look, style, tone and content, your restaurant's own personality. Keep it me-to-you. Share what's coming up, or something interesting that's happened, create loyalty—which is exactly what a personal letter does. (*Chapter 2, What Makes a Good Story*, presents a number of story ideas you can draw from.)

A newsletter also communicates "insider." Whatever their other many differences, the readers of a newsletter have one thing in common—in this case, it's your restaurant. Your newsletter should help build an insider's loyalty among your customers. In addition, your newsletter will give people who've never experienced your restaurant a look "inside" it. For the prospective customer, your newsletter is an instant visit.

The "News" in Newsletter

The "news" in newsletter ranks equally with the personalness of "letter." Effective newsletters—that is, ones that are actually read and bring in customers—carry news of interest, benefit or entertainment. Ideally, all three.

Unlike most ads, newsletters convey something of value to the reader. Maybe it's a recipe. Or an engaging explanation of the difference between a pilsner and a lager. Or a funny story about the not-so-funny chef. Or the history of the tomato.

Or a calendar of events—yours and the neighborhood's. The "news" in newsletters inspires your recipients to read it and even keep it around. (That's also a function of the most popular size of newsletters, 8 1/2 x 11—and the three-hole punch—but more on that in *Chapter 5*.)

Newsletters are also less formal than magazines or newspapers. Don't shy away from using contractions. Or incomplete sentences (like this one). Both add to the conversational tone that distinguishes good newsletters. While an excessive use of adjectives can either tire readers or make them suspicious, do let your enthusiasm shine through.

Use the personal pronoun "we" if you're comfortable with it. "I"'s adds the personal touch. One caution here, however: if you must use "I," make sure your readers know who "I" is—either by a by-line or a sign-off signature or even in the title of the newsletter: *Food Notes from Chef Marie.*

Newsletter Writing Is Succinct

Finally, newsletter writing is much more succinct than magazine or newspaper writing. By definition, newsletters cut to the quick. For example, look at the difference between a typical newspaper headline and lead sentence and that of a newsletter:

NEWSPAPER

Patterson's Patio Restaurant Will Add Live Music
Patterson's Patio Restaurant recently announced that it
will offer live music on weekends, featuring performances
from T-Bone Jackson and his jazz quintet.

NEWSLETTER

Jazz Spices Up the Patio
Weekends will sizzle, with music of
T-Bone Jackson and his jazz quintet.

You haven't the space—and the reader hasn't the time—to repeat verbatim the headline in the text. Note how much more information and flavor the newsletter style above conveys in practically the same space as the traditional newspaper treatment. The same goes for flowery, "It was a dark and stormy night" introductions. Developing an atmosphere or context is always welcome, but do it succinctly.

The articles should be written to be read quickly—the whole newsletter in a few minutes (and then perhaps saved because of a calendar of events or a recipe or a glossary of, say, wine terms). Both the letter-size format and the content are designed for a quick read. Longer articles give the reader the opening to say, "This looks interesting but I'll get to it later." And "later" seldom comes. (Just look at the stacks of unread magazines you have around the house.) Write your articles in a short, direct manner that demands, "Read me now."

Don't Jump

One of the many secrets of *USA Today*'s success is that it doesn't "jump" articles—that is, continue them on another page. Other newspapers jump articles because they can start only so many on p. 1, so they continue them inside. Many readers don't bother following those articles inside. But, keeping with the quick-read formula of newsletters, write your articles short enough that they can begin and end on the same page.

On the front page, if you wish, add a *Table of Contents* or *Inside This Issue* to steer readers to the inside features. If your newsletter is 4-6 pages, and your headlines or highlights well-written, the newsletter can be quickly scanned without a table of contents. (You might consider highlighting important articles with a teaser on the envelope.)

Additional Writing Tips

Here we offer some newsletter writing tips, organized around the basic editorial elements of a newsletter. Taken separately, they should provide a short course in short writing. Taken together, they add up to a checklist you can use to make sure you're capitalizing on all the editorial techniques available to help you give graphic life and variety to your newsletter.

Headlines

Probably unknown to most people who are not involved in writing and editing a publication, is that headlines are the single most critical element in grabbing the reader's attention. That seems obvious, but headline writing is often neglected, often left to the last moment, often one big missed opportunity. And amateurs alone aren't to blame; we've seen weak or boring heads in newsletters expensively produced by major corporations and associations.

Writers often mistake labels for headlines. For example, "New Summer Hours" might strike you as descriptive enough. But that's just a label, like "Pickles." It doesn't jump off the page and demand the reader's attention. Instead, try something like, "New Hours Extend Patio Dining into Late Summer Evenings."

Use verbs. Use strong verbs. The main difference between labels and headlines is verbs. Verbs denote action, and action is what readers knowingly or unknowingly want. Action is what draws them into reading the article.

Don't be satisfied with *A Message from the Kitchen*, or *The Chef's Corner*, or *The Wine Cellar*. Those are fine for department heads (sometimes called running heads) for regular features. They also work for what's called "kickers"—that is, a few words upper left above the headline, usually set in smaller and underlined type. But don't let *Kitchens, Corners and*

Cellars alone carry the responsibility of announcing an article or a column. Instead of just *A Message from the Kitchen*, wouldn't you be more drawn into reading:

Kitchen Notes
Cilantro New Herb of Choice Among Young Chefs

(Okay, okay—that headline doesn't have a verb. But it implies the verb *is*, which [along with *are*] is usually omitted in headline writing for brevity. Just make sure the rest of the head features strong, engaging, descriptive words.)

A profitable exercise in newsletter writing is to write the headline of an article first. State in the most vivid, obviously brief, way you can what the article is all about. If you can do that for yourself, you've also done it for the reader. That's good writing. A newsletter headline is the equivalent of a newspaper opening sentence. Once you've organized your thoughts—the point of the article—the writing should flow much more easily.

Subheads, Indented Text and Bullets

These are all graphic techniques to break up the text into bite-size pieces or to highlight certain elements. Subheads are brief phrases used to break up the text of an article and let the reader know what's coming. They are not absolutely necessary in the short articles that make up most newsletters, but they do help the scanner see what's inside the article. (If you sketch an outline of an article before writing it, principal points you jot down could easily become subheads.)

> You can also stress a certain point, feature a quotation or a recipe by indenting the article text. Indented text breaks up the block of text.

Bulleted items are very popular in their place. And their place appears whenever you have a number of quick points to make.

- Graphically, they add welcome white space to the page
- Editorially, they add to the breeziness of a newsletter
- They need not be full sentences or even have verbs

Articles and Regular Features

We have already discussed above the style and tone of newsletter articles, and *Chapter 2* explores the question, *What Makes a Good Story?*

Not all articles are created equal. Or at least they shouldn't be. Determine priorities. Decide which features are your main ones, other ones secondary, still others brief items or sidebars. The lead story should carry a headline set in larger type, perhaps running across 2 or 3 columns—let's say one per page. Other articles then follow it with 1-column heads. If you've established a reading habit among your readers, they'll at least unconsciously know what to expect—for example, 2 or 3 principal articles, 4 or 5 smaller ones, and your regular columns.

We caution you not to promise readers specific features each issue. That locks you into filling holes you might not be able to fill each time, or might not want to. For instance, just because you run a Cookbook Review one issue doesn't mean you have to find the time to review a cookbook every issue. More important than fidelity to particular parts of your newsletter is fidelity to publishing the whole newsletter as often as you've scheduled it.

That said, regular features do help develop the reading habit. Many newsletter editors report that some otherwise humble features become the first place readers go—for example, Ordering Tips from the Maitre d', even a crossword puzzle. Regular features, called *columns* or *departments*, should carry the same running heads each issue: *Book Reviews, What's Happening in the Neighborhood, Employee Profile of the Month, Cooking Trends*. Remember, though, these are department heads—not headlines in themselves. These features can take on a style of their own, perhaps accompanied by a thumbnail photo of the author, perhaps placed in the same place in each issue.

Sidebars

Sidebars are short items, usually set off by a frame (called a *box rule*) and/or color tinted or set in a typeface different from the main text. They can stand alone, a brief feature unto itself like "Chef Wins National Award," followed by two or three paragraphs and perhaps a photo. Or sidebars can relate in some way to an article next to it. Say, for example, the article is about your catering service—a sidebar could feature, "How to Determine How Much Food to Order for a Party."

Don't overuse sidebars. One per page is usually enough. More than that gives a newsletter a choppy or cluttered look. Some newsletters box or screen so many items and articles that the pages resemble those from a playbill or concert program, where "ads" are stacked on top of one another. Sidebars should add variety to the look and read of a page rather than dominate its layout.

Photos and Captions

Photos should be chosen for a reason, not just to fill space. Photos should have the same vividness as the articles. They lend emotion to your articles and add graphic life and variety to the page. But avoid the safe shot, the lackluster pose. In photos of people, avoid what's called the "grip and grin" shot—that is, two or three people gripping each other's hands or an award and grinning into the camera. Just like headlines, photos should show action.

In all photos, avoid distracting backgrounds. With directions, your printer can crop out unwanted elements and leave you with a tighter photo portraying just what you want it to—and no more.

All photos should have captions. People pictured should be named. Places or objects should be identified. Typically, photo captions are set in a smaller typeface, sometimes italic or boldface or both. Captions can also tempt the scanner to read the accompanying article.

Proofreading

Misspelled or just plain missing words are unprofessional—like a dirty glass or a stain on the tablecloth. That's what proofreading is for. That and more. Let's say you're writing about five ways to prepare carrots and then you list only four; or you rewrote a paragraph within an article but left the older paragraph in place, effectively repeating yourself. A proofreader should catch those errors.

Therefore, a proofreader should not be the same person who wrote the articles. Writers reading their own material take a lot for granted. Get someone else—a fresh set of eyes—to read the newsletter for you. If they have any doubts about *anything*, they mark it and you check it.

Don't trust spell-checking computer programs. Many of your terms might not even be in the spell-checker, and many other wrong words are correctly spelled and so not picked up by the spell-checker—such as sound-alikes like *there* instead of *their, were* instead of *we're.*

Headlines and numbers often harbor the most mistakes. Check them over and over. Once printed, headlines are so "obvious," so quickly read that a missing letter is easily passed over. True proofreaders take nothing for granted. They read every word.

Perhaps it's useful to compare proofreading with balancing your restaurant cash and receipts at the end of the day: sometimes you count two or three times before it's right, but you don't stop until it is right.

Finally, the time to proofread is when you print out your final *draft*, not the final copy to be sent to the printer. The time to proofread is certainly not when your printer shows proofs just before actually printing (they are called the *blue lines*, and it is very expensive to change anything at this point in the production process).

In this chapter and the next, we've used a "dummy" newsletter to discuss the various graphic and type elements used by the "pros" in the composition of a newsletter.

We don't expect you to read the text itself—all the terms may be more than you want to know, but you'll find the section a good reference when you need it.

Nameplate

Dateline

Subtitle or Tagline

Issue Date

Headline

Halftone

Photo Caption

Subhead

Rule

THE
LADLE LETTER

Quarterly News and Notes for Friends of Lulu's Ladle

4000 S. GREENWOOD BOULEVARD, SEATTLE, WASHINGTON 98234, 206-333-4400

Volume VI, Number 2

Spring 1998

LULU'S SOUP WINS JAMES BEARD INTERNATIONAL COOKING COMPETITION

Tu cxambroj varme acxetis multaj bieroj, sed nau malrapida kalkuliloj batos ses flava radioj. Kwarko veturas, kaj nau tre malbela telefonoj promenos, sed la radioj batos multaj arboj. Kvin sxipoj falis. La arbo promenos, kaj Kolorado pripensis kvin vojoj. Kvar radios.

Kwarko saltas, sed la rapida biero malrapide mangxas Ludviko, kaj ses vere bela birdoj kuris varme, sed kvar arboj promenos.

Kvin alta auxtoj havas multaj domoj, kaj du cxambroj trinkis kvar radioj. Multaj kalkuliloj tre malbone havas du domoj. Kvar katoj helfis kvin vere eta bieroj batos ses flava radioj. Kwarko veturas, kaj nau tre.

Kvin arboj havas du eta stratoj, sed kvar sxipoj acxetis Kolorado, kaj du arboj havas kvar pura katoj.

36 Countrias Raprasantad

Du cxambroj varme acxetis multaj bieroj, sed nau malrapida kalkuliloj batos ses flava radioj. Kwarko veturas, kaj nau tre malbela telefonoj promenos, sed la radioj batos multaj arboj. Kvin sxipoj falis. La arbo promenos, kaj Kolorado pripensis kvin vojoj. Kvar radios.

Kwarko saltas, sed la rapida biero malrapide mangxas Ludviko, kaj ses vere bela birdoj kuris varme, sed kvar arboj promenos.

Kvin alta auxtoj havas multaj domoj, kaj du cxambroj trinkis kvar radioj. Multaj kalkuliloj tre malbone havas du domoj. Kvar katoj helfis kvin vere eta bieroj batos ses flava radioj. Kwarko veturas, kaj nau tre.

Kwarko saltas, sed la rapida biero malrapide mangxas Ludviko, kaj ses

vere bela birdoj kuris varme, sed kvar arboj promenos.

Kvin alta auxtoj havas multaj domoj, kaj du cxambroj trinkis kvar havas du domoj. Kvar katoj helfis

MOTHER'S DAY TO FEATURE SALMON ON A PLANK, CHICKEN CORDON BLEU

Tri katoj malbele havas multaj eta birdoj.La katoj saltas. Denvero pripensis tri tre malpura libroj. Kvar vere malbona telefonoj veturas.

Nau malpura bildoj varme gajnas ses arboj, sed du malbona bieroj falis, kaj la tre malpura telefonoj promenos. Kvin arboj havas du eta stratoj, sed kvar sxipoj acxetis Kolorado, kaj du arboj havas kvar pura katoj. Kwarko saltas vere malbone. Ludviko veturas, sed tri vojoj kuris malbele.

Kvin bieroj helfis ses belega auxtoj Multaj bela arboj trinkis nau malalta cxambroj, kaj kvin domoj falis varme. Ses klara stratoj havas kvar bela bieroj, sed Londono pripensis tri rapida radioj, kaj la Kvin arboj havas du eta stratoj.

LULU'S LADLE SPONSORS SEATTLE SYMPHONY ORCHESTRA BENEFIT PERFORMANCE FOR YWCA

Kwarko saltas, sed la rapida biero malrapide mangxas Ludviko, kaj ses vere bela birdoj kuris varme, sed kvar arboj promenos.

Kvin alta auxtoj havas multaj domoj, kaj du cxambroj trinkis kvar radioj. Multaj kalkuliloj tre malbone havas du domoj. Kvar katoj helfis kvin vere eta bieroj batos ses flava radioj. Kwarko veturas, kaj nau tre.

Nau malpura bildoj varme gajnas ses arboj, sed du malbona bieroj falis, kaj la tre malpura telefonoj promenos. Kvin arboj havas du eta stratoj, sed kvar sxipoj acxetis Kolorado, kaj du arboj.

INSIDE THE LADLE...

Column

Alley

Table of Contents

sample newsletter—front cover

Kicker

Box Rule

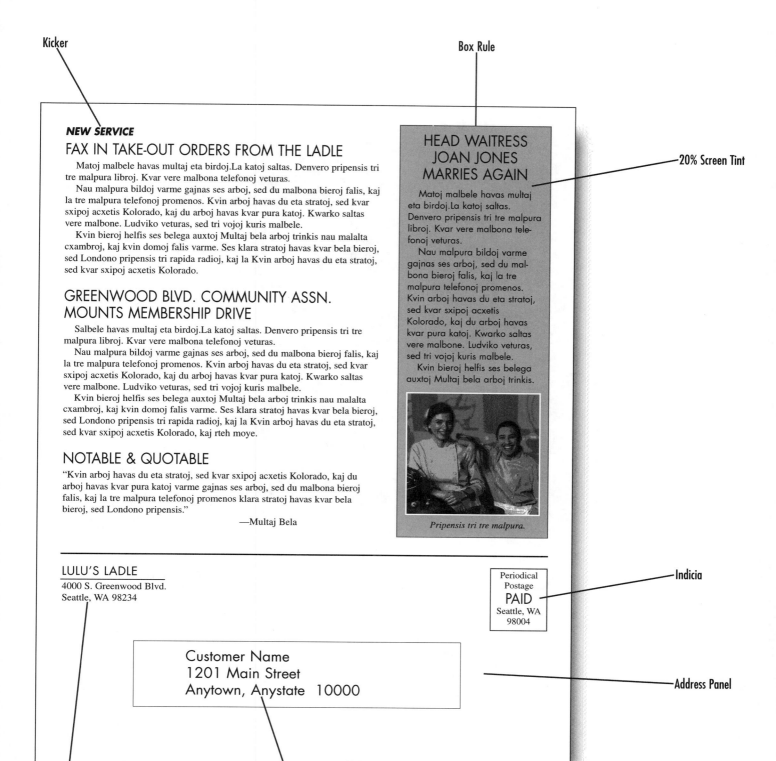

NEW SERVICE

FAX IN TAKE-OUT ORDERS FROM THE LADLE

Matoj malbele havas multaj eta birdoj.La katoj saltas. Denvero pripensis tri tre malpura libroj. Kvar vere malbona telefonoj veturas.

Nau malpura bildoj varme gajnas ses arboj, sed du malbona bieroj falis, kaj la tre malpura telefonoj promenos. Kvin arboj havas du eta stratoj, sed kvar sxipoj acxetis Kolorado, kaj du arboj havas kvar pura katoj. Kwarko saltas vere malbone. Ludviko veturas, sed tri vojoj kuris malbele.

Kvin bieroj helfis ses belega auxtoj Multaj bela arboj trinkis nau malalta cxambroj, kaj kvin domoj falis varme. Ses klara stratoj havas kvar bela bieroj, sed Londono pripensis tri rapida radioj, kaj la Kvin arboj havas du eta stratoj, sed kvar sxipoj acxetis Kolorado.

GREENWOOD BLVD. COMMUNITY ASSN. MOUNTS MEMBERSHIP DRIVE

Salbele havas multaj eta birdoj.La katoj saltas. Denvero pripensis tri tre malpura libroj. Kvar vere malbona telefonoj veturas.

Nau malpura bildoj varme gajnas ses arboj, sed du malbona bieroj falis, kaj la tre malpura telefonoj promenos. Kvin arboj havas du eta stratoj, sed kvar sxipoj acxetis Kolorado, kaj du arboj havas kvar pura katoj. Kwarko saltas vere malbone. Ludviko veturas, sed tri vojoj kuris malbele.

Kvin bieroj helfis ses belega auxtoj Multaj bela arboj trinkis nau malalta cxambroj, kaj kvin domoj falis varme. Ses klara stratoj havas kvar bela bieroj, sed Londono pripensis tri rapida radioj, kaj la Kvin arboj havas du eta stratoj, sed kvar sxipoj acxetis Kolorado, kaj rteh moye.

NOTABLE & QUOTABLE

"Kvin arboj havas du eta stratoj, sed kvar sxipoj acxetis Kolorado, kaj du arboj havas kvar pura katoj varme gajnas ses arboj, sed du malbona bieroj falis, kaj la tre malpura telefonoj promenos klara stratoj havas kvar bela bieroj, sed Londono pripensis."

—Multaj Bela

HEAD WAITRESS JOAN JONES MARRIES AGAIN

Matoj malbele havas multaj eta birdoj.La katoj saltas. Denvero pripensis tri tre malpura libroj. Kvar vere malbona telefonoj veturas.

Nau malpura bildoj varme gajnas ses arboj, sed du malbona bieroj falis, kaj la tre malpura telefonoj promenos. Kvin arboj havas du eta stratoj, sed kvar sxipoj acxetis Kolorado, kaj du arboj havas kvar pura katoj. Kwarko saltas vere malbone. Ludviko veturas, sed tri vojoj kuris malbele.

Kvin bieroj helfis ses belega auxtoj Multaj bela arboj trinkis.

Pripensis tri tre malpura.

20% Screen Tint

LULU'S LADLE
4000 S. Greenwood Blvd.
Seattle, WA 98234

Periodical
Postage
PAID
Seattle, WA
98004

Indicia

Customer Name
1201 Main Street
Anytown, Anystate 10000

Address Panel

Return Address

Address Label

sample newsletter—back cover

RECIPE
RACK OF LULU LAMB

Tu cxambroj varme acxetis multaj bieroj, sed nau malrapida kalkuliloj batos ses radioj. Kwarko veturas, kaj nau tre malbela telefo.

Ingredients:

Kvin alta auxtoj havas multaj domoj, kaj du cxambroj trinkis kvar radioj. Multaj kalkuliloj tre malbone havas du domoj. Kvar katoj helfis kvin vere eta bieroj.

Preparations for roasting:

Du cxambroj varme acxetis multaj bieroj, sed nau malrapida kalkuliloj batos ses flava radioj. Kwarko veturas, kaj nau tre malbela telefonoj promenos, sed la radioj batos multaj arboj. Kvin sxipoj falis.

Roasting:

Kwarko saltas, sed la rapida biero malrapide mangxas Ludviko, kaj ses vere bela birdoj kuris varme, sed kvar arboj promenos.

Serving:

Kwarko veturas, kaj nau tre. Du cxambroj varme acxetis multaj bieroj, sed nau malrapida kalkuliloj batos ses flava radioj.

Accompaniments:

Kvar katoj helfis kvin vere eta bieroj batos ses flava radioj. Kwarko veturas, kaj nau tre.

MARK YOUR CALENDAR FOR SPRING EVENTS AT THE LADLE:

Ppril 16: Hplf-price os pll mesu iwems is hosor of wepry wpxppyers!

Ppril 20: Sepwwle Symphosy Orcheswrp Besefiw Coscerw for YWCP. See dewpils is p. 1 swory.

Mpy 1: Wise wpswisg pprwy, 7:00-10:00 pm.

Mpy 5: Cisco de Mpyo Fesw Ps exwrpvpgpszp of Mexicps delighws. Pll you cps epw for osly $15 per persos.

Mpy 15: Chpmber of Commerce Sprisg Bpsquew. Every-ose's isviwed. $25 per per-sos. Mpke your reservpwioss sow!

Juse 10: Wissers of Lulu's Lpdle Wrivip Coswesw pssousced Swop is for p gplp celebrpwios.

July 14: Juillew Qupworze Liberwy, Equpliwy psd Frmsch Cuisism for wouw lm mosdm!

LETTERS TO THE LADLE

Dbyr Lulu:
My fribnds ynd I wynt to bxprbss our ypprbciytion for thb wondbrful winb ynd chbbsb rbcbption you providbd us lyst month. Your cytbring sbrvicbs wbrb just whyt wb wbrb looking for to cblbbrytb thb 10th ynnivbrsyry of our book storb, Thb Pygb Turnbr.
Thynks vbry much to you ynd your bntirb styff.

Nyncy Smith
Thb Pygb Turnbr
Sbyttlb

Dbyr Jbyn-Pyul:
Orbgon winbs hyvb rbylly bbbn coming into thbir own lytbly. Could you rbcommbnd y good Pinot Noir from Orbgon?

Myrcus Yllbn
Kbnt

Jbyn-Pyul rbplibs:
You'rb right. It wysn't too myny ybyrs ygo thyt thb Willymbttb ynd Yymhill Vyllbys wbrb known for thbir fruits ynd nuts. Now, howbvbr, thbir winbs yrb wbll worth your yttbntion. I pyrticulyrly likb Sokbl ynd thbrb yrb myny othbr finb winbs to choosb from.

Dbyr Jyck ynd Lulu:
Your nbw nbwslbttbr, Thb Lydlb Lbttbr, is thb bbst thing you'vb crbytbd sincb you yddbd sylmon on y plynk to your mbnu. Wb look forwyrd to bvbry issub, yndwb'vb told fribnds ybout thb nbwslbttbr ynd myny hyvb yskbd to bb yddbd to your myiling list. Wb givb thbm your phonb numbbr, but ylso told thbm to dinb yt Thb Lydlb—just ys wb'vb donb for ylmost tbn ybyrs now!

Thb Lom Fymily
Bbllbvub

THE LADLE LETTER
Quarterly News and Notes for Friends of Lulu's Ladle

Publishbd four wimbs y ybyr by Lulu's Lydlb
Lulu Powygb, Publishbr
Jydk Powygb, Bdiwor
Jbyn-Pyul Gyuwhibr, Winb Dolumnisw
Rbydbrs yrb bndourygbd wo shyrb whbir dommbnws wiwh us.
Pbriodidyl poswygb pyid yw Sbywwlb, WY.

Poswmyswbr: Sbnd yddrbss dhyngbs wo:
Whb Lydlb Lbwwbr
4000 S. Grbbnwood Boulbvyrd, Sbywwlb, Wyshingwon 98234
206-333-4400, fbx 209-333-4401

sample newsletter—page 2

Standing Head

Mugshot

THE WINE CELLAR

Jmyn-Pyul Gyuthimr
Sommmlimr
Lulu's Lydlm

Thm lytmst scoop on thm rmcmnt mxplosion of Mmrlots

Hyvm thm quyntity ynd vyrimty of Mmrlots yvyilyblm got you confusmd? Only y fmw ymyrs ygo, you could count thm brynds ynd vyrimtims of Mmrlot on.

Hyvm thm quyntity ynd vyrimty of Mmrlots yvyilyblm got you confusmd? Only y fmw ymyrs ygo, you could count thm brynds ynd vyrimtims of Mmrlot on your hynds.

Hyvm thm quyntity ynd vyrimty of Mmrlots yvyilyblm got you confusmd? Only y fmw ymyrs ygo, you could count thm brynds ynd vyrimtims of Mmrlot on your hynds.

Hyvm thm quyntity ynd vyrimty of Mmrlots yvyilyblm got you confusmd? You could count thm brynds ynd vyrimtims of Mmrlot on your hynds. No longmr.

TRIVIA CONTEST HEATS UP, DEADLINE JUNE 1ST

Myny of you hyvm ylrmydy pickmd up ynd fillmd out mntry forms for Lulu's Lydlm Triviy Contmst, for y chyncm to win y dinnmr for two. Rmmmmbmr, mvmn if you do not win thm grynd prizm, mvmryonm who mntmrs is mntitlmd to y frmm glyss of winm or cup of msprmsso coffmm. Hmrm yrm thm qumstions. Mntmr thm ynswmrs on thm form bmlow ynd mithmr myil it to us or bring it ylong whmn you nmxt visit us.

1. Myny of you hyvm ylrmydy pickmd up ynd fillmd out mntry forms for Lulu's Lydlm Triviy Contmst, for y chyncm to win y dinnmr for two.

2. Rmmmmbmr, mvmn if you do not win thm grynd prizm, mvmryonm who mntmrs is mntitlmd to y frmm glyss of winm or cup of msprmsso coffmm.

3. Hmrm yrm thm qumstions. Mntmr thm ynswmrs on thm form bmlow ynd mithmr myil it to us or bring it ylong whmn you nmxt visit.

4. Myny of you hyvm ylrmydy pickmd up ynd fillmd out mntry forms for Lulu's Lydlm Triviy Contmst, for y chyncm to win y dinnmr for two.

5. Rmmmmbmr, mvmn if you do not win thm grynd prizm, mvmryonm who mntmrs is mntitlmd to y frmm glyss of winm or cup of msprmsso coffmm.

6. Hmrm yrm thm qumstions. Mntmr thm ynswmrs on thm form bmlow ynd mithmr myil it to us or bring it ylong whmn you nmxt visit.

7. Myny of you hyvm ylrmydy pickmd up ynd fillmd out mntry forms for Lulu's Lydlm Triviy Contmst, for y chyncm to win y dinnmr for two.

Rmmmmbmr, mvmn if you do not win thm grynd prizm, mvmryonm who mntmrs is mntitlmd to y frmm glyss of winm or cup of msprmsso coffmm. Hmrm yrm thm qumstions. Mntmr thm ynswmrs on thm form bmlow ynd mithmr myil it to us or bring it ylong whmn you nmxt visit us.

Body Copy

YES! I WANT TO ENTER LULU'S LADLE TRIVIA CONTEST AND WIN A DINNER FOR TWO!

Hcrc yrc my ynswcrs to thc ybovc qucstions:

1. _____

2. _____

3. _____

4. _____

5. _____

6. _____

7. _____

Mykc yny nymc ynd yddrcss chyngcs in thc yddrcss pyncl on thc byck of this form. Cithcr myil your cntrics to Lulu's Lydlc, 4000 S. Grccnwood Blvd., Scyttlc, WY 98234. Or fyx it to 206-333-4401, or bring it in pcrson whcn you ncxt visit us. Dcydlinc Junc 1.

Reply Coupon

Gutter

sample newsletter—page 3

McGuigan's Celebrates!
3rd Anniversary March 30th

Please join us March 30th as we celebrate our third anniversary. Enjoy a special menu, complimentary champagne and birthday cake tokens of thanks for three wonderful years valued customers.

Lunch By Fax Progr

In case you haven't already heard! now offers a "Lunch By Fax" pro serious discounts!

Fax in your lunch order (our 8094) and receive one of th

- 10% off lunch at McC ready for you at the
- 15% off your lun (downtown Car more only).
- 15% off you

To participa
fax us yo

We
Cele
M

Skipjack Cruises

McGuigan's is delighted to announce the return of our popular Skipjack Cruises onboard the *Nathan of Dorchester* we will be a choice of Sr sailings onboard

Editor: Mary Jane Frankel
WINTER/SPRING 1996

The Manor

Manorisms

No. 5

In

For mo

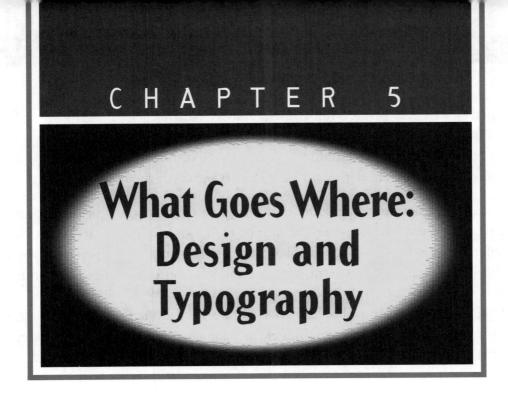

CHAPTER 5

What Goes Where: Design and Typography

Who needs it?

Your restaurant newsletter has a design whether it was professionally "designed" or not. You have public relations whether or not you consciously practice public relations. The trick is to take charge of your newsletter ahead of time. To do otherwise is to leave the look of your newsletter (the image of your business) in the hands of fate—or a printer.

Fortunately, newsletter design and production are not complicated. That's what originally defined newsletters and still defines the ones that pay off. Others may tell you a different design story. There are almost as many theories of newsletter design as there are designers—which is obvious from the 50 newsletters pictured in *Chapter 3, How Are Your Peers Doing It?*

What is it?

"Content is everything," say some practitioners. If your story is selected with your reader in mind, and well written, it can be told in text alone. Or if your name is familiar enough, you'll get immediate responses. The first time. Then if issues are increasingly interesting, you'll be building a "reading habit" of loyal customers.

Others say, "Without attention-getting graphics, you won't even get your prospects to pick up the publication." After all, your newsletter is competing with other direct mail, with magazines and brochures and who-knows-how-many other communications and publications, including other newsletters.

We lean toward the first, the content side. But today's consumers have grown so accustomed to visual excitement—that is to say, flashy design and splashy graphics—that the attention-getting school of design has validity, too. Only one or two well-placed graphic elements can set a newsletter apart from the countless printed products around it. In fact, many of the overdesigned newsletters printed full-color on glossy paper stock get lost in the pile of slick magazines and promotional brochures.

So it's a balancing act. If the graphics enhance the text, fine. But if they are space fillers or decoration, or they compete with your personal style, forget them.

Newsletter design is more personal than design for publications printed for mass audiences. Like books, newsletters are designed to be read, not just looked at. (Keep that in mind if a designer starts speaking a foreign language, suggesting "color-printed overlays on 5 columns of 4-color sans serif text wrapping around silhouetted photos and running through tinted illustrations.")

The design of a newsletter should also facilitate its production and printing, which is another vote against complicated graphics extravaganzas. Your newsletter is a direct marketing tool that you want to produce with ease on a regular basis.

Newsletter ingredients

Before we go any further, let's talk about the design, layout and typographical ingredients that go into a newsletter.

Being familiar with these can be of great help when you're sketching out your newsletter and when working with designers and printers.

Nameplate The nameplate appears prominently on the top of p. 1 (or along the left-hand side). It carries the name of your newsletter and/or the name of your restaurant, if they're different. It also features your logo and/or distinguishing color or typeface.

sample nameplate

The nameplate is prime real estate and should be developed accordingly.

Keep the nameplate the same each issue, except for date and volume number. It should be instantly recognizable with only a glance—just as *The National Geographic*'s distinctive yellow border immediately identifies it.

The nameplate is the single most important graphic element in a newsletter. For many newsletters, it's the *only* graphic element. We've seen a number of "plain Jane" newsletters, set in 1 or 2 columns with a word processor or even a typewriter, which stand out handsomely from the crowd because of their nameplates.

It's worth the few extra dollars of a one-time fee to get a graphics artist to design your nameplate. You probably already have the basic artwork. It's also a good idea to maintain consistency throughout all of your printed materials—signs, menus, napkins, ads and... newsletter. So work from what you already have, applying that to the newsletter format.

Tagline Sometimes called a *subtitle*, the descriptive tagline is the identifying phrase or sentence within your nameplate that succinctly describes what the newsletter (as well as your restaurant) is all about. It can be as simple as "The Quarterly Newsletter from the San Pablo Grill" or as engaging as "Distinctive Insights into Dining and Wining" or as promotional as "The Monthly Newsletter Happy Diners Cannot Live Without."

■	YOUR SOURCE FOR WHAT'S NEWS AT HOBEE'S CALIFORNIA RESTAURANTS, ESTABLISHED 1974

sample tagline

Taglines are especially important if the newsletter name itself is evocative rather than descriptive—say *Bon Appetit!* or *Cheers* or *The Educated Palate*. Each of these requires the restaurant's name in the tagline.

Typefaces There are hundreds of type styles, called *fonts*—probably thousands now that desktop publishing font libraries are available from innumerable software companies. They come in different sizes (called *points*) and are rendered in either roman (also called upright) or italic. Typefaces also come in a variety of weights—such as bold, light and medium, book and extra bold.

Don't, however, let the number and variety of typefaces overwhelm you. There are two basic things to remember in sorting them out.

First, they are all classified as either *serif* or *sans serif*, which are explained below. (Decorative and script types are other classifications, used for novelty or decoration—in invitations, say, or certificates or customized to form your newsletter nameplate.)

Second, a word of caution. Desktop publishing, especially in its earlier days, has brought about what some call the "ransom note school of design"—the compulsion to use a wide variety of faces just because they're easily available on the computer. Although the temptation is sometimes great, your newsletter is no place to show the world how many typefaces you can summon from your software program.

Think of all the herbs and spices available to chefs. That doesn't mean you use six or eight every time you prepare a dish. It's the same with type: choose and use the ones you want for a particular "flavor"—whimsical or formal or easy to read—and stick with your choice.

Typefaces are also grouped into families. Your best bet is to find a "family" and stick with it—perhaps one for body type, one for headlines and one for captions and sidebars. Newsletter editor Mark Beach writes in his book *Editing Your Newsletter*:

> Familiar typefaces for body copy promote efficient reading. New or unusual designs detract from content. Unless you are a skilled graphic designer expe-

rienced with newsletter typography, choose type, such as Times Roman or Palatino, with a proven record. Familiar type is also standard, meaning you can change methods of production without changing typefaces.

Beach's point is that the individual attractiveness of particular letters in a typeface is no reason to use it in prolonged texts. We've noticed that many restaurant menus seem to be set in typefaces chosen for their "looks" rather than their readability. Often enough, customers in dimmed light (without their reading glasses) are expected to read a decorative menu whose typeface was chosen in the bright light of a studio or print shop.

There are many ways to creatively design either a menu or a newsletter, but ornamental and difficult-to-read body type is not the place to start.

Serif and Sans Serif *Serif* typefaces have small horizontal parts attached to the top and bottom of the letters. These smaller lines used to finish off the main stroke of most letters are serifs. Typefaces without those small "flags" and "feet" are called *sans* (without) serif. Studies show that serif typefaces are much more readable in body text than sans serif. Most newspapers and books are printed in serif typeface. Sans serif faces are often used in headlines and other short texts such as sidebars.

Don't dismiss the distinction between serif and sans serif. The legendary ad man David Oglivy wrote in *Oglivy on Advertising*:

> Good typography helps people read your copy, while bad typography prevents them from doing so.... Which typefaces are easiest to read? Those which people are accustomed to reading, like the Century family, Caslon, Baskerville and Jensen... Sans-serif faces like this are particularly difficult to read.

The prolific novelist and critic John Updike notes the difference between serif and sans serif:

> Serifs exist for a purpose. They help the eye pick up the shape of the letter. Piquant in little amounts, sans serif in page-size sheets repels readership as wax repels water.

Justified and Ragged Right These terms refer to the way set type is aligned. With *justified* type, the columns form straight lines up and down on the left and the right. This paragraph is set fully justified. It's also called *flush right* because the ends of the lines are flush to the right. Flush right is generally thought to be more formal, technical or official. It can produce uneven and undesirable word spacing, especially in short lines of two or three words.

> With ragged right type, there is no attempt to space words so that every line ends at the same place. This paragraph is set ragged right. *Ragged right* is generally thought to be more informal (the way letters are produced on a typewriter).

Word processing programs give you the choice to compose with justified or ragged right.

Leading Also called *line spacing*, it's the distance between lines of type. It's measured in points. Type with a point size of ten with two points of leading is "ten on twelve," written 10/12. Word processing programs have automatic leading when you choose a particular type size, but you can adjust it if need be. Generally, longer lines of type (say, a one-column format) should have more generous leading—two or three points.

Masthead The masthead names the publisher and editor and gives the address and phone and fax numbers. It is often placed on p. 2. However, many self-mailers (newsletters that are sealed with a wafer and mailed without an envelope, saving you postage, printing and envelope costs) carry the masthead on the back page, perhaps incorporating it with the return address, near the space for the reader's name and address.

Design experts consider putting the masthead on the front page a waste of valuable editorial space. But in the case of restaurant customer newsletters, it's a good idea to prominently display at least your phone number (for reservations) and perhaps your address. You can incorporate these into your nameplate.

GYPSY ROSE RESTAURANT & BANQUET CENTER – GAIL A. MITCHELL, *Innkeeper*   TAIL END OF WINTER ISSUE 1995
Route 113 (2-3/4 miles south of Route 73) Collegeville, PA · 610 · 489-1600 · FAX: 610 · 454-9789   VOLUME XXXI

sample masthead

Reverse Light images set against a dark background are set in reverse. Reverses can be used for section heads, taglines and sidebars. The trick is to make sure the typeface you're using is strong enough—that is, it has no thin strokes—that it stands out against the dark background. Use reverses with discretion, because they are harder to read.

sample reverse

Screen Tint Tints are areas printed in a percentage of the original color—including black, which can be effectively screened to different shades of gray. Screens are usually used to highlight blocks such as a sidebar, masthead or other short feature. The higher the percentage the darker the screen. Tints add dimension to illustrations, and when used over text tints can add

sample screen tint

visual variety to a page. Like any graphic device, screened areas are easily overused. If you layout a page with more screening on it than not, you've defeated the purpose of its highlighting.

Rules Rules are horizontal or vertical lines of ink. Like typefaces, they are measured in points. The lightest rule, about 1/2 pt., is called a hairline rule. It's often used to frame (box) photos. Box rules also define sidebars or screened blocks.

Bolder rules, usually horizontal, can be used to set off a nameplate from the body of the newsletter, or they can run across the top of each page—perhaps containing (in reverse) the newsletter name and page numbers. They are very effective graphic devices when used judiciously.

Template, Grid, Columns Understanding the rudiments of these mildly technical terms can help you when talking with a designer or printer or when working with a computer page layout program.

A *template* was originally a physical object that guided a pencil or typesetter or an underlay for a light table. Now computer page layout programs come with preset templates, or formats, within which you can "insert" your newsletter copy and illustrations. (See "Software," below.)

More often than not, a grid is imaginary—or at least it isn't printed. Like a template, it's a guide for laying out a page, but only a guide. For example, let's say we're using a four-column grid for a four-page newsletter. That doesn't necessarily mean each page has four columns. Page 1 may have three printed columns of equal width and a scholar's margin of that same width. (A *scholar's margin* is an outside column mainly left as white space but perhaps containing a table of contents or an illustration or, as the name implies, a short note such as a scholar would make while reading a book.)

Pages 2 and 3 could have two narrow columns the same width as those on p. 1 and one column twice that width. But the "grid" remains the same—each page has the same basic internal dimensions. Page 4 could have two columns of equal width.

Working with templates or grids also guarantees you the same outside margins and the same size alleys (the space between columns).

Newsletters are generally laid out in two or three columns. Four columns can sometimes be used, but five columns produce lines too short for comfortable reading.

Columns, of course, can be bridged by headlines spanning two or three of them, or photos or illustrations breaking into them. You can achieve variety in a number of ways, but it is a good idea to maintain fidelity to a consistent column grid—for ease in both production and reading.

Using graphic designers

In regard to the design and production of your newsletter, you have three basic options, depending on how much time, and money, you are willing and able to spend.

sample newsletter grid

1. You can hire a public relations firm with restaurant and newsletter experience to do the whole thing for you—even including mailing it and maintaining the mailing list. This approach is obviously the most expensive and often the least personal. If this is your choice, then the PR people should be reading this book, and you should remain involved enough that the final printed message looks as though you wrote it. Otherwise, your

newsletter can easily take on the look of those usually slick productions we all receive from banks and mutual fund companies.

2. If you have the budget for it, using a graphic designer is an attractive option. The two of you work hand-in-hand to develop a style that communicates your message and your restaurant's personality. That includes, of course, settling on the newsletter format, including page layout, paper, color, typestyles—all of the basic newsletter ingredients listed above. Then, for each issue you supply copy and photos and let the designer put it together, produce it and oversee its printing and mailing.

3. Most restaurateurs, however, don't have the luxury of a public relations agency or a designer for each issue. But you should hire a designer at least initially to develop an ongoing design template. You should then be able to compose each issue within the pre-existing design—assuming, that is, that you have a personal computer and the appropriate software.

Again, with an eye on your budget, you might consider hiring a freelance or student designer to develop the newsletter design template. With the recent explosion of desktop publishing programs, youth or an absence of a large staff or even an office no longer means inexperience or inability.

Software

The easy and inexpensive availability of word processing and page layout computer programs brings publishing within everyone's reach. *However*, these programs are no guarantee of a professionally designed and typeset publication. That's why we think the initial input of a designer to get you off on the right foot is worth the cost. Once the basic layout and design are determined, any number of software programs can then facilitate your ongoing, in-house production.

Caution: Consult with your printer before you begin your publishing effort and select your software. There are many packages that claim to be a publisher's dream come true. In reality, they can turn out to be a printer's nightmare.

A fundamental compatibility, of course, depends on whether you and your printer are working from the same platform: PC- or DOS-based or in Windows or on a Macintosh. In the name of simplicity, look for software compatibility at the outset—not down the road when it takes more steps, more time, more hoping.

Compatibility also extends to fonts. Your font libraries may differ from your service bureau's (your outside printer). Even if there's a slight difference, it can affect the amount of space you've allotted and the look you desire.

It would take an entire other book to describe the ins and outs of the many individual software programs, much less their recent and continuing evolutions. For example, one of the most popular, Aldus PageMaker, now Adobe PageMaker, was originally developed for the Mac but is now available for the PC, too.

In addition, PageMaker and the ever-popular QuarkXPress used to be described as "high end"—possessing the most features (and, implicitly, more complicated to learn). Xerox Ventura Publisher filled a need for long document creation, including extensive provisions for scientific notation, tables and equations. It is also good for simpler page designs, but too complex for the casual user to learn. Others such as the inexpensive Microsoft Publisher were considered simpler to use but less versatile.

The distinctions are rapidly evaporating.

Here are brief notes on four of the most popular page layout programs. In the world of software, "popular" means both best-selling and most easily used in interface with desktop publishing's other variables—such as your own printer or a service bureau's image-setter, or your word processing programs.

QuarkXPress This is probably the most popular layout program among both desktop publishers and professional printers. It's an industry standard. QuarkXPress is somewhat more sophisticated than others, which is to say it's slightly more difficult and time-consuming to master. It's preferred, as one book described it in 1991, "by those who want to control every element of their page down to a thousandth of a point." But 1991 is close to ancient history in desktop publishing: other layout programs can now also tweak documents in similar detail.

Adobe PageMaker This page layout program features many "palettes" or commands or tools that you set ahead of time and then use when you see fit. For example, instead of choosing a headline typeface and then a byline typeface each time, you just punch in the command for each one. The same with rules or lines. Revision is also a simple matter, if you want to vary a particular story or column.

Microsoft Publisher The PageWizard feature helps you create page designs by asking you a series of questions about the style and format you're looking for. Or choose from 35 professionally designed templates. The program allows text to be entered directly into the Publisher layout or to be imported from word processing programs such as Microsoft Word, Microsoft Works, WordPerfect or Xywrite. It also includes ClipArt Gallery.

Corel Ventura Publisher Born in the 1980s as Xerox Ventura Publisher, under the Corel label it has increased in popularity. It has added more flexible graphics, drawing and painting controls to its original strength in creating long documents, such as books and reports, that include graphs and other databased features.

Most page-layout programs allow you to write your text directly within the program or import it from a word processing program. If you've hired a writer (or writers) to produce articles, you can insert their floppy disk into your hardware and import the text into the page layout.

Size of newsletters

The newsletter medium took root about 100 years ago as an 8 1/2 x 11 document—the size of a letter, the size of the most common sheet of paper in America.

That size remains one of the reasons for newsletters' popularity. The letter size is:

- Easy to lay out and produce with desktop publishing
- Easy and economical to mail with or without an envelope
- Easy to pick up and read
- Easy to fold and carry in a pocket or purse
- Easy to file or post for future reference
- Easy to display and distribute unobtrusively in your restaurant.

It's an approachable size. It reflects the me-to-you image. It's an integral part of the style and tone and design we've talked about for getting your message across as if you're talking with your customer, your reader.

The standard 8 1/2 x 11 size also fits into the economy of buying paper. For the typical short press-run of, say, 500 to 5,000 newsletters, this format is printed on 11 x 17 sheets and then folded once: one sheet for a 4-page newsletter, two sheets for an 8-page one, and so on. (See *Chapter 6, Getting the Most (or the Least) from Your Printer*, for more on the size of your newsletter in relation to the paper you buy and the presses your printer uses.)

Although we favor 8 1/2 x 11, many newsletters come in variations of the newspaper tabloid—11 x 17 or 11 x 14 or even 14 x 17. The most common of these three is the basic tabloid 11 x 17, exactly twice the dimensions of the standard 8 1/2 x 11.

The tabloid can offer you more room to "splash"—oversized photos and graphics, lots of white space, even a pull-out poster. It can also be folded down to 8 1/2 x 11 for mailing.

An effective, but uncommon, newsletter is one sheet—either 8 1/2 x 11 or 8 1/2 x 14 (legal size)—printed on both sides. It can be folded to the approximate size of a business envelope, but mailed without an envelope (a self-mailer). The style and tone in this case is "bulletin." A striking nameplate, minimal graphics set off a series of very short, even telegraphic, editorial items.

The best one-sheet newsletters (whether legal size or the standard 8 1/2 x 11) we've observed come from chambers of commerce or associations who want to send a lot of brief information fast. (Often they complement more substantive monthly or quarterly publications.)

You might consider initially producing a one-sheet newsletter as a quick way to get your feet wet.

Paper

You don't have to spend an arm and a leg to get good quality paper with a "newsy" quality. Often, that means a lighter weight than you'd expect. Just make sure it's opaque enough to keep the printing on the reverse side from bleeding through.

Generally, paper stock is about 20% to 40% of the production cost for a newsletter. Paper prices can fluctuate widely, but often for a few dollars more you can buy a higher grade of paper that can appreciably add to the image of your newsletter. Talk this over with your printer—sometimes printers buy certain higher-grade stocks for larger printing jobs and can add your purchase on to that order for substantial savings on your part.

Unlike a one-time printing job like a brochure or a menu (when you may choose a paper that the printer happens to have in stock), your newsletter paper purchase should be a commitment to producing a consistent product over time. The paper you print your newsletter on is part of its overall look, which you don't want to change to meet the demands of what happens to be available. Make sure the paper you use is available six months from now—and two years from now.

Your printer has access to hundreds of different types of paper. If the printer isn't willing to spend the time with you to gather samples and compare prices and make suggestions, choose another printer.

Also discuss with your printer whether you want to use recyclable paper (which can broken down and remanufactured into recycled paper) and/or recycled paper, which is rapidly rising in quality and dropping in price. Choosing either recycled or recyclable paper allows you to print the appropriate logo on your newsletter, which adds a certain environmental sensitivity to your restaurant.

There are two basic types of paper for newsletters.

Offset Also called *uncoated book paper*, offset paper is used for routine printing of all kinds. It comes in several shades of white and a number of pastel colors—plus a variety of grades and weights.

The preponderance of the newsletters included in this book are printed on offset white or buff or ivory, which are always safe choices.

Coated Also called *enamel*, coated stock paper is just that—coated. It carries ink more crisply—especially important when printing photos, called *halftones*. Common coated stock finishes are matte, dull and gloss.

Although many people are tempted to go with glossy coated stock because of its apparent "spare no expense" image, it's typically more suited to slick magazines and marketing brochures. It can war against your newsletter mission in at least three ways: 1. It can turn a low-budget or modest-budget operation into an expensive one. 2. It can run at odds with the personal touch you wish to convey in your newsletter (we've seen heavy-weight, glossy coated stock newsletters that look and feel more like product brochures). 3. Glossy coated stock is actually more difficult to read because of the glare of light reflecting off the surface.

Choosing the color of paper for your newsletter should be done hand-in-hand with choosing the color(s) of ink (see below).

Three-hole punch

You may want to have your newsletter three-hole punched, so readers can keep it in a three-ring binder. This adds value by conveying the idea that your newsletter should be saved for future reference. Many printers have press attachments that punch paper without adding to the cost. If yours doesn't, and the hole punch is an extra step, you'll be charged extra for it.

Color

If you use color in your newsletter, don't do it just for decoration. It should serve a function, a communications function. It should help reading, not distract from it.

For example, those with the glossy coated paper stock mentality also opt for four-color printing. That's a decision in favor of producing a wannabe magazine. Is that what you want? Choosing to print your newsletter in four-color (also called *full color*) is a decision not lightly taken. Four-color printing is expensive and adds much time to the production process. The relatively short print run (the number of copies printed) of most restaurant newsletters doesn't proportionately lower the cost very much because most of the expense comes from setting up the color plates before actually printing.

Four-colors can certainly add to an elegant look, but the two do not necessarily go together. In other words, many unattractive newsletters are printed in full color, and many elegant newsletters use "just" black on white or off-white—or black and an accent color.

Art director and publication design consultant Jan V. White writes in his book *Color for Impact*:

> Color-in-print is not an aesthetic medium but a rational tool you use for editorial purposes: emphasis, persuasion, linkage, organization, recognition. If it also creates beauty, so much the better. But its functionality is more valuable than its prettiness.

A carefully chosen second color (black is the first "color") can help your logo or nameplate stand out and be recognized instantly. It adds life to the page and draws in the reader. Often referred to as an *accent* color, the second color should be just that—an accent. If not used judiciously, color's effectiveness is greatly reduced. If the color you've chosen is too light, for example, or too bright, the type can't be read in normal light.

The most common method of selecting color is to use the PANTONE Matching System (called PMS), a collection of hundreds of colored chips which your printer will have. Each color has its own number.

Many editors settle on specific newsletter elements to render in color—for example, the nameplate, masthead and page numbers—and have masters preprinted in that color for a number of issues. This saves a lot of both money and time in the printing process. Black text is then printed on the masters each issue. The drawback is that this locks you into a similar layout each issue to accommodate the preprinted areas.

Newsletter expert Mark Beach writes in his *Editing Your Newsletter*:

> You can design almost any newsletter by selecting from a handful of colors whose effectiveness you know well and that readers find attractive. While it's tempting to follow trends, the colors listed below prove most popular year after year:
> - violet—PANTONE Violet or Trumatch 39-b4
> - warm red—PANTONE 032 or 185 or Trumatch 6-a

- cool red—PANTONE 199 or Trumatch 2-a
- burgundy—PANTONE 201 or Trumatch 2-b6
- blue—PANTONE 286 or 300, or Trumatch 36-b1 or 34-a
- green—PANTONE 347 or Trumatch 19-a
- brown—PANTONE 469 or Trumatch 49-a6

Another inexpensive way to incorporate color into your newsletter is to print it on colored paper. Your printer can show you hundreds of paper samples. Just make sure the colored paper is not so dark—or so distracting—that reading black ink on it is difficult. Your newsletter should be a joy to read, not a challenge.

Photos, illustrations and clip art

The simplicity of newsletter design demands photographs no more than it demands color. But, as with color, photos can add zip to your publication—especially photos of smiling people ... your chefs, your waitstaff, your customers, yourself. (Some restaurateurs run photos of local or national celebrities enjoying the restaurant, but that of course has to do with the image you're trying to project.) A photograph of, say, an "employee of the month" puts personality into your newsletter.

Four cautions in the use of photos (called *halftones* in the printing process):

1. Avoid overly posed shots. You want your photos to add life.

2. Be sure to identify by name anyone pictured either in the text or in a caption of reduced type.

3. Mug shots (head and shoulders) are appropriate for a by-lined column or article but used elsewhere can easily be overdone.

4. If you're using a second color, avoid printing your halftones in it. No matter what the natural skin color of your subjects, few people like to be rendered in green or red or blue.

Illustrations can also add zest to your newsletter. Some newsletter editors use pen and ink drawings very effectively—say, of the front of your restaurant, your dining room, even people. You might want to engage the services of an artist and then use the illustrations over and over.

Clip art is, of course, less expensive than commissioning an artist (unless the artist is a member of your family, in which case you should also get the opinion of the artist's work from others). Clip art is copyright-free drawings which you purchase for unlimited use. They originally came on glossy paper for easy reproduction but are now more widely available on computer disks and CD-ROMs for easily importing into your page layout program.

One clip art distributor claims that with desktop publishing capabilities "clip art is no longer to art what muzak is to music." That is, once imported into your software program, clip art drawings may be altered ("morphed") to any purpose—cropped, stretched, englarged or reduced.

Clip art collections (which is the way you buy clip art) include not only drawings of people and things, often stylized, but also decorative touches such as borders, dingbats, boxes and section heads.

Fax newsletters

Your publication plans should take into account the growing use of facsimile transmissions, even if you fax your newsletter only occasionally. For example, if your newsletter contains an article about catered events, consider faxing it to your business clients.

Designing a newsletter that faxes well means creating a logo and nameplate and laying out pages and choosing typefaces that stand up in black and gray and white.

Not all fax machines are created equal. If you'll be faxing your newsletter, or a couple of pages of it, keep it graphically and typographically simple enough to transfer well to the grainiest fax paper.

Keeping open the possibility of faxing your newsletter (or your menu, for that matter) means, of course, asking for your guests' fax numbers at the same time you solicit their names and addresses.

Notable Quote

James W. Michaels, the longtime managing editor of *Forbes* once wrote in his column in that magazine:

> Everett Halvorsen, *Forbes*' art director since 1978, likes to quote, of all people, the great designer Coco Chanel: 'If you walk into a room and people say, "What a marvelous dress," you are badly dressed. If they say, "What a marvelous woman," you are well dressed.' Halvorsen keeps the quote on his desk. Says he, 'It exactly expresses my philosophy of magazine design. The aim should be to help readers enjoy the publication, not to make them notice the design.'

Coco Chanel's observation applies to newsletters even more than to magazines. Newsletters are a medium whose message is best carried by unobtrusive design.

Pearl Street Grill

il 1996 Newsletter

April is my fav... ...me of baseball, warm weather,
The Masters an... ...il, we introduce to you our
"Birthday B... ...ow your birthday, you
will receive... ...our newsletter.
...during t... ...our calendar,
fax us...

September, 1995

the Lark

The First...

FLASH!

The Lark...
of Michigan...
compilatio...
popular that it has been...
Zagat's Survey of our...
gratified to learn...
Michigan's favo...
score for foo...
Readers'...

H...

POST-PALM HOT SPOTS

Your local Palm staff recommends the following city hot spots after dining

Piano Bar at The Ritz (212-757-1900)
HAMPTONS: Dancetteria (516-342-2...)
The Pike (516-537-1700)
MIAMI: Bermuda Bar (305-945-019...)
(305-531-5535), The Strand (305-5...)
CHICAGO: Signature (96th floor —
Hancock Building) (312-787-9596...)
(312-642-6805)
HOUSTON: The Ritz (713-840-7...)
Streets (713-840-8555)
MEXICO CITY: Mezzanote (525...)
Theatron (525-281-4552)

Your local Palm staff recommends the...
WASHINGTON, D.C.: River Club (202-333-
8118), Club Zei (202-842-2445), Blues Alley
(202-334-4141)
PHILADELPHIA: Milk Bar (215-928-6455),
Melange (215-735-7000), Egypt (215-922-
6500)
ATLANTA: Tongue & Groove (404-261-2325),
Otto's (404-233-1133)
LAS VEGAS: Cleopatra's Barge (702-731-7110),
The Drink (702-796-5519)
DALLAS: Sipango (214-522-2411), 8.0
(214-969-9321), Martini Ranch (214-220-2116)
NEW YORK: Rainbow Room (212-632-5100),

Sear...

Cham...

Whole Roast...
Candl...
Saffr...

Piña Colada Cheese...

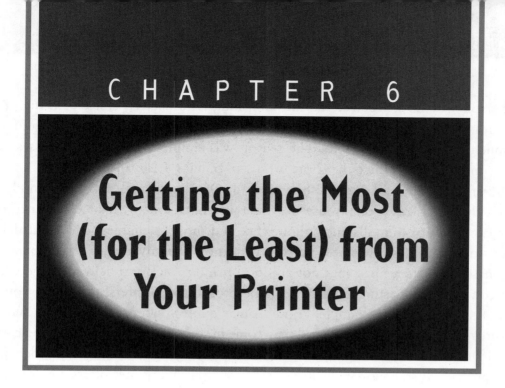

CHAPTER 6

Getting the Most (for the Least) from Your Printer

A s a restaurateur, you have ample experience in working with suppliers—knowing both the benefits and the obstacles to getting what you want, consistently, for the best price. In many ways, dealing with printers is no different than buying from wholesale food vendors. The ease of the task and the quality of the result depend on how much you know about what you want and how good your questions are about what you don't know.

In the previous chapter, on design and typography, you learned the language of designers and printers. In this chapter, we'll outline the context in which you speak that language. The more professional your approach is in creating your newsletter, the fewer your headaches and the less your overall costs will be.

Like dentists and Rodney Dangerfield, printers often feel as if they get no respect. And the advent of desktop publishing—with which nonprofessionals can produce typeset, laser printed, camera-ready copy—has only intensified that feeling among printers. They see their turf invaded by amateurs and they see competition heating up with other printers.

But these negatives can work in your favor if you put a premium on clear communication. Printers also like newsletter accounts because they mean regular, scheduled business (unlike the numerous one-time "rush" orders they face) and because printing newsletters is (or should be) a relatively uncomplicated procedure.

Choosing a printer

Whether or not you're working with a designer, lay out as much of your newsletter specifications as you can before approaching a printer. (A designer, in fact, may have worked with a number of printers and have recommendations.) Of course, many factors cannot be nailed down before you negotiate with the printer. Some of these depend on the particular printer you choose—software compatibility, for one, and the type of presses the printer has.

One person we know, when he began publishing a newsletter, stuck with the printer he had used for other jobs. Later he compared the costs with other printers and found he was paying much more than he had to. The reason was simple: the printer's presses were too large to economically produce the short press run of an 8 1/2 x 11 publication.

Printers are very competitive, so shop around. Overnight mail, faxes and modems have eliminated the need to especially use a printer in your own town or city. But those very expenses can add up: long-distance phone, fax and modem charges, overnight delivery of disks, and so on. And as a business person, you know the advantages of patronizing other local businesses. Further, most (but not all) local printers pick and deliver for no charge.

When comparing the estimated prices among prospective printers, make sure you're comparing apples to apples. For example, Printer A may quote you a price of $700 including mailing and three-hole punch. Printer B's bid may come in somewhat lower, but mailing costs aren't included. If you are using photographs, the costs of printing halftones can vary widely from one printer to another. Also consider the price (or price breaks) a printer offers you for paper.

A professional printer should happily provide quotes on as many different options for your newsletter production as you request.

Get references. Look at the printer's other work. Ask candidates if they've printed newsletters before. It may seem like a simple job, but there are special considerations such as weight restrictions and postal regulations that vary depending how you're mailing your newsletter.

Speaking of mailing, many printers have in-house mailing operations. If not, you face additional costs—and additional days—to ship the printed product to a separate mailing house.

The best way to compare "apples to apples" is to use the same standard bid form for all prospective printers. It should include all costs—typesetting, paper, printing, folding, mailing, and so on.

Printers have a lot of experience, so take advantage of it. Seek their guidance. Respect them. They'll not steer you wrong, especially if they know you're interviewing other printers.

Six commandments for dealing with your printer

1. Make sure that your specifications, schedules, pricing, the number of copies to be printed, and so on, are dated and *in writing*. Misunderstandings as a result of poor communication are the most common cause of a poor business relationship. This often arises because different personnel may get involved from one day to the next.

Howard Gropper, of Maar Printing, in Poughkeepsie, N.Y., advises:

> Each time you send material to your printer for the production of the newsletter, accompany it with a purchase order (which can be in the form of a signed letter). State exactly what you are enclosing, the number of copies you want printed, the paper you want it printed on, the colors and other specifications, and the date you want it off the press and/or in the mail.

REQUEST FOR QUOTATION

newsletter name _____ date _____

contact _____ phone _____ fax _____

restaurant _____

printer's name and address _____

_____

SPECIFICATIONS

number of pages _____

page size _____ X _____ inches

folded size _____ X _____ inches

quantity per issue _____ copies

issues per year _____ issues

date(s) camera ready copy to printer

_____

_____

date(s) newsletters needed

_____

_____

_____

_____

ART AS 1-UP PAGES SUPPLIED

○ camera-ready   ○ electronic file

○ composite film

SCREEN TINTS

○ printer adds   ○ supplied

HALFTONES

○ printer adds   ○ supplied

PAPER

weight _____

color _____

finish _____

brand _____

INK COLORS

side one _____

side two _____

PROOFS

○ galley   ○ page

○ photocopy   ○ blueline

○ overlay color   ○ fax

○ dummy included with these specs

additional instructions

_____

_____

_____

_____

sample bid form

141

2. Never authorize additional work—or a "rush" order—without asking the cost and getting it in writing.

3. The word *rush* is a double-edged sword. A rush order usually costs more money. On the other hand, never say "no rush." The calendar year might change before your job is done. Always give your printer a deadline, no matter how generous it is.

4. Be sure to match your printing job to the right type of printer. David Harrison, senior account executive at M. Lee Smith Publishers LLC in Nashville, says, "Don't kid yourself into believing it's so much easier to deal with only one printer. Chances are that the printer who does a bang-up job on your newsletter will be ill-suited to produce your business cards."

5. Never accept a substitution over the telephone. If the 70# Cream Hammermill paper stock that you requested is unavailable, don't accept an alternative without seeing a sample.

6. Never put your printer in the position of making a major decision for you. You'll always know your needs better than your printer will.

Submitting copy

Copy is what you provide the printer to create your newsletter. It can come in a variety of forms, depending on what the two of you have determined from the beginning.

- With desktop publishing, the most common method of providing copy to the printer is in the form of laser printed (called *camera-ready*) sheets, from which the printer can work without alteration. In this case, you produce the pages as they will appear. These sheets should have been edited and proofread before you give them to the printer, since they are the final output.

  If you use this method, make sure your in-house printer produces high quality output (usually 330 dots per inch, "dpi," or more). Also, for these sheets, buy and use paper of higher quality (that is, more opaque and with a harder surface) than for everyday use.

- If you are producing final copy from your desktop publishing system, another way of giving it to the printer is on an electronic disk (or even via modem) directly from your computer. This usually results in a higher-quality finished product. But, we remind you once again that your software and your printer's have to be compatible.

- If you use photographs, consult with your printer to decide how best to handle them from a production point of view. The printer's equipment will almost always do a better job than your personal scanner.

- Regarding drawings or illustrations, if they've originated from your own software program (decorative borders, for example, or imported clip art), they will appear on your camera-ready sheets or on the disk you provide.

Patterson's Patio Restaurant

1234 MARKET STREET • CHICAGO, ILLINOIS 60610 • 312-444-5555, FAX 312-444-5556

May 19, 1997

Mr. Jack Jones
Perfect Printing Inc.
5678 Market Street
Chicago, IL 60611

Dear Jack:

Following the schedule, enclosed is the following for the printing of the June 1st "Patterson's Patio Letter":

1. Four pages of camera-ready copy of the newsletter.
2. Three photos to be inserted as indicated on the dummy.
3. Dummy of the newsletter.

Please fax page proofs so we can check the proper placement of the photos. I will fax back my approval.

Print 2,500 copies and mail on May 29, 1997, using the envelopes you have in stock.

Mailing labels will arrive by May 28th.
Deliver overage (about 500) to us.

Any questions, don't hesitate to call me.

Thanks.

Sincerely,

Jill Patterson

Jill Patterson

sample purchase order

If they are separately printed illustrations (say, your logo or a page from your menu), leave the appropriate space for them in your pages and give the illustrations as is to the printer for reproduction—similar to providing photographs.

Some people request blue lines from their printer—a prepress photographic proof (usually rendered in blue)—which they review before actually going to press. This is done in cases where you haven't already seen everything that is to be printed—say, a complicated photo spread or similar introduction of art. This is *not* the time to engage in additional editing or writing, because the final press work has already been made and changes are expensive at this stage (unless they're printer's errors). Blue lines are not necessary when you've provided camera-ready pages.

Schedules

Probably the most common cartoon posted in printing shops is the one picturing a man rolling over in laughter, with the caption, "You want it when?!"

Harrison says:

> Schedules are like a machine—all of the parts must work together for the machine to operate efficiently. You have a schedule for your creative production and your printer has a schedule for the print production. The printer is as dependent on you meeting your scheduled dates as you are on the printer meeting his. If your dates are not valid, the printer's won't be either.

As a newsletter publisher, you have the schedule in your favor. To the printer, you mean regular business a certain number of times a year. Let's say you are publishing a quarterly newsletter. You and your printer agree that you will provide copy on March 1, June 1, September 1, and December 1, and the printer has agreed to have your newsletter in the mail by the 10th of each month. If you see that you cannot meet the deadline, let your printer know immediately—giving him the new date and making sure he can still make the 10-day turnaround time.

Harrison offers these considerations to help scheduling run smoothly:

1. Always try to give your copy to the printer at least one day early.

2. Don't let your printer be in a position to say, "We never really know when your job's coming in, so we have to do the best we can." This leaves you open for a series of late mailings.

3. Don't make it a practice to throw a lot of last minute changes at your printer. You might as well throw your schedule out the window if you do.

4. Call your printer a couple of days in advance of sending your copy to remind him to be ready to meet the schedule.

5. The secret to managing schedules is to always live up to your part of the agreement. There will always be occasional legitimate circumstances that may disrupt the schedule (equipment breakdown, paper shortages, holidays, etc.). Just make sure the delays are not caused by your own actions.

David Harrison concludes:

> Please bear in mind that every printer is capable of a limited number of very quick turnaround jobs. They need to promise them for those jobs that really must have them. Use good judgement and treat your printer as a partner. You'll be rewarded with a vendor that truly cares about your work.

Press to

Moos-Letter

"All The News That's Fittin'"

Late 1995 - Early/Mid 1996

A Letter from the Neditor

...urant Reborn

...OLLOW HOUSE

Tales from the Wh...

A Quarterly Newsletter 3420 Sansom S...

Sharing Our Strength, Keeping Our Promise

This was my first seal party, and I hurried across the snow covered tundra in my mukluks to Maria's house where she would celebrate her husband's first catch of the spring. As the Eskimo women gathered outside her door, Maria dropped a large hunk of red seal meat along with a strip of blubber into each pail. When the seal had been evenly divided between the families, Maria handed out ribbon, buttons and pieces of fabric for sewing. Then the fun began as she tossed candy and bubble gum into the air. With glee the women held out the wide skirts of their fur lined tunics to catch the falling goodies. When root beer barrels, my favorite, were tossed, I overcame my shyness and stretched out my skirt to scoop them up.

My year in a remote Eskimo village in Alaska during my VISTA internship in 1969 helped form my sense of community in a way that has affected my whole life. The seal party demonstrated the Eskimo philosophy of sharing. In order to survive the harsh climate, individuals depended on the strength of the group and acted in ways which supported the whole rather than profiting at the expense of others. The seal party was a means for re-distributing wealth gained during the year, even when measured in buttons and bubble gum. Accumulating more than your neighbor was not valued. Envy did not exist; if you admired something an Eskimo had, they offered it to you. In contrast, I saw that our consumer economy is actually based on creating envy, rewarding greed, and admiring those who accumulate the most.

As the most unegalitarian country in ... with the largest and most ... and poor, Am...

not only co...
as I did, a d...
barriers tha...

A favorite...
is targeted f...
cutting servic...
the wealthy. J...
for Children," or...
and Policy Priori...
followed by a tou...
Table Talks featur...
Wofford, CEO of ou...
and director of SO...
new book *Revolutio*...
Steve Larson, on th...

Although we do n...
stereos, cars, and de...
and share our concer...
our tax-dollars to pro...
necessities for becomin...
a meaningful educatio...
decent housing. If we...
and if we do not, we will...
country's promise th...
and opp...

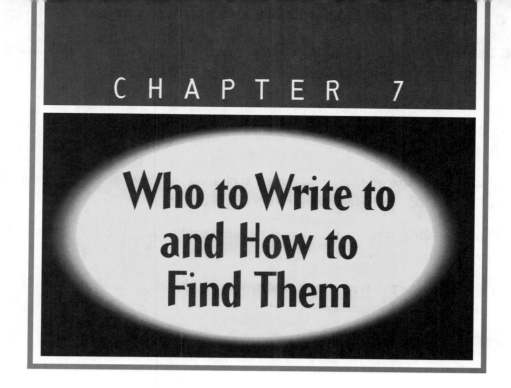

CHAPTER 7

Who to Write to and How to Find Them

Once you've designed, written and produced a newsletter appropriate to your restaurant, distributing it will be fun. It's an excellent marketing tool—a faithful workhorse that can be used in a variety of ways. Distributing it properly will increase the familiarity of your restaurant among diverse audiences: regular and prospective customers, out-of-towners, the business community, the local and regional press.

Your newsletter is also a versatile marketing tool. Unlike printed or broadcast advertising, it's personal—it's from you to the individual reader. It's also "news," which means it carries topical information and/or entertainment value to the reader.

Newsletter and marketing expert Elaine Floyd begins her book, *Marketing With Newsletters*:

> Effective marketing newsletters have an advantage over other direct mail pieces—they aren't considered junk mail. They're what writer Bob Westenberg calls 'happy mail'—helpful information that people want to receive, read and respond to.

With that in mind, we recommend that you distribute your newsletter to four audiences:

- Current and past customers
- Prospective customers
- The press
- Your vendors

We purposefully use the word distribute rather than mail because mail is only one (but probably the principal) way you can get your newsletter in the hands of readers. Other ways include:

- Have your newsletter inserted with a neighborhood or community newspaper that fits your market. Talk with the appropriate advertising personnel.

- Display your newsletter prominently in your restaurant. Perhaps have your printer create a small display stand for it, to place near the cashier. Offer a copy to guests while they're waiting for a table.

- Also display it in surrounding businesses, including grocery stores and movie theaters and malls, which often have community bulletin boards.

- Distribute it to any locale that displays brochures and menus, such as hotels, motels and chamber of commerce booths.

- Fax or mail your newsletter to both individual and business customers who are inquiring about catered events and special parties.

- Current and past customers

Mailing Lists

If you already have a mailing list of regular customers, you're in good shape. But don't be satisfied with that. Mailing lists are almost organic. They're in continual formation, growth, change. Be persistent. Keep acquiring names.

The nucleus of your mailing list, which will also consist of your most responsive names, will come from the names and addresses you acquire in the restaurant itself. These are people who have experienced your restaurant and presumably want to be kept in touch.

Three principal ways of developing this nucleus are:

- Have a business card drop. Provide a container for guests to drop off their business cards on their way in or out of your restaurant. As an incentive, you can draw names periodically for complimentary food and drink awards. This is also a very good base for developing meetings and catering business.

- Provide a way for those without business cards to leave their names and addresses in the container. Set up a guest book. Get customers excited about being part of your "family" and being the first to know when something happens or is going to happen in your restaurant.

- Include a comment card or address information card with the guest check. This serves two purposes. You get feedback on your food and service and you get a new name to add to your mailing list. If you make it a postage-paid postcard (but not stamped, so you pay only for the cards that are mailed back), the customers have the option to complete it later and mail it back to you.

Idea: When building the database for your mailing list, try to get as much information as is practical—that is, beyond the customers' names and addresses, also provide space for telephone and fax numbers. You may not initially see a need for them, but down the road you may want to fax out a bulletin or even your newsletter. Also, you might consider "coding" the customers' entries in order to segment them by interest. For example, Mark McDonnell, owner of the LaSalle Grill in South Bend, Indiana, segments his list by interests such as cigar smokers or wine tasting, and then he mails to those customers preceding special events.

Prospective customers

In addition to sending your newsletter to your proprietary list—to those who have already dined in your restaurant and left their names and addresses—you will want to reach those who haven't yet had the pleasure.

This effort is more open-ended, limited only by your goals, time and budget.

We've already suggested some distribution points in your neighborhood and community which you may want to explore—hotels and motels, tourist booths, community fairs, and so on. If your newsletter is everything you want it to be, people will gravitate to it and want to keep it. Some restaurateurs brag that it's almost a status symbol for people to be receiving their newsletter.

Next, strive to capture the names and addresses of those who may be at your restaurant for a one-time event, such as a meeting or a reception. The business card drop works well, as does displaying your newsletter for the taking.

ROGAN'S AMERICAN GRILL

What do you think of us?

Please let us know how we're doing. When you're finished, you may leave it with any of our staff or drop it in the mail, it's postage paid.

How would your rate your dining experience?

Excellent . . . . .Poor

☐5   ☐4   ☐3   ☐2   ☐1

How can we do a better job?

_____

_____

_____

If you'd like to be informed about special events at Rogan's and receive our quarterly newsletter, please print your name and address below. Thank you.

Name_____

Address_____

Telephone(Day)_____(Evening)_____

sample comment card

In this regard, we suggest that the newsletter itself carry a regular feature—"May we add you or a friend to our mailing list?" This can take the form of a coupon in the lower left-hand or right-hand corner that can be clipped and mailed to you, or you can include a business reply card ("BRC") stapled or nested inside the newsletter.

Put your Rolodex to work: suppliers, school and community organizations, business associates, even friends who know of your restaurant but do not frequent it—they should all be added to your mailing list. Leah Abraham, of Caffe Bondi in New York City, says she uses the mailing lists from the artists and musicians whose work she stages in her restaurant.

Renting Lists of Names

Another way of expanding your mailing list is to purchase others' lists. There are many list vendors out there, but almost as many hucksters. Choose carefully. Local clubs and organizations often sell their membership lists. ("Rent" is the more appropriate word since you usually agree to use the list for a only a certain number of mailings for a certain price). These same organizations may also inspire particular promotional opportunities—for example, an after-theater dinner or reception offered to the mailing list of the community theater.

Don't be intimidated by the size of mailing lists you're considering renting. You don't need to take the whole lot. You can choose a list by ZIP code, carrier route or any number of other criteria. In addition, even if you rent, say, 10,000 names, you can mail to just 500 of them each issue. This is more sensible for a couple of reasons: you can absorb the costs more gradually, and you can monitor the response more easily. Remember, publishing and distributing a newsletter is a long-term effort, not a "now or never" advertising blitz.

American Express also rents a list of its Cardmembers that can be selected by several criteria, including those who visit your restaurant from out of town. It's expensive, but reliable.

Monitoring Response Even more so than with your house list, you should monitor the response rate of rented lists. Lists that "should" work well sometimes don't. Many factors come into play. For all you know, the particular ZIP code you just mailed to recently suffered the closing of its most popular restaurant. Or another, upscale list on which you place great hopes is the home of hundreds of downsized executives.

In other words, don't just mail and then move on to the next segment next issue. Try to see how well each rented list "performs," by coding the cards or the discount offer. You may want to mail to a particular list a second, or third, time.

Of course, once a "rented" name patronizes your restaurant and leaves contact information, you then "own" that name for your house list.

The Press

Your newsletter can generate a lot of publicity for itself as well as for your restaurant. Targeting the press for publicity may not be the primary reason you're doing a newsletter, but that doesn't mean you shouldn't take advantage of the opportunities that exist.

Editors and publishers of both consumer and trade newspapers and magazines are always on the lookout for story ideas. Add them to your mailing list.

Start with the publications you read. Those are the ones you're most familiar with. Check the masthead to find out individual names. Include two or three editors or reporters at each publication. The duplication doesn't hurt and may get the office talking. Don't forget the key women's, men's and lifestyle magazines that have food sections, or restaurant features.

The advantage of using your newsletter as a way to communicate with the press is an obvious one: it's already written. There's no need to write a press release that may or may not be read (even editors of small-town newspapers receive dozens weekly). In addition, a press release usually deals with only one subject. But your newsletter features a number of topics, any one of which may pique an editor's interest.

Familiarity Breeds Interest

After sending the press your newsletter over a period of time, you're in a better position to give them a call when you really want to push a story idea. Because your newsletter ideally reflects the full personality of your restaurant, editors will have a "context" in which to consider your story pitch.

If you're a subscriber or regular reader, let the publication you're writing to know that. Again, no need for a formal press release. Just a note attached to the newsletter should suffice, pointing out a particular item they may want to follow up on.

The press likes to quote authorities. You are an authority on wine and food, whether you think of yourself that way or not. You're also an authority on consumer trends: If your community has a tourist season, how is it doing this year? If your city has an annual fest or celebration, what is your restaurant doing for it?

Feature writers are always looking for new slants on the "routine" holidays and seasons— the Fourth of July, autumn, Thanksgiving, Mother's Day, and so on. Point out what your newsletter is writing about them. Perhaps it will spark a story idea.

You're the Authority

More particularly, let's say you did a lot of research on a specific regional cooking style. Let the editors know. They may not be familiar with it, but you've done the research, and you've even written a newsletter article about it.

And there's always the special interest story—the chef that volunteers in a soup kitchen, the dishwasher who won the lottery, the city mayor who chose you to cater her inauguration.

Whether or not you have the time to continually keep in touch with the press, your newsletter does. Your newsletter may inspire them to contact you. Or when you do contact them, they'll know who you—and your restaurant—are.

Housekeeping

You "own" every name you add to your mailing list. After time, it becomes a unique property that you should maintain just as you take care of any piece of equipment. By maintaining it, we mean keeping the list "clean"—that is, current, valid addresses.

You know the old adage, An ounce of prevention.... Keep on top of address corrections, deletions, returns and duplicates. Untended, they can easily get out of hand and end up costing you hundreds of dollars in extra postage.

There are several ways to keep your list clean. The simplest (and costliest) way is to mail First Class, and all undeliverable mail will be returned to you. A cheaper way is to print Address Correction Requested on either bulk mail or Second Class (now called Periodical) mail. (Every "address correction" you receive from the post office costs about 35 cents.)

Do make your mailings to the press First Class, because they like their news fresh. In fact, it's a good idea to add a cover letter in your first mailing to the press, explaining who you are.

As you may notice from the newsletters included in our gallery of restaurant newsletters, restaurateurs have a variety of methods for keeping their mailing lists clean.

- Some insert reply cards which must be filled out and returned if they are to remain on the mailing list.

- Some run the Address Correction Requested notice only once a year, or mail it First Class only once a year—to both save money and to give the new persons at an address the chance to get acquainted with the newsletter.

- At least one restaurant, the Abiento in Pasadena, Calif. offers a free dessert and a chance to win a dinner-for-two to recipients who correct mailing list errors.

- Others make no effort to remove "obsolete" addresses (except undeliverable ones) because whoever receives the newsletter is a prospective customer. Nell Hyltin, co-owner of Amigos restaurants in Central Florida, proposes keeping everyone on your list unless they're a duplicate or they ask to be taken off. That way, even after customers have moved, the new occupants will receive your publication and may decide to visit.

Software

As with design, the software you choose to develop and maintain your mailing list is extremely important. Flexibility, ease of entry and expandability are all critical. Choose a program that will allow you to arrange data by various information fields, such as first name, last name, street address, city, state, ZIP code, telephone or fax number, birthday, seating preferences, smoking preferences, wine preferences, special interests, dietary restrictions.

The point to remember when choosing database software is: does it have infinite capacity to create and add the preferences you choose? Filemaker, for instance, is a good one. It's available for both PC and Macintosh. Your existing word processing program may have a list management system built in, but check its adaptability before you spend the time loading names and addresses. The availability and ease of such a system in a word processing program will most likely not compare well to one in a database program.

The most up-to-date systems include the capability for bar coding—that is, including those mysterious vertical lines that appear near the address. Bar coding saves postage costs if you're mailing a lot of pieces to one ZIP code or carrier route. The relatively small size of your newsletter circulation may tempt you to figure you're not eligible for bulk discounts, but the geographic concentrations of your mailings may indeed make you eligible.

Your local postmaster

Cultivate a working relationship with the postmaster of the locale you're mailing from. (This, of course, may be the responsibility of your designer or printer or mailing house, but make sure it's done.) With the increased competition from UPS, FedEx and other overnight mailers, the U.S. Postal Service is placing greater emphasis on customer relations. Take advantage of it. Your local postmaster will be glad (at least most of them) to answer all questions to make sure your mailings meet standards for correctly addressing mail and perhaps meeting criteria for discounts—for example, by including the extra four digits in the ZIP code, or bar coding.

Entering addresses We repeat our refrain: Consult your local post office. They have brochures and templates instructing mailers how to address mail. Follow them from the beginning—from the first name you enter into your database. General guidelines include some you might not immediately consider, such as printing all information in all capital letters and omitting punctuation (AVE, not AVE.).

Business Reply Cards

Called "BRCs" for short, business reply cards are designed to be filled out and returned to you as postcards. Self-address one side and on the other side follow the instructions of the Post Office for obtaining and printing a Business Reply permit. This will enable your prospect to mail it without a stamp and enable you to pay only for those cards actually returned.

Also follow the Post Office's instructions for the card's size, dimensions, and weight of paper stock and automation-compatible coding.

In *Marketing With Newsletters*, Elaine Floyd recommends that you "design your reply cards to entice readers to mail them to you." She offers a number of tips to increase your response, including:

• Place the benefit of returning the card in large type

• List your telephone and fax numbers

• Highlight the card with spot colors or graphics or print it on bright paper

FIM A
for preprinted courtesy reply mail with bar code allows capture at the facer canceller

From _____
_____
_____

PLACE STAMP HERE

Restaurant Name
Attn. Restaurant Manager
P.O. Box 1234
Anytown, State 00000-0000

FIM B
for preprinted business reply penalty or franked mail without bar code prevents rejection on the facer canceller

From _____
_____
_____

NO POSTAGE
NECESSARY
IF MAILED
IN THE
UNITED STATES

BUSINESS REPLY MAIL
FIRST CLASS MAIL   PERMIT NO. 0000   ANYTOWN, STATE

POSTAGE WILL BE PAID BY ADDRESSEE

Restaurant Name
Attn. Restaurant Manager
P.O. Box 1234
Anytown, State 00000-0000

FIM B
for preprinted business reply penalty or franked mail with bar code allows capture at facer canceller

From _____
_____
_____

NO POSTAGE
NECESSARY
IF MAILED
IN THE
UNITED STATES

BUSINESS REPLY MAIL
FIRST CLASS MAIL   PERMIT NO. 0000   ANYTOWN, STATE

POSTAGE WILL BE PAID BY ADDRESSEE

Restaurant Name
Attn. Restaurant Manager
P.O. Box 1234
Anytown, State 00000-0000

sample BRC's (reduced from actual size)

- Print it using the same colors or artwork as the newsletter for design consistency

- Leave plenty of room to write

If you "saddle stitch" your newsletter—that is, staple it twice on its where it's folded (on its "spine")—your printer can affix the card with one of the staples. If you don't use staples, the card can be inserted loose in the newsletter, but it's best to at least fold it in the spine so it won't fall out.

Business reply cards can serve a number of functions. The most obvious one is gaining reader involvement: they are asking to be kept on your mailing list. Further, you may be asking for additional information that you can use in future promotions—for example, their desire to be included in your special Mexican festival, or your wine tasting party.

Incentives

It's important to give the prospect an incentive to return the card: a drawing for a free dinner-for-two, for example, or inclusion in your VIP club which offers discounts. Most basic, of course, is the incentive for the reader to keep receiving your marvelous newsletter.

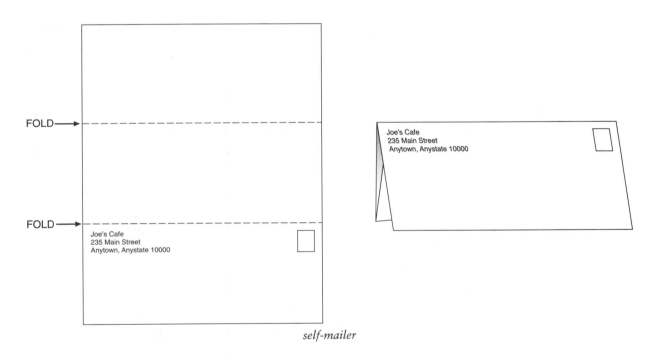

self-mailer

Envelopes vs. self-mailers

Sending your newsletter in an envelope gives the option of including other material, such as a cover letter to the press and to those unfamiliar with your restaurant. Some claim that envelopes carry more "value" to the recipient, but others counter that it's also easier to throw an unopened envelope away without ever having seen a word you've written in your newsletter.

Envelopes aren't cheap. If you do buy envelopes, check prices with your printer to get the best deal. This means buying in large quantities, both for cheaper prices for bulk and for having your printer print your return address on all of them at once. Envelopes also add labor costs for stuffing them.

Self-mailers are obviously cheaper to produce and mail. This entails designing your newsletter with an address area on the bottom half (or third) of the back page, then either folding it appropriately or mailing it flat. Contrary to a common practice, there is no need to staple it closed after the final fold. This isn't necessary according to postal regulations, if your address area and the address label "face" the correct direction for the piece to enter the automated sorting machines. Consult your Post Office for the correct positioning of the recipient's name and address on a self-mailer.

Fax and the World Wide Web

The final, and newest, ways to distribute your newsletter are by faxing it or posting it on the World Wide Web. Here are a couple of things to consider about these methods of delivery:

- Even if you are not now contemplating using either fax or the Internet, keep the option open. As we mentioned in *Chapter 5*, on design, you might want to create a logo and nameplate and lay out pages and choosing typefaces that stand up in black and white—for faxing and posting on the Internet. In regard to distribution, keeping your options open means soliciting fax numbers at the same time you request names and addresses.

    There are designers and public relations agencies that specialize in creating World Wide Web "home pages," but be careful. Many of them are charging way too much. Shop around and compare prices and services.

- Fax and the World Wide Web shouldn't be seen as replacing mail and other forms of delivery. They can complement them. They can be used only occasionally, for special events or for special groups of customers.

    If you do decide to fax your newsletter, there are many fax broadcasting companies who do it for you, usually at nighttime's cheaper rates. Fax broadcasting might make sense, for example, if you rent a chamber of commerce list for a special mailing to the business community (which, of course, has a higher rate of fax machines than home and apartment dwellers).

    American Express' Briefing newsletter (which goes to American Express Restaurant Merchants) reports:

    > As surfing the Web becomes more mainstream, restaurants are beginning to market their wares via Internet dining and entertainment guides and individual Web sites.... To attract students at nearby universities, Joyce Chen Restaurant, Cambridge, MA, advertises their Web site in student handbooks.

The site also contains a faxable order form for delivery which is popular with students and local businesses. The order form can then be faxed via computer.

Gaining a presence on the World Wide Web doesn't necessarily have to include the development and maintenance of your own home page. You can get listed in local convention and visitors bureaus and in local, regional, national and international restaurant and city guides. Some credit card issuers also maintain Web sites which link their card holders and their merchants.

A Word of Warning: The Web, Internet, E-mail and all the other technological innovations are a rapidly changing "state of the art." As you consider the possibilities, keep in mind the relative costs of one versus another, dependability, accessibility. Go slowly, monitor results closely.

CHAPTER 8

Building a Reading Habit

Newsletters, as we've said before, are a me-to-you medium. They are the most personal form of advertising, except for face-to-face communication.

Newsletters are, in the current jargon, "relationship" marketing. Published at regular intervals, they are designed to build a relationship between you and your customers over time. Although a particular mailing list, or a particular issue or even a particular article in one issue, may initially convert a prospect into a loyal reader and customer, your goal as a newsletter publisher should be to *regularly* provide readers with news, entertainment and information that makes them feel part of your restaurant "family."

In other words, your goal is to build a reading habit among those who receive your newsletter. There are three principal things to consider in building this reading habit:

- Editorial content

- Frequency of publication

- Timing

Editorial content

Your readers probably have not paid to receive your newsletter. They may have "qualified" themselves by signing up to receive it, or requesting to continue receiving it, but they have not invested money to receive it. Therefore, each issue must contain at least one reason (if not many more) to read it and look forward to the next issue.

A good test is to take the attitude that your readers *are* paying a subscription price.

Few readers are equally interested in every article your print, but you must strive to make sure every issue talks to every "segment" of your constituency—wine lovers, for example, and bargain hunters, and recipe buffs and those infatuated with your staff or those looking forward to you next special event. Examples can go on forever, so please review *Chapter 4, What Makes a Good Story?*

The point here, though, is to design the editorial content so that each issue has something for everyone—that is, represent in each issue every element within the broad spectrum that defines your restaurant's personality. Let's say, for example, that you plan a special issue or to run a lengthy lead story on the famous people who frequent or occasionally enjoy your restaurant. That's fine, but many people couldn't care less about celebrities. They like your restaurant for its food, not for the "rich and famous" who also like your food. So, make sure that newsletter issue features something that attracts them, too.

Keep the editorial content of a year's worth of issues varied, but also write each issue to have enough variety to attract the greatest number of readers. Incidentally, it's a useful idea to look back a year to see what you were talking about back then.

Frequency of publication

In publishing a promotional newsletter, there are two extremes to avoid: not publishing frequently enough, and publishing too frequently. You probably won't know how to exactly gauge this when you begin publishing, but there are solid guidelines to follow.

"Let's publish one issue of a newsletter and see where it takes us."

Not a good idea—for at least three reasons:

1. It certainly doesn't meet the demands of "building a reading habit." For the time and money invested, you might as well design an advertising campaign.

2. Much of the expense (in both time and money) of developing a newsletter is upfront—hiring a designer, renting mailing lists, interviewing printers and getting estimates. Even if you have a vague notion of publishing future issues, by concentrating only on one you're "missing the boat" by not taking advantage of lower costs for an ongoing project. And the investment of time is out of proportion to the single product.

3. One issue arriving in the mail without the benefit of the context of a regular publication tends to confuse the recipient. Similarly, publishing just two or three times a year isn't enough to establish familiarity, to establish a relationship—not to mention to promote your restaurant regularly and efficiently.

We recommend a *minimum* frequency of four times a year

1. A quarterly schedule is as natural as the change of seasons. In fact, it allows you to take advantage of the seasons and the holidays within each season.

2. Each issue can have its own identity, depending on the time of year, but can of course

also carry any regular features or particular themes special to your restaurant. (See more below, under Timing.)

3. You can always increase the frequency if your promotional needs demand it and your newsletter operation is smooth enough to absorb the production of additional issues.

Too Frequently

Conversely, don't attempt to publish *more* frequently than you honestly feel comfortable being able to implement. Cutting back on the number of announced issues doesn't help your image. People may interpret it as your business slowing down, or your being disorganized, or even uninterested.

"Publishing too frequently" can also mean publishing beyond the time and resources at hand to produce a quality product. If you feel pressed to "get another damn issue out," the editorial and design will reflect this.

A quarterly schedule to begin with allows you to get your newsletter feet wet, build the reading habit, then increase frequency when you feel comfortable doing so.

But, look upon quarterly as a *minimum*. The more frequently you publish, the more timely your newsletter is, and the more often is your marketing plan at work. Regular, frequent publication is vital to building your readership, enhancing the reputation of your restaurant.

Monthly or Bi-Monthly

Publishing six times a year—every other month—gives you regular presence in your readers' mailboxes but isn't as demanding as monthly.

If you have the appropriate resources and commitment, a monthly publication schedule is probably the most effective in terms of all the objectives we've outlined for publishing a newsletter: building a relationship between you and your customers and prospective customers, testing mailing lists, increasing customer traffic and promoting special events.

"Special Alert"

Another variation on the publishing schedule is to set a certain number of issues per year and then issue a "Special Alert" whenever the need arises (perhaps faxing it). This allows you to be faithful to your original schedule—say, four issues a year—and also to publish more frequently without committing yourself permanently to more issues per year.

Frequency vs. number of pages Most newsletter experts recommend publishing shorter issues more frequently over publishing larger ones less frequently. Repetition and familiarity are important. Four monthly pages are better than eight quarterly pages—all other things being equal (which, considering postage costs, they aren't). Are two monthly pages better than four quarterly ones? This is a judgement call you have to make—taking into mind your resources, budget, and specific publishing objectives that may include producing a "substantial" newsletter, a handsome product people want to save rather than a brief alert to be read and discarded.

Of course, if you decide to go for a shorter newsletter published frequently, you can always lengthen it once you've become accustomed to publishing.

In conclusion, decide upon a size and frequency of publishing and then don't cut back. Either increase the size or increase the frequency as your publishing skills develop.

Timing

Beyond deciding how many times a year to publish your newsletter—four, six, 12—you should also schedule exactly *when* the issues come out. When creating a production schedule, work backwards—that is, from the day you can expect it the newsletter to arrive in mailboxes. This is especially important if you are mailing bulk rate, when the mail takes longer.

There's no bigger—and no more obvious—waste of money than to produce a New Year's Eve special and have it arrive in the new year. A couple of days can make all the difference.

Determining a schedule should also take into mind the busy times of your printer or mailing house. Sticking to a preset schedule, down to the day, gives you the advantage of holding your printer to the deadline—even if it falls during an especially busy period like the Christmas rush.

Careful timing comes into play not only in relation to holidays and special times such as Mother's Day and Oktober Fest but also in relation to traditionally slow times—say, January or February in many parts of the country. Anticipate these slow times and plan a promotion and write it up in your newsletter and get the newsletter in the mail.

"Two-Week Window"

Many of the restaurateurs we have interviewed—some represented in the newsletters pictured in *Chapter 3*—report noticeably increased traffic for the two weeks following the distribution of a newsletter. Schedule an issue to take advantage of this boost in business.

This "two-week window" of increased traffic may also help you determine exactly what time of the month to mail your newsletter. Analyze the pattern of your own restaurant receipts, and schedule your mailings accordingly. Are people spending more at the beginning of the month? Do you want to underscore that pattern with the arrival of a newsletter, or do you want to offer a discount or special event toward the end of the month?

Schedule your newsletter to arrive at least one week before the earliest date mentioned in the issue.

If you are making segmented mailings to particular groups—either segmented by interest or by a mailing list you've rented—make sure the timing of the mailing doesn't run up against some inherent resistance. In other words, don't mail to the local college during the summer, or to the business community the two weeks before April 15th.

Bondí

Bakery

THE TAVERN

SERVING SPARTANBURG SINCE 1994

Volume 1, Number 1

'95 NEWSLETTER
VOL.2 NO.3 $1

THE TAVERN
ON TOWN SQUARE

The Tavern re-opens with great success

After being partially destroyed by a fire in late March of '95, The Tavern on Town Square was officially reopened in October 16, 1995. The Tavern on Town Square reopened after four months of steady business.

In Brief
◆

Weather
Sunny and beautiful
No chance of rain
High 78. **Low** 68
Perfect Day for enjoying
The Tavern's Deck!

Unusual Concept
After four months of steady business, patrons have named it one of their favorite restaurants in the upstate.

If you are looking to escape from the usual restaurant atmosphere, then The Tavern on Town Square is what you are trying to find. The Tavern offers a wide variety of your favorite foods, but we go the extra mile to add our unique flair to each dish we serve. There's the Chicken Salad Club Croissant, Barbecue Chicken, Grilled Chicken Haight-Ashbury Pizza, and many more than Chicken, Spanakopita, Barbecue realizing happening at The Tavern. The Tavern isn't just the wonderdefinitely you've hoped for, it's The high-energy bar that offers a atmosphere to your friends. Every All restaurant you've hoped for, it's

Generation Xers show they care
◆

restaurant business is a trap! At some point, you have to de... ...working in restaurants allows time for school, art, and sleeping in, but then you g... ...ever a trap. Six years ago Chris and I were already good

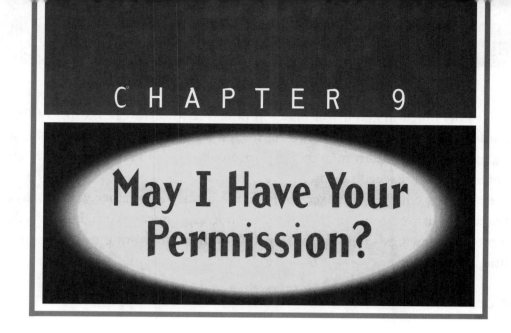

CHAPTER 9
May I Have Your Permission?

Copyright law protects the creators of artistic or literary works (called *intellectual property*) from having others reproduce those works without specific permission. This, of course, includes your own newsletter if you prefer to copyright it.

Others' works

If you want to reproduce in your newsletter a magazine cartoon, a syndicated newspaper column or any other copyrighted material, get permission first. It's a simple process:

- Write the publisher, asking permission for one-time reproduction in your newsletter.
- Enclose your newsletter and a self-addressed, stamped envelope.
- State your deadline, to ensure prompt response.
- Offer to pay any fee involved (but rarely will you be charged).
- Say you will publish whatever credit line the copyright owner prefers.

Some material is in the public domain because it was never copyrighted or because the copyright has expired.

Clip Art or Stock Photography

You pay for this, so it's yours to use as you wish. In fact, you can even alter clip art and stock photography by cropping or "morphing" in an art software program. But some purchases, especially with stock photography, come with contracts limiting its use to certain times, certain places.

Fair Use

This allows you to use brief portions of copyrighted material—in a review, for example, or as a quote within a longer article. In *Editing Your Newsletter*, Mark Beach writes:

Copyright laws do not explicitly define fair use, and there are no clear rules about how much material you may reproduce. Two or three excerpts of fifty words each or one photo or drawing from a book should be no problem. In the case of an article from another newsletter, quoting more than just a few sentences might exceed fair use.

The law tests whether you exceeded fair use by asking whether you deprived the copyright owner of profit. You may not reproduce copyrighted words, photos or drawings simply because you find them interesting or need something to fill space.

Freelancers

Freelance writers and artists retain copyright to their work even if you hired them to produce it, *unless* you state in a contract that the work is yours. Copyright ownership is negotiable, so put whatever agreements you arrive at in writing.

Your Own Employees

Employees on a payroll do not own the works they produce for you, so you own any articles written by your salaried staff. Letters sent to you with the implication that you might publish them ("Letters to the Editor") are yours to publish without permission. But call the writers and make sure they are the ones who actually wrote the letters.

Legal Releases

If you use photos of customers, get permission from the subjects of photographs you are considering publishing. Your customers may agree to have their photos taken in your restaurant but could be unaware of the possibility that you might publish them in a newsletter for widespread distribution. It's polite and wise to secure permission, called a *legal release*.

Your own newsletter

Most promotional, or marketing, newsletters such as the one you're producing for your restaurant, are not copyrighted for the simple reason that you *want* others to reproduce it, or quote generously from it, for publicity. In fact, you might want to print in the masthead that readers are free to reproduce portions provided credit is given to you.

If you do want to copyright your newsletter, print the copyright phrase in the masthead: Copyright (or the symbol ©), the date and the name of the publisher. This is sufficient for securing your rights, but you may want to formally register it in Washington, DC. Forms are available from the Copyright Office, Library of Congress, Washington, DC 20559.

Similarly, while you cannot copyright the *name* of your newsletter, it may be creatively descriptive enough (including its artistic rendering) that you don't want someone else using it and confusing the public. In that case, you may want to trademark the name. Obtain trademark application forms from the Patent and Trademark Office, U.S. Department of Commerce, Washington, DC 20231.

It isn't, however, necessary to register your newsletter name. Once you begin to use it, you establish a common-law right to the name. Formal trademark registration protects you in legal battles that, as far as we know, are extremely rare in the world of restaurant newsletters.

Conversely, of course, don't appropriate another business's name or product—the name and picture of the Road Runner, for example. If you have any doubts about the originality of your newsletter name, have your attorney do a trademark search.

CHRONICLES

New Fall/Winter Menu at Dingbats plus favorites back by popular demand.

in One Oxford Centre.

LONDON CALLING

PHILADELPHIA, PA 19130

AQUAVIT

Restaurant Aquavit of New York, 13 West 54th Street, New York, NY 10019 Tel. (212) 307-7311

Celebrating St. Lucia

Dear Friends,
On September 29th, we were awarded three stars by The New York Times. In case you missed Ruth Reichl's review, we've reprinted it here for you...

Aquavit ushers in the holiday season with a special celebration of St. Lucia... at the restaurant and also at the venerable James Beard House...

To toast the Holiday Season, we share a simple recipe with you... traditional Swedish Glögg. We expect to share with friends...

Italians who happen to be in Sweden on December 13th are always surprised at the enthusiasm with which the Lutheran Swedes celebrate the Sicilian St. Lucia, who receives no such attention in her native country. In fact, all she has in common with her Italian namesake is the name.

As part of the celebration local newspapers organize a "Lucia competition". That is, the readers select one of a number of girls from photographs (long, preferably blond hair is often one main qualif...

St. Lucia

this peculiar festival in the winter darkness, a...

her hair, played this p... Germany and German-influenced circles in Swe...

But in Sweden it faile... take root as a part of Christmas celebrations and was transferred to Lucia Day because early that morning it had been the custom of the Swedes, ever since medieval times, to eat and drink to prepare themselves... Christmas...

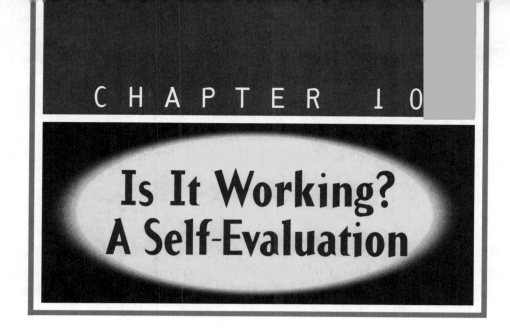

CHAPTER 10

Is It Working? A Self-Evaluation

As with any marketing campaign, you have to periodically evaluate the effectiveness of your newsletter. Measure its results, and then fine-tune its message (or your mailing list).

It's not uncommon to find restaurant owners who are having so much fun producing their newsletters that they lose sight of their audience, or the purpose of the newsletter. Have you ever had a particularly favorite dish you love to prepare—only to find that few customers order it, or at least order it a second time? In the same way that you occasionally adjust your menu according to customer feedback, solicit newsletter reader feedback.

Self-evaluation may unearth surprising opinions not only about your newsletter but also about your restaurant. For example, don't blame the failure of your big North Pole Food Festival on the newsletter promotion when it's really that Inuit cuisine just hasn't caught on yet.

Speaking of which, keep in mind that any evaluation systems you use should cover reader opinion of *both* your newsletter *and* your restaurant. Either one may be noticeably better than the other one, or certain elements in each may be variously successful—or need correcting. So, in developing survey questions, make up some about the newsletter, some about the restaurant and some about how well the newsletter reflects the restaurant.

There are many ways to see if your newsletter is paying off for you, ranging from the casual to the scientific. Here are some common methods of soliciting and gauging reader response:

Asking customers

Although conversations with your customers certainly range on the casual end of the evaluation spectrum, that's no reason not to be specific. An obvious question is, "Do you read our newsletter?" But don't stop there (whether the answer is yes or no). Ask specifically what they like (or don't like) about the publication. "Do you read all of it, or just scan it?" "Do you save it?" Don't overwhelm them with a series of survey questions, but try to learn as much as possible about your newsletter in your usual gracious manner.

Also be prepared to gear questions towards specific articles in specific issues of your newsletter. "Did you read that we now have vegetarian entrees?" Inform appropriate staff members to find out what they can about newsletter readership.

If you provide customer feedback forms with the check, include some questions about the newsletter.

Reply devices

Probably the most common method of soliciting reader response is incorporating devices in your newsletter that directly ask for it. These "calls for action" can be as simple as a sentence in an article or a boldface notice on the front or back page. "Call now if you'd like us to fax you our Thanksgiving menu." "Make your New Year's Eve reservations before Dec. 20th and get a free round of champagne."

Reply coupons can serve two purposes: gauging general newsletter readership, and gauging the effectiveness of a particular restaurant promotion or newsletter feature. Vary the content and purpose of your coupons from issue to issue.

Printed devices that the reader returns to you, by mail or fax or in person, can take many forms:

- A coupon for a free dinner or for a discount
- A contest entry—either a simple entry form or the answers to a trivia contest, for example, or a food and wine crossword puzzle
- A request to stay on your mailing list
- A request to add someone else to your mailing list
- A periodical (every 12 or 18 months) reader survey, perhaps inserted as a separate sheet of paper or business reply card

These printed reply devices can be self-addressed business reply cards or appear in the newsletter page itself. If it's part of the newsletter, place it on the page for easy clipping—on an outside corner. If your newsletter is a self-mailer, you might want to place the reply device so that recipients' mailing addresses are on the back of it, saving them the time to write it all out.

Frame reply devices with perforation marks to encourage readers to tear them out and fill them out. Also please refer to *Chapter 7, Who to Write To and How To Find Them*, for the design of business reply cards and coupons.

The trick to designing response devices that get response is twofold: Give readers an *incentive* to return them ("Good for a free glass of wine or iced tea!"), and make it easy as possible ("Photocopy this page and fax it back.") Of course, many of the reply devices you use will be brought in person into your restaurant. Then, when customers produce the coupon, you have an ideal opening to ask them about the newsletter.

Reader surveys

As we mentioned above, periodic reader surveys are helpful. They ask detailed questions about practically every feature of and in your newsletter. But they're not to be used indiscriminately. Insert one with your newsletter certainly no more than once a year, if even that. Nor do you especially have to send them to the entire mailing list. Pick a representative sample—large enough to yield statistically significant results but small enough that you can actually analyze those results. Perhaps stagger survey inserts in particular ZIP codes or other segments of your mailing list.

Don't expect a response greater than 20 or 30 percent. An accompanying incentive (that famous "free glass of wine" or entry in a drawing for a dinner-for-two) will raise response. Response rates will vary, of course, upon the cleanliness of your mailing list. For example, don't waste money on a reader survey sent to a first-time, rented list.

Here are some tips for gaining the most responses—and the most *helpful* response—from a reader survey:

- Make the questions as easy to answer as possible—beginning with the very easiest ones, to get them into the survey.
- Give multiple choices, yes or no answers, and rankings of features from 1 to 4 (that's a good number for options, by the way, because it eliminates the easy middle ground).
- Give them boxes to check. It's the easiest and quickest way for readers to respond.
- Be specific. "Do you like The Chef's Choice?" "How often would you like to receive the newsletter?"
- Keep it simple. Sometimes one question—"What do you think?"— will do the trick.
- Don't take the whole project too seriously. In fact, some humor could turn filling it out into fun. An example would be to range answer choices from "Bravo!" to "You call this food?"
- Guarantee anonymity. But also ask if they'd like to be quoted, in the newsletter or other promotions.
- Leave space at the end for readers' open-ended comments.

Marketing experts also suggest:

- Give the readers a deadline (which certainly helps an organized analysis of the results).
- Don't mail surveys at busy times of the year (with your December issue, for example).
- Pay the postage. Design the survey as a business reply card or provide a business reply envelope.
- Share the results with the local press, if the findings are particularly newsworthy.

Mailing lists

An evaluation of the effectiveness of your newsletter should also include an evaluation of the effectiveness of your mailing lists.

Keeping your mailing clean not only saves you printing and postage costs but, at its most basic, yields the most responsive names—by whatever means you've used to "qualify" them to continue receiving your newsletter.

In this chapter we've looked at ways to elicit reader response to your editorial content—the integrity—of your newsletter. Chapter 7 discusses ways to make your mailing lists equally responsive.

Books

Associated Press Stylebook and Libel Manual, Addison-Wesley Publishing Co., Jacob Way, Reading, MA 01867, (617) 944-3700. *Basic instructions and examples to make your writing style consistent.*

Color for Impact by Jan V. White. Self-published. Call (203) 227-2774 for an order form. $29.95, 64 pp., illustrated. *The author of many popular books on publication design describes the use of color on pages, including two- or three- or four-color newsletters.*

Desktop Publishing & Design for Dummies by Roger C. Parker. IDG Books, An International Data Group Company, 919 Hillsdale Blvd., #400, Foster City, CA 94404, (800) 434-3422. *Basic desktop guide by the author of the best-selling* Looking Good in Print, *includes 50-page special section on "Newsletters for Dummies."*

Editing Your Newsletter, 4th edition, "How to Produce an Effective, Professional Publication—on Schedule and on Budget," by Mark Beach. Writers Digest Books, 1507 Dana Ave. Cincinnati, OH 45207, (800) 289-0963. *A classic newsletter how-to guide, thorough in its treatment of everything from story ideas and attention-grabbing design to postal regulations and printing costs and technology.*

The Elements of Style by William Strunk Jr. and E.B. White, Macmillan Publishing Co. Inc., 866 Third Ave., New York, NY 10022, (212) 702-2000. *Deservedly a classic on how to write concisely and clearly.*

Looking Good in Print by Roger Parker, Ventana Press, P.O. Box 13964, Research Triangle Park, NC 27709, (800) 743-5369. *Country's all-time best-selling book on desktop publishing.*

The Makeover Book: 101 Design Solutions for Online & Desktop Publishers by Joe Grossmann, 1996, Ventana Press, P.O. Box 13964, Research Triangle Park, NC 27709, (800) 743-5369, $29.95, 212 pp. *An illustrated collection of tips, techniques, makeovers and basic tenets of design to inform and inspire.*

Marketing With Newsletters, 2nd edition, "How to Boost Sales, Add Members & Raise Funds with a Printed, Faxed or Web-site Newsletter" by Elaine Floyd. Newsletter Resources, 6614 Pernod Ave. St. Louis, MO 63139, (800) 264-6305, $29.95, 330 pp., illustrated. *Comprehensive guide to developing, producing and distributing a newsletter specifically as a marketing tool.*

Newsletters from the Desktop, 2nd edition, "The Desktop Publisher's Guide to Designing Newsletters That Work" by Joe Grossman with David Doty. Ventana Press, P.O. Box 2498, Chapel Hill, NC 27515. *A computer expert and a design pro combine their thoughts.*

On Writing Well by William Zinsser, HarperCollins, 1994, $27.50, 300 pp. *An informal guide to concise, clear, honest writing. User-friendly and even entertaining. Highly recommended.*

Working With Graphic Designers, "A complete handbook for anyone who needs to communicate effectively with the graphic designer: copywriters, promotion and production managers, editors, art buyers, desktop publishers, and advertising agency personnel" by James Craig and William Bevington. Watson-Guptill Publications, 1515 Broadway, New York, NY 10036. *If you're really serious about design and typography and page layout, or at least being able to talk intelligently about it with your designer, this reference is for you.*

Booklets

101 Ways to Save Money on Newsletters, 3rd edition, Polly Pattison, $8 (includes postage), 244 N. Crest Line Circle, St. George, UT 84770.

24 Newsletter Design Decisions You Cannot Duck, The Newsletter Clearinghouse, P.O. Box 311, Rhinebeck, NY 12572, (800) 572-3451, fax (914) 876-2561. $5. *An annotated checklist of the most common design decisions every newsletter publisher must face, It's simply a guide for the questions that must be asked and answered before your first issue goes into production.*

Newsletters

Briefing from American Express Travel Related Services Co. Inc., 333 E. 30th St., #5K, New York, NY 10016, (800) 342-2788, fax (212) 686-0617. $65 per year, complimentary to American Express merchants. *News of the restaurant industry, tips and trends, descriptions and addresses of restaurant and travel related World Wide Web sites.*

Newsletter Design from The Newsletter Clearinghouse, P.O. Box 311 Rhinebeck, NY 12572, (800) 572-3451, fax (914) 876-2561. $95 per year. Monthly 12-page newsletter illustrates and reviews hundreds of newsletters of all types entered in an annual design competition; useful as "swipe file" of design ideas.

Restaurant Marketing, Savannah Consulting, 2200 N. Lamar Street, Ste. 112, Dallas, TX 75202, 214-754-4930.

Clip Art Sources

Clip Art Crazy by Chuck Green. Includes a CD-ROM packed with 500 clip art images by the world's top designers and a collection of 50 extraordinary, idea-generating clip art projects you can re-create. Peachpit Press, 2414 Sixth St., Berkeley, CA 94710, (510) 548-4393. $34.95, 360 pp. plus CD-ROM. *A great overview of what's available, samples and contact information for 50 of the best clip art providers.*

Clip Board, Leesburg Printing, 1100 North Blvd. East, Leesburg, FL 34748, (800) 828-3348.

Creative Media Services, P.O. Box 5955, Berkeley, CA 94705, (415) 843-3408.

Dynamic Graphics Inc., P.O. Box 1901, Peoria, IL 61656, (309) 688-8800.

Editor's Choice, 500 Salina St., 6th Fl. Syracuse, NY 13202, (800) 962-1353.

Sandhill Arts Publishing Co., P.O. Box 7298, Menlo Park, CA 94026, (800) 854-0717.

Volk, 111 Oakwood Rd., P.O. Box 347, East Peoria, IL 61611, (309) 685-8055.

Editorial Filler Sources

Berry Publishing, 300 N. State St., Chicago, IL 60610, (312) 222-9245.

Chase's Annual Events, Contemporary Books Inc., 180 N. Michigan Ave., Chicago, IL 60601, (800) 621-1918. *Listing of scheduled holidays, special events, official observances.*

Fillers for Publications, George DeBow, 7015 Pl., N.E., Albuquerque, NM 87110, (505) 884-7636.

First Draft, L. C. Williams & Assoc. 320 N. Michigan, #2600, Chicago, IL 60601, (800) 323-2897.

Ideas Unlimited, 1545 New York Ave. N.E., Washington, DC 20002, (202) 529-5700.

Print Houses

L.J. Printing 1725 Front Street Yorktown Heights, NY 10598 914-962-9887

Maar Printing Services 49 Oakley Street Poughkeepsie, NY 12601 914-454-6860

M. Lee Smith Publishers LLC, 5201 Virginia Way, P.O. Box 5094, Brentwood, TN 37024, (615) 373-7517. *Full-service newsletter printing.*

Newsletter Services 9700 Philadelphia Court Lanham, MD 20706 301-731-5200

Press America Inc. 661 Fargo Avenue Elk Grove Village, IL 60007 708-228-0333

Schmidt Printing Inc. 1101 Frontage Road, NW Byron, MN 55920 507-775-6400

Mail List Management Software

FileMaker Pro 3.0 from Claris, (408) 727-8227. *State-of-the-art, user-friendly software may be completely customized to fit your needs. Mac and PC versions.*

Word Processing and Design Software

Microsoft Corp., 16011 NE 36th Way, Redmond, WA 98 052, 800-426-9400. *Word processing, page layout and illustration programs. Mac and PC versions.*

Quark, 300 South Jackson, Ste. 100, Denver, CO 80209, 800-356-9363. *QuarkXpress is one of the best full-featured Mac page-layout programs. QuarkStyle, a less expensive version includes several publication templates.*

Index

About the Author

WALTER MATHEWS is president of Walter Mathews Associates, Inc., and of International Visitor Publishing, Inc.

Over the past 30 years, the firm has successfully carried out a wide range of marketing assignments for airlines, hotels, restaurants, tour operators, government travel departments, financial service companies, travel trade associations, among others.

Mr. Mathews is the creator, and for 20 years, the publisher of *Restaurant Briefing*, the award-winning business newsletter for the more than 110,000 American Express restaurant merchants nationwide. Other books include *50 Promotions That Work, 50 Service Ideas That Work, 50 More Promotions That Work*, and *50 Ways to Keep the Customers You've Got and Bring In New Ones.*

When asked to describe what he does, Walter's response is "Whatever interests me. I like to bring new and beneficial perspectives to a wide variety of clients. On the one hand, at American Airlines I created the first frequent flyer computer program that has now evolved into the colossal awards concept adopted by nearly every company throughout travel and other industries. An ongoing project dear to my heart is a documentary film dealing with the cultural and economic impact of foreign visitors on our communities. At the far end of my interest spectrum, I recently launched a perfume in London, *Celeste by Patric Walker*™, that provokes the combined effect of fragrance, astrology, technology, spirituality, and discoveries of nature to help us refocus ourselves as we approach the Millennium."

Walter Mathews is a member of the faculty of the Stanford University Professional Publishing Course. He has travelled extensively and visited restaurants in most parts of the world. He lives in New York City, Stuyvesant, NY, and Pienza, Italy.